THE BIBLE AND THE PALESTINE-ISRAEL CONFLICT

The Bible and the Palestine-Israel Conflict

First Published 2014
ISBN 978-965-7409-06-0

Printed and bound by Emerezian Est., Jerusalem
www.emerezian.com.

Cover photo: The wilderness east of Jerusalem (photo by Gerard Horton)

THE BIBLE AND THE PALESTINE-ISRAEL CONFLICT

Edited by
Naim Ateek, Cedar Duaybis
and Tina Whitehead

Sabeel Ecumenical Liberation Theology Center — Jerusalem
2014

DEDICATION

We dedicate this book to the founders of Sabeel:
Abuna [later Archbishop] Elias Chacour, Assis [later Bishop]
Riah Abu El-Assal, Samia Khoury, Jean Zaru, Cedar Duaybis,
Jonathan Kuttab, and Assis Naim Ateek,
who through their tireless work over the past 25 years
have strived for justice and liberation
and sought freedom and peace
based on the liberating power of the Gospel.

CONTENTS

EDITORS' NOTE

Sabeel is grateful to the many contributors who donated their time and energy to the 9th International Conference and the assembly of this book. Many of the papers were transcribed from video recordings taken during the conference, and therefore retained a conversational, rather than purely academic, tone. Due to space constraints, we occasionally shortened the papers, but tried to preserve the central message and the presenter's unique voice.

We attempted to maintain an overall grammatical style for the papers to ease the job of the reader, but allowed for regional spelling and capitalization differences; indeed, we believe this book should retain the diversity of experience of the Sabeel community.

Where appropriate and when the authors indicated, we have included footnotes to clarify topics.

All opinions and views expressed in this compilation belong to the contributors and do not necessarily reflect the position of the Sabeel Ecumenical Liberation Theology Center.

ACKNOWLEDGMENTS

First and foremost, Sabeel wishes to thank our friends around the world who encourage us and each other to work for peace and justice in Palestine and Israel. Without such support, Sabeel could not have reached 25 years of dedicated service to the Palestinian community. Special thanks go to the participants and speakers at the 9th International Conference, whose presence with us was a great encouragement and a wonderful witness in the face of the principalities and powers of this world as we continue to strive for justice and liberation.

This conference would not have been possible without the commitment of our local and international staff and volunteers who offered help along the various stages of preparation. Many thanks go to these dedicated individuals for their invaluable help in organizing a successful conference.

A few of these deserve special mention:

- Dr. Paul Parker, who spent six months of his sabbatical year from Elmhurst College volunteering at Sabeel, and laid the groundwork for the conference. Without him it would have been difficult to do the initial preparations, including the contact of speakers and the building of the program. Sabeel is immensely grateful to Paul for his friendship and dedication to Sabeel's work and ministry.
- Jim and Jean Strathdee, conference participants, who graciously stepped in and enriched our worship time with their gift of music.
- Jessy Hampton, for the tremendous effort exerted in the transcribing and editing of the conference papers and this book. Jessy works at Sabeel as the Mennonite Central Committee's SALT (Serving and Learning Together) placement.

- And for the second conference in a row, we wish to express special thanks to Mr. Robert Maynard for generously underwriting the cost of the production of this book.

We would like also to express our thanks to the many organizations, churches, and individuals around the world which gave and continue to give financial support to the ministries of Sabeel, without which this conference could not have occurred. We also wish to thank the many local organizations which contributed to the participants' understanding of the cultural and political issues in Palestine and Israel, and to the local guides and representatives from these organizations. And, of course, our work will always depend on the support and steadfastness of the Palestinian Christian community.

Above all, we give thanks to God for the ministry of Sabeel and we pray that we can remain steadfast and faithful in the work of justice and peace.

CONTRIBUTOR BIOGRAPHIES

Ms. Maha Abu-Dayyeh is founder and general director of Women's Centre for Legal Aid and Counselling (WCLAC). She is engaged in responding to the political, legal, social, and cultural needs of Palestinian women. Born and raised in Jerusalem, Ms. Abu-Dayyeh is a recipient of the French Republic Human Rights Award (1998) and the 2002 Ms. Woman of the Year Award. Abu-Dayyeh serves on the boards of several local Palestinian and international human rights organizations that promote democracy and civil society.

Rev. Dr. Naim Ateek is cofounder and director of the Sabeel Ecumenical Liberation Theology Center in Jerusalem. As early as 1989, he articulated a Palestinian theology of liberation in *Justice and Only Justice: A Palestinian Liberation Theology* and again in his more recent book, *A Palestinian Christian Cry for Reconciliation.*

Dr. Mustafa Barghouti, MD, is Secretary General of the Palestinian National Initiative and member of the Palestinian Legislative Council. He was a candidate for president of Palestine in 2005 and nominee for the Nobel Peace Prize, and he writes extensively on civil society, democracy, and health policy for Palestinians living under occupation.

Dr. Hala Khoury-Bisharat has been a longtime member of the Board of Directors for Adalah, the Legal Center for Arab Minority Rights in Israel, and is now also the Chairperson of the Board. She is a lecturer in criminal procedure, law of evidence, public international law, and international criminal law at Carmel Academic Center-Haifa.

Dr. Gary Burge is Professor of New Testament at Wheaton College, with forty years of experience among Christian communities in Israel, Palestine and Lebanon. He has written extensively about West Asian Christians, land theology, and Zionism.

Ms. Diana Buttu, JD, is an attorney based in Ramallah. She is also Research Fellow in the Middle East Initiative of the Belfer Center for Science and International Affairs at the Harvard Kennedy School of Government as well as an Eleanor Roosevelt Fellow in the Human Rights Program at Harvard Law School. She specializes in negotiations, international law, and international human rights law and is a former spokesperson for the Palestine Liberation Organization.

Dr. Mohammed S. Dajani Daoudi is the head of the American Studies Program at al-Quds University and founder of the Wasatia movement of moderate Islam. He serves as a visiting scholar at The Washington Institute and is Founding Director of the Jerusalem Studies and Research Institute.

Rev. Dr. Peter Du Brul, SJ, is a professor and the first chairperson of the Religious Studies Department at Bethlehem University as well as having been the former chair of the Humanities Department.

Ms. Rania Elias Khoury is Director of Yabous Cultural Centre, which supports revival of cultural life, and is also Director of the Jerusalem Festival. She is on the executive committee of the Palestinian Campaign for the Academic and Cultural Boycott of Israel, as well as on the board of several local organizations.

Mr. Bo Forsberg is the General Secretary at the Swedish NGO Diakonia and the Chairman of the Foundation for Human Rights. He has written hundreds of articles about democracy and human rights as the basis for equitable distribution of resources to work for peace. He is also a longtime Friend of Sabeel.

Dr. Mads Fredrik Gilbert, MD, is a Norwegian physician and professor specializing in anesthesiology and emergency medicine. He has volunteered as a medical solidarity worker for Palestine since 1981, most recently serving in Gaza at al-Shifa Hospital during the 2008–2009 and 2012 Israeli bombardments. He is the coauthor with Dr. Erik Fosse of the documentary book, *Eyes in Gaza*, which describes the situation on the ground during Israel's "Operation Cast Lead."

Professor Mary Grey is a Roman Catholic liberation theologian and former professor at St. Mary's University College in London and the University of Wales. Her present theological focus is on reconciliation, including reconciliation with the earth. She is Trustee of Living Stones of the Holy Land, a core member of the Balfour project, a Patron of Friends of Sabeel UK, and a longtime Friend of Sabeel.

Dr. Jeff Halper is an anthropologist, author, lecturer, political activist, nominee for the Nobel Peace Prize, and cofounder and director of the Israeli Committee Against House Demolitions. His books include *An Israeli in Palestine* and *Between Redemption and Revival: The Jewish Yishuv of Jerusalem of the Nineteenth Century.*

Mr. Gerard Horton is a cofounder of Military Court Watch (MCW) and has worked on the issue of children prosecuted in the Israeli military court system for over six years. Gerard has authored a number of reports on the subject for nongovernmental organizations and UN agencies, as well as three UN shadow reports to CAT, HRC and the CRC. Prior to cofounding MCW, Gerard worked for Defence for Children International and practiced as a barrister in Australia at the Sydney bar, specializing in commercial and criminal law.

Rev. Dr. Gregory Jenks is an Anglican priest, biblical scholar, and the Academic Dean at St. Francis Theological College in Brisbane, Australia. He is also the co-director of the Bethsaida Excavations Project in Israel and coordinator of the Jesus Database project.

Rev. Dr. Pietro Kaswalder, OFM, is a professor of Old Testament Exegesis and Archeology at the Studium Biblicum Franciscanum in Jerusalem and the author of many highly influential works, such as *Biblical Archaeology and the Origins of Israel*.

Rev. Dr. Yohanna Katanacho is a Palestinian evangelical Christian who serves as Professor of Biblical Studies and Academic Dean for Bethlehem Bible College. He is one of the coauthors of the Palestinian Kairos document and has written several books, including *The Land of Christ: A Palestinian Cry*.

Mr. Jonathan Kuttab, JD, is a leading Palestinian human rights attorney in Israel and Palestine. He is also a cofounder of Al Haq, Sabeel Ecumenical Liberation Theology Center, and the Palestinian Center for the Study of Nonviolence. He continues to serve as Chairman of the Board of Bethlehem Bible College.

Mr. Gordon Matthews is a lifelong Quaker who recently served for three months as Resident Friend at Claridge House, a Quaker centre for rest, renewal and retreat in Dormansland, Surrey. He works as a freelance translator and has recorded a CD of his own songs in the folk tradition. He is an associate tutor of Woodbrooke Quaker Study Centre and recently did a short spell as Joint Representative at the Quaker Council for European Affairs.

Rev. Dr. David Mark Neuhaus, SJ, is an Israeli Roman Catholic priest of the Jesuit Order and serves as Latin Patriarchal Vicar for Saint James Vicariate for Hebrew Speaking Catholics in Israel. He teaches at Bethlehem University and at the Seminary of the Latin Patriarchate of Jerusalem. His most recent book is entitled *The Land, the Bible and History: Toward the Land That I Will Show You*.

Rev. Dr. Nancy Cardoso Pereira is a Brazilian Methodist pastor, community organizer, member of the Land Pastoral Commission, and Professor of Ancient History, Porto Alegre Institute of the Methodist Church, Brazil.

Professor John B. Quigley, LLB, is the President's Club Professor of Law at Moritz College of Law at Ohio State University, where he teaches International Law and Comparative Law. Professor Quigley's numerous publications include works on human rights, international law, the United Nations, war and peace, the Arab-Israeli conflict, and the State of Palestine.

Dr. Rosemary Radford Ruether is a leading feminist theologian and Visiting Professor at Claremont Graduate University in the United States. She also specializes in liberation theology and is a longtime Friend of Sabeel.

Mr. Raffoul Rofa is Executive Director of the Society of St. Yves of the Latin Patriarchate of Jerusalem, which promotes human and civil rights by providing legal assistance, counsel, and advocacy to the politically oppressed Palestinian population in Jerusalem and the southern West Bank.

Mr. Moriel Rothman is an American-Israeli activist, writer and poet. He was born in Jerusalem, raised in Ohio, and now lives in Jerusalem. He was imprisoned for publicly refusing to serve in the Israeli military. He is a member of All That's Left, a diaspora collective against the occupation, and writes a regular blog.

Rev. Dr. Donald E. Wagner is an ordained Presbyterian minister (PCUSA) and the National Program Director of Friends of Sabeel-North America. Formerly Professor of Middle Eastern Studies and Director of the Center for Middle Eastern Studies at North Park University and National Director of the Palestine Human Rights Campaign, he is the author of four books on the Israeli-Palestinian conflict, including *Anxious for Armageddon* and *Dying in the Land of Promise: Palestine and Palestinian Christianity from Pentecost to 2000.*

Dr. Deborah Weissman is a Jewish educator, a founder of the Kehillat Yedidya Synagogue, and actively involved with feminist and peace activism. She is President of the International Council of Christians and Jews, and has lived in Jerusalem since 1972.

Mr. Joakim Wohlfeil works as Policy Officer for Conflict and Justice for the Swedish NGO Diakonia. He has studied theology and human rights at the Stockholm School for Theology and has performed several studies regarding the role of both financial and religious factors in armed conflicts.

Dr. Sami El-Yousef is Regional Director of the Jerusalem field office of the Pontifical Mission for Palestine. After a long academic career, he now devotes his efforts to humanitarian projects via the churches, believing that maintaining the Christian presence in the Holy Land depends upon strengthening such institutions, which serve all Palestinians without any form of discrimination.

Ms. Jean Zaru is Presiding Clerk of Ramallah Friends Meeting in Palestine and a founding member of Sabeel Ecumenical Liberation Theology Center. She is the author of the influential book, *Occupied with Nonviolence: A Palestinian Woman Speaks*, and was actively involved with the World Council of Churches.

FOREWORD

Naim Ateek

Twenty-five years ago (1988), a movement was born—Palestinian Liberation Theology (PLT). It was nourished by a small group of Palestinian Christians who struggled to find a relevant faith in the midst of occupation, dispossession, and oppression. Over the years, PLT has reached Palestinian Christians throughout the Holy Land as well as people around the world who together share a vision of justice, peace, and reconciliation under the sovereignty of a loving, inclusive God. During this conference, we celebrate 25 years of this vision and movement.

In the years following World War II, Zionist ideology clothed itself in two garments. The first was a secular garment that succeeded in creating the State of Israel in 1948; the second was a religious garment that was slowly stitched together after the 1967 war. But the clearly identifiable threads of Zionist ideology were sewn into both garments: to establish a Jewish state in Palestine with a dominant if not exclusively Jewish population, despite the thriving presence of the Palestinian people.

After World War II, secular Zionism made use of the Christian West's guilt for the holocaust to cloak the aggressive Zionist acquisition of the land of Palestine. Zionists callously exploited the horrible suffering of the holocaust in such a way as to ostracize and condemn as anti-Semitic anyone who disagreed that the Jewish holocaust should be used to justify the dispossession of another people. On the one hand, Western powers sacrificed Palestine as a burnt offering to falsely absolve their consciences of the guilt of hundreds of years of Christian anti-Semitism, including biblical anti-Jewish misinterpretations. On the other hand, Western states accepted the Zionist arguments that the Christian West must compensate Jews for their near total destruction and protect them within a state of their own from the threat of future catastrophes, even if that state was built on the ashes of another people.

While we agree that Christian anti-Semitism and anti-Jewish biblical misinterpretations are wrong, totally untenable, and are to be rejected wherever they happen, we do not believe that the Palestinian people have to pay the price for the guilt of the West. Yet, on the ashes of Palestine and of millions of holocaust victims, secular Zionism triumphed.

While the 2013 international conference presupposes the secular Zionism of the nineteenth and twentieth centuries, as well as holocaust Zionism, the foci of this conference are, first, the religious and more specifically the biblical garment that hides the brutality of Zionism and, second, the question of human rights and international law that are buried beneath today's Zionism.

Israel's 1967 victory over Egypt, Jordan, and Syria, which resulted in its possession of Gaza and the West Bank, including East Jerusalem, was proof for most religious Jews that Zionism and the State of Israel were God's redemption of God's chosen people. Whereas most Western Jews up to this point had been equivocal about the State of Israel, now Western Jewry offered unmitigated support to Israel and its Zionist project.

Once God was invoked in the conflict, it became the responsibility of religious Jews to wash secularism out of Zionism so that all that remained was the "God of Israel" acting in history to return "God's chosen people" to the Promised Land. It was their religious duty to reclaim God's promise of the land; anything less would be infidelity. But just as Zionist ideology/theology is rooted in biblical "holy war," tribalism, exclusion, inequality, and domination, Zionist ethics have justified war, assassination, terrorism, land theft, ethnic cleansing, home demolitions, eradication of villages, and the uprooting of thousands of olive trees. The holocaust was no longer necessary to justify the possession of Palestine and the dispossession of Palestinians. The Bible replaced the holocaust as a far more potent tool to dominate and expel Palestinians and to control and appropriate their land. The new Zionist ideology set in: "We are not here because of the holocaust; we are here because God gave us this land and the Bible is our title deed. Don't talk to us about international law or the human rights of the Palestinians; we have divine rights to this land. The Palestinians must go."

This is today's theology of the religious Zionist extremists, both Jewish and Christian, and even the so-called secular Zionists. The Hebrew Bible—the Christian Old Testament—has become a weapon by which Palestinian Arabs, including Palestinian Arab Christians, are denied their internationally guaranteed rights to their lands, livelihoods, culture, and self-determination. Hence the theme of the 9th International Conference: "The Bible and the Palestine-Israel Conflict." Moreover, although the Bible has been part of the problem and must be part of the solution, Sabeel's vision is that the political solution to the conflict must be based on the universal principles of human rights and international law. The world must find a way to come together regardless of differing and even competing ideologies and religions.

In light of the above, Sabeel Ecumenical Liberation Theology Center has organized the 9th International Conference, 2013. We hope that you will find it intellectually stimulating and an invaluable experience that will energize your commitment to continue the pursuit of a just peace for all the people of Palestine and Israel.

INTRODUCTION

Naim Ateek

Sabeel's 9th International Conference focused directly on the issue of the Bible. It has taken us many years to arrive at this point: to address squarely the use, misuse, and abuse of the Bible. Finally the hour has come.

A quick look at the last 25 years shows the rich variety of themes Sabeel has chosen for its nine international conferences. Every one of them has been relevant to the life and wellbeing of the Palestinian people who have suffered since the creation of the state of Israel over 65 years ago, and have been living under the illegal Israeli occupation for close to 50 years.

1st conference, March 10-17, 1990 - Tantur. "Palestinian Liberation Theology." The Book: *Faith and the Intifada.*

2nd conference, January 22-29, 1996 - YMCA East Jerusalem. "The Significance of Jerusalem for Christians and of Christians for Jerusalem." The Book: *Jerusalem: What Makes for Peace!*

3rd conference, February 10-15, 1998 - Bethlehem University. "The Challenge of Jubilee: What Does God Require?" The Book: *Holy Land Hollow Jubilee: God, Justice and the Palestinians.*

4th conference, February 21-24, 2001 Jerusalem, Notre Dame. "One New Humanity Where Justice is at Home." No book was published.

5th conference, April 14-18, 2004 - Notre Dame, Jerusalem. "Challenging Christian Zionism." The Book: *Challenging Christian Zionism: Theology, Politics and the Israel-Palestine Conflict.*

6th conference, November 2-9, 2006 - Notre Dame, Jerusalem. "The Forgotten Faithful: A Window into the Life and Witness of Christians in the Holy Land." The Book retained the title as the conference theme.

7th conference, October 12-19, 2008 - Nazareth & Jerusalem. "The Nakba: Memory, Reality, & Beyond." Pre-conference publications: *I Come from There ... and Remember* and *A T i m e to Remember; Palestinian Towns and Villages.*

8th conference, February 23-28, 2011 - Bethlehem Hotel, Palestine. "Challenging Empire: God, Faithfulness and Resistance." The Book retained the conference theme.

9th conference, November 19-24, 2013 - Notre Dame, Jerusalem. "The Bible and the Palestine-Israel Conflict." The Book retained the conference theme.

Sabeel, as a center of Palestinian liberation theology, has obviously used the Bible and theology extensively during all of these conferences, but it was not until the 9th conference that it became the focus, primarily due to the increasing misuse and abuse of the Bible, especially by both right-wing Israeli settlers and right-wing Christians.

Sabeel's 9th International Conference was held at the Notre Dame Convention center in Jerusalem, November 19-24, 2013. The workshops and focus groups were held at the Freres School within the walls of the Old City of Jerusalem. On-site visits were arranged to the Negev as well as to Hebron and the Bethlehem area. The conference ended with a celebration of 25 years of Palestinian Liberation Theology at the Inter-Continental Hotel in Jericho where we were joined by several busloads of people from Nazareth in the Galilee. The attendance ranged between 250 locals and internationals in the Jerusalem venue and 500 in Jericho. The participants came from 17 different countries.

Sabeel and its global friends represent a broad range of Christian backgrounds that span the major Christian denominations, namely, Orthodox, Catholic, Protestant, and Evangelical, also including a good number of people who have no specific religious commitment but see themselves as secular. Due to this diversity, it was important to address the theme of the conference in such a way that it could speak to those who come from faith perspectives as well as those who do not.

Furthermore, since Sabeel is an ecumenical organization and our friends come from a wide theological spectrum, ranging from the liberal to the conservative and from the Evangelical to the Catholic, we had to design a special format for most of the sessions. We were determined to expose the participants to various theological perspectives of Bible reading, interpretation, and understanding.

We have always maintained at Sabeel that the Bible, when rightly interpreted and understood can inspire Christians to reject violence and war and work for justice and peace for the oppressed. But when wrongly interpreted, the Bible can arouse and motivate us to use violence and to even kill others in the name of God and the Bible. Therefore, we felt that we cannot promote the resolution of the Israel-Palestine conflict on the basis of the Bible and the way it is understood and interpreted, especially by extremists. Moreover, in some parts of the Bible there are texts that reflect violence and terror that are attributed to God[1] and are therefore open to misuse, especially in our existentially troubled societies. It is easy for such texts to be abused by extremists as they, indeed, are.

Where then is the place and role of the Bible? To begin with, it is important to discover the authentic message of the Bible. We believe that in both the Old and New Testament, the heart of the message is that of love and mercy, justice and peace, liberation and nonviolence, forgiveness and reconciliation. Any message that does not emphasize these and similar characteristics cannot be a message from God to us.

I am convinced that in the twenty-first century it is mandatory to resolve intractable world conflicts on the basis of international law. At Sabeel, we have always maintained that ultimately the resolution of the Israel-Palestine conflict must be based on the principles and demands of international law. We believe that international law is not biased towards any one country or any one religion or ethnic group. Since the adoption of the United

---

1 For more on this subject, read Naim Ateek, "Bible Study: Land of Promise," page 113 of this edition.

Nations Charter in 1945 and the Universal Declaration of Human Rights in 1948, we have seen the emergence of a "set of universal requirements for the legal and administrative order of every state. Matters previously within the domestic jurisdiction of each state have now become subject of international concern and regulations. International supervisory bodies have emerged to push for compliance with universal norms."[2]

Tragically, however, we have not yet seen the full realization and implementation of international law, but I believe that it is only a matter of time. International law is not prejudiced against the State of Israel and the Jewish people nor is it prejudiced against the Palestinians and the Arabs. It is prejudiced and biased towards truth and justice. It upholds and promotes justice and peace among nations.

We therefore designed the conference program in such a way as to have it climaxed by referencing international law clearly as the foundation for a lasting peace. On the one hand, international law should be used to determine and to adjudicate the injustices committed by both sides—the Israeli government and the Palestinian government. On the other hand, international law should be the basis on which the future peace is constructed. We believe that it is the only foundation that can guarantee longevity and permanence. We are sure that no peace imposed by Israel can last if it is not built on justice as interpreted and administered by international law and democratic principles that ensure the equality of all people. Such a peace needs to be cultivated and nurtured by a system of education that can build a culture of democracy, peace, and nonviolence.

At Sabeel, we believe that sooner or later the leaders of the world will insist on finding ways to foster the respect and implementation of international law by the countries of the world and to demand the compliance of all. What is needed is the *will*

---

2 Eide, A. (2000). Citizenship and international human rights law: Status, evolution, and challenges. In N.A. Butenschon, U. Davis, & M.S. Hassassian (Eds.), *Citizenship and the state in the Middle East: Approaches and applications.* (88-122). New York: Syracuse University Press.

on the part of the international community to take a conscious and intentional stand and to execute its own UN resolutions. The possibility of peace for the people of Palestine and Israel is real. People's dreams for peace and prosperity can be realized in our lifetime.

Long ago the formula for peace was laid down by the prophet Isaiah. But what could not be realized at the time of the prophet has a greater chance to be realized in the twenty-first century due to the presence of international law. Isaiah wrote, "The effect of justice will be peace and the result of justice quietness and trust forever" (Isa. 32:17). When peace is based on justice and justice is defined by international law, it stands a good chance to succeed. The spirit of the Bible can then coincide with the principles of international law; both Palestinians and Israelis can share the land and can live together in peace and trust.

Our immediate and urgent responsibility is to be actively engaged in peacemaking so that we can challenge world leaders to do justice. "Blessed are the peacemakers for they shall be called children of God" (Matt. 5:9).

PART I
THE OCCUPATION OF THE BIBLE

OPENING SERMON

"Today the Scripture is Fulfilled"
Naim Ateek

"The eyes of all in the synagogue were fixed on him. Then he began to say to them, 'Today this scripture has been fulfilled in your hearing.'" (Luke 4:21, NRSV)

On behalf of the Sabeel Center, I would like to welcome you all to our 9th International Conference. I thank God for your safe arrival and for your presence with us. I hope and pray that our time together will be blessed and fruitful. I pray that this conference will energize us and renew our commitment to continue the struggle for a just peace for all the people of our land. Although it is my hope that this conference will raise important questions about the Bible and the way it has been used and abused in our land, we will be giving special attention to the importance of international law and human rights for the resolution of the Palestine-Israel conflict. Due to biblical abuse from Jewish and Christian Zionists and, inadvertently, from many well-intentioned ordinary Christians, the Bible that can lead us to salvation has become itself in need of saving. In other words, many of our people are being killed and oppressed by the way the Bible is being used and interpreted. Tragically, this is not new in the history of our faith.

The Bible has been used to justify slavery, war, apartheid, silencing of women and many other things, and now the oppression and killing of the Palestinians. How did Jesus use the Bible? Can Jesus guide us? I believe he can. Let us look at Jesus' encounter in his hometown Nazareth as recorded in Luke 4.

31

We know from the Gospels that Jesus was brought up in a small town called Nazareth in the Galilee. What do we know about this town? Not much. But New Testament scholar Kenneth Bailey, a good friend of some of us, has written, as a result of his research, something very interesting. It seems that the northern part of Palestine after the Exile (sixth century B.C.E.), including the Galilee, was largely inhabited by non-Jews. The prophet Isaiah, writing several hundred years before Christ, refers to the Galilee as "the Galilee of the Gentiles," i.e. non-Jews. Nazareth, according to Dr. Bailey, started as a settlement for Jews, probably built in the second century B.C.E. by Aristobulus the Maccabean, who conquered the Galilee and wanted to judaize it. Nazareth, therefore, was a settlement town and it was inhabited, to begin with, by settlers, many of whom were nationalists.

We also know that there is no mention of Nazareth in the Old Testament. One of the theories as to why Joseph and Mary chose to go to Nazareth after their return from Egypt was the availability of employment in that area. About three miles northwest of Nazareth, King Herod Antipas was building and beautifying Sepphoris (*Saffouria* in Arabic) as his first capital. Joseph probably sought employment there, and so chose to live close by. If this is the case, then Jesus grew up in a settlement.

We know from the Gospels that when he was 30 years old, Jesus went to the Jordan River and was baptized by John the Baptist. Sometime later he returned to Nazareth, and on the Sabbath went to the Synagogue to pray. The *khazan*, the attendant, handed him the scroll of Isaiah. From the text we deduce that it was Jesus who chose the passage that he wanted to read:

> *The Spirit of the Lord is upon me,*
> *because he has anointed me to bring*
> *good news to the poor. He has sent me*
> *to proclaim release to the captives and*
> *recovery of sight to the blind, to let the*
> *oppressed go free, to proclaim the year of*
> *the Lord's favor.* (Luke 4:18-19, NRSV)

He rolled up the scroll, gave it back to the attendant and sat down. Then the text reads:

> *The eyes of all in the synagogue were fixed on him.*
> *Then he said, "Today this scripture has been*
> *fulfilled in your hearing."*
> (Luke 4:21, NRSV)

There are several important points that we need to remember as we look at this event:

FIRST: The Isaiah text from which Jesus reads is chapter 61. This text has found fulfillment in the coming of Christ. In his reading of the Isaiah passage, Jesus said, *"Today this scripture has been fulfilled in your hearing."* As Christians we recognize that Jesus Christ is the goal, center, and climax of our biblical faith. In him the scriptures have been fulfilled.

SECOND: The text which Jesus read in the Nazareth synagogue expresses God's concern for the poor and oppressed. It talks about God's good news to the poor, good news of liberation for the prisoners and the oppressed, and healing for the sick and the diseased. The heart of the message, which the prophet Isaiah conveys to the people in exile, is about justice and that God is their liberator. They are words of comfort and hope for people who were broken by years of oppression.

THIRD: What is significant is the fact that Jesus did not read the Isaiah text verbatim; he edited it. He omitted some words and added others from another section of Isaiah. By doing so, he made it more relevant to his hearers. His hearers were not living in exile; they were living under the Roman occupation. Jesus contextualized the message and made it relevant. Is this an important hint for those who use the text literally? Jesus did not hesitate to edit the text. For him, the liberative message was more important than the literal words.

FOURTH: Moreover, Jesus did something more radical with the Isaiah text. He stopped midsentence and did not finish the reading of the passage. What did he leave out? The whole sentence reads,

To proclaim the year of the Lord's favor,
And the day of vengeance of our God.
(Isaiah 61:2, emphasis added)

The year of the Lord's favor is the Year of Jubilee when justice is restored to the poor and oppressed in the community. This Jesus read, but he left out "the day of vengeance of our God."

In one of my first visits to Hebron years ago, I saw that the Palestinian shops were closed and that the settlers had written on the doors the Hebrew word *neqama,* "vengeance" or "revenge," the same word as the Arabic *naqma.* The Hebron settlers were calling for vengeance against the Palestinians.

Jesus refused to call for God's vengeance on the non-Jewish enemies. He refused to read what for him was theologically offensive and unacceptable. I realize that some biblical scholars have given various interpretations, but I believe that it was Jesus himself who, due to his theology of God as a loving parent, could not call for God's judgment on their enemies. In my understanding of the text, Jesus felt free to critique Isaiah's words; Jesus refused to read words that reflected racism and bigotry. Jesus' hermeneutic of God's love for all caused him to stop in midsentence.

Remember, Jesus was speaking to a settler community who would love to hear that their God was standing with them and would pour out wrath and vengeance on their enemies. Jesus refused to give them that pleasure. For me, the lesson is clear: whatever does not agree with the hermeneutic of God's love for all people has no authority for us and must not be read, even if it is written in the Bible.

FIFTH: Jesus showed great courage by standing before a group of nationalists and confronting their bigotry. When we look at the rest of the chapter, we see words that can only be described as racist. What are some of the words that Jesus did not read?

Strangers [non-Jews] shall stand
and feed your flocks, foreigners shall till
your land and dress your vines; but you
shall be called priests of the Lord, you
shall be named ministers of our God; you
shall enjoy the wealth of the nations, and
in their riches you shall glory. (Isaiah 61:5-6, NRSV)

In October 2010, the late Israeli Sephardic leader Rabbi Ovadia Yosef, the spiritual leader of the Shas Party and a former chief Sephardic rabbi of Israel, said, "*Goyim* [Gentiles] were born only to serve us [Jews]. Without that, they have no place in the world; only to serve the People of Israel. . . . Why are Gentiles needed? They will work, they will plow, they will reap. We will sit like an *effendi* [aristocrat] and eat." I am certain he had the Isaiah text in mind. It is important to mention that a number of Jews condemned his words. But he was using the Hebrew Bible. Zionism made hewers of wood and drawers of water out of the Palestinians. Isaiah was describing a community after the Exile when societal roles would be reversed; the exiled Jews would become masters and the Gentiles would be their servants, and Jews would feast on the wealth of nations and be proud that it was theirs. I believe that Jesus could not subscribe to such a theology.

Such words are found in the Bible even on the lips of Isaiah, but it reflects bigotry and xenophobia. It is contrary to the spirit of a loving God who loves and cares for all. Again the lesson is clear: when using the Bible, we can critique those exclusive texts found in the Bible because they do not reflect the God of Love. Some Christians try to rationalize and justify them, but they are best disregarded as it is difficult to whitewash them.

SIXTH: In order to drive home his message, Jesus used two examples from their Hebrew tradition.

1. In order to care for the prophet Elijah during a period of famine, God sent Elijah to a Phoenician widow from Lebanon, a Gentile who looked after Elijah for three years.

The pagan widow had faith that the God of Elijah would provide for her and her family as well as the prophet. Jesus was emphasizing a strong and clear theology of God when he chose a foreign widow as a model of faith for the Nazareth settler community.

2. Jesus struck at their racist nerve when he referred to how Elisha the Prophet healed Naaman, the Syrian general, who was a Gentile. God chose pagans as models of faith. God's love and care is not restricted to one small ethnic community.

SEVENTH: Jesus had a hermeneutic of God's love for all people and Isaiah's words did not comply with that criterion. The people of Nazareth did not like the preacher Jesus. They wanted to hear words that would satisfy their bigotry against foreigners, but Jesus was not willing to play their game or give them that pleasure. He confronted them and gave them a lesson in theology.

The God Jesus talked about is a liberator God. If God is biased, God shows bias toward the poor and the oppressed. Jesus shattered their exclusive concept of God and critiqued their understanding of the scriptures. Just because it is in the Bible does not mean it is correct or its theology is sound.

By doing this, I believe that Jesus gives us an important lesson about how to relate to the Bible. Brothers and sisters, imagine the scene: Jesus stands in the Nazareth synagogue and courageously confronts his nationalist hometown folks. Jesus was not seeking popularity and admiration; he sought to be faithful to God. I believe Jesus gave us an example of how to read scripture.

What does it mean for us to say scripture is fulfilled?

- Like Jesus Christ, we can only say scripture is fulfilled when we are proclaiming justice and liberation for all the people of the land regardless of their ethnic, racial, or religious background.
- We can only say scripture is fulfilled when we witness to God's love for all people; and for us Christians, God's love is seen and exemplified in the love of Jesus Christ.
- To say scripture is fulfilled is to take a stand for justice

and to struggle and confront injustice, racism, violence, discrimination, and everything that corrupts and dehumanizes people.

- To say scripture is fulfilled is to critique any misuse of scripture that justifies the theft of people's land, the demolition of people's homes, the uprooting of people's olive and fruit trees, and the oppression of the people of the land.
- To say scripture is fulfilled is to believe that God's word for us is always a word of life, peace, love, and joy. It is a word of hope and strength for all people.
- To say scripture is fulfilled implies a challenge for us. It challenges our narrow and exclusive theology. It challenges us to become more compassionate and Christ-like people.

May God give us the strength and the wisdom not only to challenge the powers that be, but to remain faithful in our work and witness for justice and peace!
Amen.

BIBLICAL AUTHORITY

Gary Burge

First of all I want to thank the leadership of Sabeel for inviting me to be here. I also want to say that Naim's early writing, his work on the subject of Israel-Palestine, was formative for me in my early years when I began to be introduced to this. So I say thank you to Sabeel and thank you to Naim.

I'm grateful that the subject of the Bible is on the agenda for this Sabeel meeting. I have had countless conversations about the conflict during the course of my last 30 years, and the Bible always seems to come up. I have heard variations of a conversation that include, "Why are you doing this? God has given me this land." Then all arguments lead to Genesis 12 or Romans 9-11. If you happen to be in the Evangelical world like I am, you have to be adept at knowing what to do with Genesis 12-17 and Romans 9-11. When we have a conversation about the Christian Church and the land, we certainly have to be adept at how we use the Bible.

This is an extremely complex subject but let me begin by giving five foundational principles that I think will help us to lay a groundwork for what we think about when we think about the Bible.

First of all, we believe in a God who acts and speaks. This speaking from God is unique to the three Abrahamic faiths; therefore we talk about the Torah and the Prophets. We talk about Jesus' speech as *extraordinary* speech. God even speaks in conferences like these, which are not lost in history. Exodus 17, for instance, has the first instruction in the Bible to make a record of what God has said. The Amalekites attack Israel, but Israel is victorious, so God instructs his people to "write this down, because the writing of it will be your later salvation" (Ex. 17:14). In Exodus 20-24, a covenant is *written*; the Decalogue (the Ten Commandments) is placed in stone before us.

Consequently, we have this idea within the Church that what we call verbal or spoken revelation is essential to our faith and it is natural to what we mean when we talk about the God of the Bible. For instance, in John 10, Jesus disputes with the temple leaders and he says, "Scripture cannot be broken" (John 10:35). Therefore, there is this instinctive reflex in Jesus that says Scripture is a binding guide by which we must discuss these matters. In Matthew 5 in the Sermon on the Mount, Jesus says, "Not one iota of the Scriptures or the law can be changed" (Matt. 5:18). In 2 Timothy 3:16, Paul declares his own view by describing these sacred writings as "God breathed."

So my first principle is that *written revelation* in the Church is not a marginal idea; it has always been essential. Consequently, we tend to cite Scriptures such as 1 Corinthians 10:11 where Paul summarizes the Old Testament story and states, "These things were written down for our instruction." In other words, the Old Testament story is not a simple historical archive; it is written for us in our time so that we might be instructed. We believe in a God who speaks, and this is not a marginal idea.

Secondly, we affirm that scripture requires careful use. Throughout the history of the Church, the teaching office of elder or scholar has always been critical, and today this has led to a fairly sophisticated area of study that scholars refer to as hermeneutics, or the "science of interpretation." We need hermeneutics because the meaning of Scripture has not always been clear. When the written Gospel moved into the Greek and Latin worlds from the Middle East, much was lost. Anyone who is bilingual understands that natively. In other words, the Gospel message is imbedded in a language and a context that is foreign to every successive era. Therefore anyone who reads the Scriptures today, in the West especially but also in the Middle East, reads these texts as foreigners.

My students regularly ask, "Why are hermeneutics necessary? Wouldn't it have been better if God had spoken directly to us in our own time and place? Creatures, however, necessarily have to see and hear God *indirectly*. As John 1:18 says, "No one has ever seen God, only the incarnate Son has actually seen and heard God." We, as creatures, only hear things indirectly. God speaks from a burning bush. God speaks to us through an incarnate Son. Therefore indirect speech necessarily adopts the context of our culture so that we might understand. As a result, we need help when we read the Scriptures, which is why translations of the Bible came rapidly in the history of the Church. Skilled copyists needed to bring Old Latin, Syriac, and Coptic Scriptures to a new place and time. The need for hermeneutics also brought the evolution of Christian scholarship to boost our confidence in understanding the Scriptures. When we do read Scripture, we must do so with care.

My third principle is that we must embrace what I call interpretive humility. We must have hermeneutical humility. God does not wear our clothes, yet we consistently dress God in the fashions and politics of our day. From Byzantine algorists to Renaissance artists who barely understood that at the Lord's Supper no one was wearing knickers, to modern theologians, we find in Scripture what we want to find. We read Scripture with sinful eyes. Therefore when we read Scripture, we also have to remember that we are reading from our own perspectives. Am I male or female, and how will that affect what I see and hear? Am I African or Arab or White or Jewish or Brazilian? Am I rich or poor? I come to Scripture with a perspective; I look at Scripture through a lens, and that lens brings distortion. Therefore, we must not fall victim to hubris and arrogance, because interpretive confidence requires humility.

There is a frailty in all that we do with the Scriptures, which explains the frequent abuse and misuse of the Bible throughout history, as well as the frequent frustration and despair that often accompanies Biblical interpretation. I wonder how many times I have been at a theological conference or with laity, and people will take a copy of the Bible and say, "You know, people will take this Bible and make it say anything they want it to." A wash of despair consequently falls over the Church. I imagine this is nowhere more evident than in Israel and Palestine, where the Bible consistently serves special interests, or as a friend of mine once said to me, "The Bible has been weaponized."

My fourth principle is that this despair has eroded Biblical authority. Especially since the Enlightenment in Europe in the early eighteenth century, religious authority has moved away from the Bible, and in some cases Biblical authority has been discredited altogether. The twin gods of the Enlightenment, reason and individualism, demanded that we sacrifice both the Church and the Bible on the altar of the Enlightenment. The Enlightenment led some theologians to seek revelation in other places. They have looked away from the Bible, and they have sought to hear the voice of God someplace else. In particular, people in the last 200 years have sought to find God in the human soul, the progress of civilization, or guidance, perhaps through common grace, in the governments of the world. Other people have found some key theme inside the Bible that they felt they could excavate. They thought they could take that thematic relic of the Bible, excavate it, hold it aloft, and say, "This is the one theme for which the Bible stands."

Adolf von Harnack, a late nineteenth century theologian extremely popular in Europe who died in 1930, epitomizes this second position. In his book *What is Christianity?*, published in 1901, which is one of the most famous and popularizing theological books ever written, he basically states, "The message of the Church is not that we promote the Church, not that we promote Christ. It is simply the love of God, and the brotherhood of humanity. That is all that we believe to be Christians."

My fifth and final principle is that theology that lives and works without the Bible has failed. It was Karl Barth who made this observation in the first half of the twentieth century. Karl Barth had been formed through nineteenth century theological liberalism, and when his theological teachers, especially Adolf von Harnack, promoted the love of God and the brotherhood of all humanity and then endorsed German war aims in 1914, Barth was crushed. He then abandoned the liberal theological project of the nineteenth century because the ideas he had so treasured had succumbed to political ambition and corruption. As he stood in the ruins of a decimated Europe in 1919, he wrote the most devastating commentary on the Book of Romans that we possess today, and which has since undergone many editions. Barth declared what we often forget: the human project cannot be done on its own. We need a penetrating, authoritative word from outside. We need to place ourselves *beneath* the Scriptures and not *above* them. We need a word, not just of love, but of judgment and redemption. Redemption, according to Barth, had to come from the outside, from above, and the key to this redemption was revelation, a word from God, written in Scripture.

Barth was conservative because he regained a notion of revelation. Barth believed, and the Church today believes, that we require a word: a word from God and a word of God. We need a word to which we are subordinate, because without an authoritative word from God, without a theology that is shaped by the Scriptures, the Church runs the risk of collapsing under the weight of the political and economic fashions of our day.

BIBLICAL AUTHORITY

Nancy Cardoso Pereira

This panel is about "Biblical Authority." While Gary Burge talked about the biblical perspective, I would like to discuss the topic from the perspective of authority.

The problem of biblical authority is not reduced to the interpretation and application of the text, but in my opinion, the problem is within the Western hegemonic format of Christian theology, or better, North Atlantic Christianity. The emergence of indigenous and contextual theologies, especially feminist theology, in the last century, has raised a number of important methodological and epistemological issues which strongly demand the deconstruction of the paradigms of the epistemological and cultural theological enterprise—and I'm using enterprise here for a specific reason. Christian theology emerged in its historical context as apology, as a rational defense, after the first enculturation whose prototype was the incarnation of the *logos* in the Eastern Semitic culture. Crucial theological enculturation took place in the Greek-Roman culture and empire, with all the consequences for the development of the emerging theology. Thus some concepts, totally foreign to the biblical cultures, entered the Christian theological vocabulary, and began to occupy an important place in the formulation of the dogma and the links of the new religion. As examples, the concepts of person, transcendence, absoluteness, essence, nature, being or nothing.

This first theological enculturation emerged from a real contextualization with the dominant culture of the Roman Empire. However, what had been part of the context quickly became faith itself. It became part of faith. The result was a radical realization of the new Christian faith, and Romanization of ecclesiastical and legal expression. What is problematic is not the process of enculturation and contextualization—that's natural—but the movement from above, the pontification and absolutism of the economic context. This is the problem. The contextualization became the message, paralyzing the need for permanent critique. And from then on, Christianity became a customer, and acquired a taste for hegemonic forms of power.

And then a second important moment happened in shaping modernity: a hegemonic, Western, North Atlantic, historical interpretation of salvation and mission led to a powerful and painful combination of Western-North Atlantic history and culture, with a socioeconomic system as the dominant and mainstream way of understanding and living our Christian faith in the world. The combination of Western-North Atlantic Christianity with Western-North Atlantic capitalism has shaped the last five hundred years of human history. The Christian missionary message was so attached to capitalist intervention that even now, North Atlantic Christianity cannot live and understand faith apart from capitalism. And we, the historical receivers ("Third World" receivers) of the Good News of the double "C"—Christianity and capitalism—live in second-class citizenship in both Cs.

Biblical fundamentalism and Zionism are also possibilities within the hegemonic theological scheme, leading to extreme potential in an apologetic vision of domination that permits both the religio-economic enterprise and the political-economic enterprise of capitalism. Biblical fundamentalism and Christian Zionism are the unconditional defense of the West as a totalitarian program. The fact that they are more or less liberal-reading does not diminish the capacity of aggregation, aggression, manipulation, and alienation of Christianity as part of the Western political domination in the world. At the end, what we call biblical authority was and is a practice trying to hide its own belonging, trajectory, and program; it can be a church hierarchical authority, a North Atlantic scientific authority, or the authority of the market creating religious commodities to be bought.

The hegemonic discourse on biblical authority is, today, a reinforcement of capitalist and imperialist practice, an expression of Western-North Atlantic moral reserve against the world's resistance and search for alternatives for another possible world. Yes, there is life outside of capitalism. The irrationality of capitalism leads us toward a disaster of still incalculable proportion. The signs of this disaster are already visible and are called by many names: greenhouse effect, nuclear waste accumulation, deforestation, extinction of species and reduction of biological diversity, food crises, overcrowding, and endless war. And don't say that this is normal. And don't say that this is necessary.

Israel enjoys support in the U.S. not just because of the Israel lobby, with its bribes and treats, or because Americans imagine that they have rescued European Jews. Israel is supported in the U.S. as an ideal. Like the U.S., it is an ideal of White Europeans invading a country far from home, declaring it to be empty, and then emptying it of its original inhabitants, and proclaiming that it is all God's will.

This link is clear in G4S's rise. G4S, a UK security company, is indicative of two worrying aspects of neoliberal capitalism in Israeli apartheid: the ideology of security and the increasing privatization of what have been, traditionally, state-run sectors. Security as the context does not imply security for everyone, but rather when one looks at the major clients of G4S security—banks, governments, corporations—it becomes evident that when G4S says it is "Securing your world," as the company slogan goes, it is referring to a world of exploitation, oppression, occupation, and racism.

In the pride of its heart, capitalism says:

"I am a god. I am a god. I sit on the throne of a god, in the heart of the seas." You think you are wise, and no secret is hidden from you. By your wisdom and understanding, you have gained wealth for yourself and amassed gold and silver in your treasuries. By your great skill in trading you have increased your wealth, and because of your wealth your heart has grown proud. You think you are wise, as wise

as God. . . . Through your widespread trade you are filled
with violence and you sinned. Your heart became proud on
account of your beauty, and you corrupted your wisdom
because of your splendor. By your many things and amassed
trade, you have desecrated your sanctuaries.
(Ezekiel 28: 2-5, 16-18)

The Ezekiel prophesy is saying simply and directly, "You are only human. You are not God." Who today knows how or is able to produce such theology or prophesy? Who is able to condemn and combat the spiritual aura conferred to a socioeconomic phenomenon? We need to choose the difficult option and learn to say again: By your many things and dishonest trade, you have desecrated sanctuaries and you have desecrated the biblical text itself. The world and its living beings—peoples and their cultures, the earth, water, and seeds, everything that moves—are sacred, like the Bible, and so economic systems that produce injustice, dishonor, and theft cannot be blessed, legitimized, or tolerated in the name of God.

So, some tasks for us: First, denounce current and historical connections of Christianity with hegemonic capitalism and all forms of oppression. Second, break spiritually, culturally, and politically with capitalism; join together in the construction of another possible world. Third, denounce all worship of capital, in the media and in our churches. Fourth, deny all use of Christian faith and the Bible as justification for war, for the destruction of other religions, and legitimization of systematic forms of exploitation of human labor and nature. Fifth, understand ourselves as one religion among others. That's what we are: one religion among others. A people of faith among other people of faith. And we commit ourselves to do justice, to embrace faithful love, and to walk humbly with our God. Finally, trust in God's liberating grace. We do believe in a free Palestine. Deep in my heart I do believe, and I will do what is asked. We shall overcome, and here comes the day. Let's do it!

BIBLICAL AUTHORITY

David Mark Neuhaus

I would like us to think about the challenge that Nancy Cardoso Pereira has enunciated so clearly to authority, and how we can think of authority differently, whether we're talking about biblical authority or any other kind of authority. I'd like to remind us again of that first text that talks about authority, in the Gospel of Mark, when Jesus comes into the synagogue of Capernaum and his *exousia,* his *shiltona,* imposes itself, not through a hegemonic use of force, but through the coherency of his person. Perhaps that's a very useful exercise to engage in before trying to address the authority of the Bible: to sweep our vocabulary, our thought process, our very being from the temptation, almost a satanic temptation, to turn authority into some kind of hegemony of violence and destruction.

I'd like to reformulate, perhaps in very different language, some of what Gary Burge was speaking about: in what sense is the Bible an authority? I want to give just four points about why I think it is authoritative in our lives. Again, I'm trying very hard to keep in mind Nancy's prophetic warning.

First and foremost, I think the Bible is authoritative in my life as a Christian because it teaches me how to speak. It is, in fact, a vocabulary, a grammar, and a syntax, teaching me how to speak about God and my community, and myself and my community through the eyes of God.

Second, it provides me with a narrative about where I'm coming from, and most importantly, what God has done in order to lead those who are my ancestors, my mothers and my fathers in faith, through the centuries. In that sense, of course, both in providing language and in providing a sense of where I'm coming from, the Bible is an authority when it comes to my identity. Who am I, and who am I in the sight of God?

Third, the Bible does indeed provide guidelines for how I am to maneuver myself and my community in the present. How should I walk in the midst of the world that God has created as a subject of God? And, of course, that is not an "I" that is only personal; it is foremost an "I" that is communitarian, a "we."

And fourth, where are we going? Where are we headed? Where are we headed in a future that is formulated by the promises of God? That's sometimes the hardest of all the exercises because it means we need to deconstruct the language, the understanding of the past, the maneuvering of the present that this world offers us, with all of its hegemonic use of power and violence. How can we conceive of a future as the prophets conceived of a future?

In all these senses I would say that the Bible is indeed an authority. But there is, of course, a problem, and this is a very fundamental problem that has already been implicitly addressed by Gary and explicitly addressed by Nancy. The Bible needs to be conceived of as different from the text Gary held up and shook. The book, full of words. The Bible is not only that. The Bible is not only an instrument to impose some kind of vision on the world. The Bible has to include the act of reading; the reader and the text must go together. The text has a context, the word exists in a world, and revelation is always given in time, in history. Very often those who are manipulating, in some sense suffocating the word through their manipulation, are using the word without the world, the text without a context, and revelation without history.

In my own tradition, scripture must go together with the community that reads scripture, the community that is reflecting on the word and being challenged by the word. We know in this particular context how the text is used to justify the user of the text, when, in fact, the primary relationship between reader and Bible is the relationship in which the reader is challenged by the Bible and not self-justified by the Bible. Again here, going back to that original image of Jesus in the synagogue at Capernaum, the authority imposes itself because of its coherence. In that sense, the Bible can only be authoritative if its message challenges our perception of the world. Thus, the text is not only read within a context, but that word, that text, must challenge the context, taking consciousness of "*Who am I as reader and in which world am I reading the text?*" That word must challenge the world. That revelation must challenge the historical processes that the reader is witnessing.

I would say that the Bible cannot be divorced from tradition. I think that's what Gary was saying, perhaps in very different words. However, there is an understanding of *sola scriptura* that changes the *scriptura* into a text that offers a clarity that is, in a certain sense, satanic, because it is a seductive clarity. A clarity offered gnostically, Hollywood-ily, a division of the world into the forces of good and evil where I am always part of the good. And this is a betrayal of what the Bible ultimately is, written by a people engaged in a very, very honest and harsh look at itself. First and foremost this recognition is humility enacted. The Bible humbles us. Humbles us as we realize that we as the community of readers, whoever we are, are not living up to the word that is challenging us in our world. Again, this is a very different kind of authority than the transformation, the distortion, the perversion, of the biblical text into an instrument of self-justification, into a weapon.

And finally, tradition and scripture must go together, but there is also a magisterium, a teaching authority, which must also follow that same authority of Jesus. A teaching authority that serves rather than dominates, a teaching authority that first models itself on that critical word that challenges the world, that shout of revelation that does not simply justify historical process but attempts to change the march of history, that does not simply seek to harmonize the text with context, but seeks to unravel context and reform it. This teaching authority that serves the people of God is the very necessary meeting between the word and the needs of a world crying out in anguish because of its separation from the Lord. I think that here are the challenges that have been clearly formulated by Gary and Nancy, to think differently about Bible and authority, and to offer a reflection that can help the Church understand a concept that is fundamental to her march in the world as a body of priests, kings, sages, and prophets building up the Kingdom of God that is already here.

THE OCCUPATION OF THE BIBLE

Gregory Jenks

One of the things I have learned to do when speaking in Australia is to always bring greetings from the Church and the Christian communities in Palestine. But when I am somewhere else, I find myself discovering a deeper sense of my own country, or unique place in the world. As someone who has been out of my own "country" (an indigenous Australian term for the specific place where a person is born) for most of my adult life, I am learning to appreciate how the Christian Scriptures are used and misused in terms of Palestine, Israel, and the conflict.

I begin from the assumption, of course, that the Bible has immense authority for this conversation. We have already begun to explore this with the earlier panel. Because of the authority that the Scriptures have, and however we understand that authority, the Bible will inform and shape the ways that we address issues of justice, peace, and reconciliation for all the communities that live in this land.

So far as process is concerned, my working assumption is that this will require an active and open-ended engagement with the sacred texts. It will also require us to be involved with the historical processes that have led to the present situation in this land. As we have already heard, we need to be paying attention to our own perspectives, our own locations, and our own points of view.

I actually think we had a fine example of that in the opening sermon that Assis Naim Ateek gave in the Melkite Church. However, I want to go out on a limb and indicate one of the places where I would probably differ significantly from some of the other members of the panel, and particularly the previous panel.

I am one of those liberal or progressive scholars who look at the way Scripture functions in terms of the Palestine-Israel conflict. This is one way of working around the issue of how the Scripture impacts the claims made for land by both Jewish and Palestinian communities.

So as the sermon began I said to myself, "This could be hard." While I love Assis Naim very much, I could see that he was going to take the story very literally. And that is not what I would do. As the sermon unfolded, I was delighted, then more delighted, and more pleased. I found myself drawn along. I loved it and entirely agreed with the way he unfolded the text. I mention this because saying that I do not begin with the assumption that the Bible is simply a record of something that happened can frighten the camels; it can scare the horses. Choose whichever metaphor works for you.

But even if we start from different positions as we engage with Scripture, my experience has been—and this perhaps goes to the question of the role of the Spirit in this whole process—that no matter from what position we start, if we engage the Scriptures with open hearts and minds then God is able to speak to us.

So what I saw yesterday was someone who took the Gospel story at face value in a way I would have difficulty doing, and yet deftly avoided some of the traps that I might imagine when people say they are taking the Bible literally, at face value. What I saw yesterday, and what I am committed to myself, is engaging with Scripture in a way that offers the Bible the best of our critical engagement. We are called to love God not only with heart and soul and strength, but also with our minds. I believe we are called to engage with Scripture in that same diverse way: with the best of our mind, the best of our soul, the best of our heart, and the best of our strength.

The Bible, I suggest, deserves and requires the best of our critical engagement, rather than naive readings which perhaps are predicated on the assumption that we should defer to Scripture. I think Scripture—like God in the Book of Job—is strong enough, powerful enough, and robust enough to take our questions, to take our confrontation, and then to take us further into the journey that God has for us.

With all that in mind, I take this panel to be an invitation to explore some of the ways the Bible has been exploited to justify the occupation of Palestine to the benefit of some people and the simultaneous detriment of others, rather than serving—as I think it *could* and *should*—as a prophetic text that might challenge both the occupiers and the dispossessed.

This gets me thinking about the significance of the location and agenda of the reader when using Scripture in the context of occupation. Clearly a Jewish settler would read the Bible differently than a displaced Palestinian, and neither would read the Bible from the same perspective as me. I am a white, male, Anglican, academic, priest. And a colonialist, or at least a descendant of colonialists. And someone who benefits from the dislocation and displacement of the indigenous peoples of my own country.

There are other variables as well, including those between someone like myself, who reads the Bible from a consciously critical and humanistic perspective, and others who may read the same Bible from different perspectives, some of which we heard in the panel on Biblical Authority. My experience has been that beginning with different perspectives does not prevent us from discovering common ground and hearing common wisdom.

I invite us to think about how the Bible's three different "worlds" are captured in this occupation of the Bible, these worlds being the *world behind the text* (the historical realities that we presume to be behind the text, how we imagine the ancient past), the *world within the text* (the stories, the context of the Bible as it is), and the *world in front of the text* (those places in which we exist as we engage with Scripture).

The World behind the Text

I think of the historical dynamics of ancient Palestine that witnessed the emergence of ancient Israel and Judah and, at some point in that process, the suppression of non-Yahwistic Canaanite communities with their rich cultural fabric. As an academic and as a follower of Jesus, I find myself wondering how many of those ghastly stories of ethnic cleansing and religious violence reflect events that actually happened. To what extent do they represent the imagination of later religious scribes—the Taliban of ancient Jerusalem—who were expressing how they felt about their experience of marginalization and their threatened fragile existence, and found comfort in fantasies about total conquest, excluding the other, ethnic cleansing, and the belief that God gave this land to no one but me and my own kind?

So there is a whole set of issues regarding claims made and assumptions embraced in terms of the historical veracity of the biblical narrative. You might have already picked up, in case I have not made it clear enough, that I am actually a minimalist and I think there is very little historical value to the biblical narratives. (So get the tar and feathers ready!)

The World within the Text

The second world is the world within the text. This is the story world that Naim and I both find in Luke 4. Whether or not there was a synagogue in Nazareth for Jesus to attend during the first three decades of the first century, and whether or not Jesus was literate are beside the point. These are narratives by first and second century Christians, and the sermon created for Jesus by Luke now serves as a sacred text that calls us to faithfulness.

Whether we think of the Old Testament or the apocalyptic fantasies of the New Testament, the ethnic violence of the Bible, real or imagined, inscribes and reinforces patterns of fear, suspicion, and violence that are presumed to have divine legitimacy. The Bible drips with blood, whether that be the blood of Jesus (whose death is often understood in Christian tradition as expiating an angry, potentially violent, and dangerous God), the blood of the little ones who are crushed by empire, or the blood of those whose religion is different from ours and are thus doomed to destruction by our God. The Book of Revelation is certainly a classic text in that respect.

The World in front of the Text

Then, of course, there is the world in front of the text. This is the world in which we live, the world in which we attempt to shape lives that are holy and true.

Looking at the text from where I stand and from among the communities to which I belong, I discover that I am in an ambiguous space. I belong to a religion that has incarcerated, tortured, and killed its opponents, whether they be internal dissidents or external infidels. My religious community has drunk deeply from the well of violence. I am a citizen of a nation that has dispossessed and literally hunted down the indigenous community. I benefit from an economic system that continues to use violence to sustain itself.

So neither the text nor this reader of the text is innocent. Yet all the same, both are open to be used by God and to serve God's purposes of justice and peace. The occupation of the Bible can come to an end, just as the Bible can encourage us to resist the occupation of Palestine until it also comes to an end.

THE OCCUPATION OF THE BIBLE

Yohanna Katanacho[3]

One bad biblical interpreter could be more dangerous than one hundred terrorists. We have an Arabic proverb that says one foolish person drops a stone in a well and one hundred wise people cannot get it out. It is easier to destroy or to confuse than to build or clarify, and this is exactly our experience as Palestinian followers of Jesus. We continually encounter dangerously bad interpreters who spread death instead of life. These interpreters have thrown the Bible into a deep well of confusion, and we hope that the wise people of our generation can rescue the Bible from interpretations that produce death. Elsewhere I have argued that, among Palestinians, we have at least four different approaches: liberation theologies, reconciliation theologies, narrative theologies, and an apologetic reading of the Bible.[4] I would also add the Kairos reading of the Bible. I hope to point out a few major hermeneutical approaches, including the hermeneutics of the Kairos document, and a few implications for reading the Bible in the Palestinian-Israeli context.

Historical Critical Approach

In "Historical-Critical Approaches," John Barton explains that many interpreters read the Bible with the following genetic

---

3 The essay is based on a published paper. Yohanna Katanacho, "Approaches to the Bible." *Al-Liqa' Journal* 37(2011): 36-41. I have modified it and added few additional items.

4 Yohanna Katanacho, "Palestinian Protestant Theological Responses to a World Marked by Violence." *Missiology: An International Review* 36(2008): 289-305.

questions:[5] when and by whom were the books written? What was the intended readership? The interpreters look for the original meaning. They try to reconstruct the history with a hermeneutic of suspicion. Moreover, they distinguish between what really happened and what the authors want readers to believe. These interpreters also affirm that the best reading strategy is to have a neutral, objective, disinterested reader.

Many of the genetic questions are related to identity: who is the "true" Israel? Should we adopt a maximalist point of view of biblical history and believe in the historicity of Abraham, Moses, David, Joshua, and others? Should we accept that the biblical events are actual historical events? Other interpreters prefer a minimalist perception of biblical history and point out that many biblical stories are simply ideological, political, literary, or mythological depictions. Many Israeli archeologists strive to establish a particular reading of biblical history in order to gain political advantage. Names of modern places are changed to ancient biblical names. Such reading strategies put the Palestinian Church at a disadvantage, as the community is often perceived as the biblical Canaanites or Philistines. Some Palestinians are tempted to engage this history game, and they argue that they were in the land before the ancient Children of Israel, as if an ancient historical presence is the basis for contemporary human rights, including the right to own your home, inherited from a grandfather or grandmother.

Social Scientific Approach

In continuity with the historical critical method, several scholars wanted to reconstruct the pre-textual social world in order to understand and interpret the Bible properly. They emphasized the importance of sociology and anthropology, greatly enriching our understanding of the text. However, many scholars in this school focused on Israel and its social world, overlooking other inhabitants of the land. The social world was constructed through

5 John Barton, "Historical-Critical Approaches," in *Biblical Interpretation* (ed. John Barton; Cambridge: Cambridge University Press, 1998), 9–20.

the eyes of the privileged community, and the marginalized nations in the land were overlooked or considered ethnically and religiously inferior. Such depictions created a social conceptual grid that encouraged segregation and ethnocentricity. The current State of Israel continues to suffer from the latter. Admittedly, social scientific approaches are not the reason for Israel's ethnocentric perception, but these approaches facilitated the acceptance of such beliefs.

Literary Reading
After failing to reconstruct the pre-textual reality, several scholars rightly moved into focusing on the text itself. New approaches appeared, questioning the relationship between different texts, i.e. intertextuality. Several Israeli and Palestinian scholars highlighted the different literary dimensions of parts of the Bible. This literary approach freed readers from the concerns of the absent author(s) or redactors. The synchronic study dominated the diachronic one. Then the interest in the readers and their concerns escalated, which paved the way for post-structuralist and postmodern readings. One of the important consequences for the Israeli-Palestinian context is a political reading of the Bible.

Political Reading
The literary reading led many scholars to question the ideology embedded in particular texts. The feminist scholar Phyllis Trible, for example, says that "in the interaction of text and reader, the changing of the second component alters the meaning and power of the first."[6] The time was ripe to challenge not only an historical critical reading of the text, but also a pietistic reading rooted in separating the church from the state, claiming they have two different spheres of responsibility and that the only goal of reading the Bible is to develop a personal relationship with God or worship God in our small communities. In short, some decided

---

6 Phyllis Trible, "Treasures Old and New: Biblical Theology and the Challenge of Feminism," in *The Open Text: New Directions for Biblical Studies?* (edited by Francis Watson; London: SCM, 1993), 48–49.

to expose the violence of power and authority by deconstructing false assumptions and worldviews. Others wanted to consider the response of a community in the Bible and extrapolate its correspondences for a contemporary community in a similar political situation. The main goal is not to interpret the Bible, but to interpret life with the help of the Bible.

The Kairos Reading of the Bible

It is fitting now to argue that the Palestinian Kairos document develops this political reading of the Bible into an ecumenical post-liberal theo-political reading.[7] It is obvious that the Kairos document is interested in the contemporary reality. It begins by describing the current painful reality of the Palestinians and even alludes to anti-Palestinianism, which is not a private prejudice but an ideological, political, and theological issue. The description of the contemporary reality is done in biblical categories, neither in a naïve exegesis which abuses the text nor in a modern exegesis which defers the interests of the reader in the name of finding authorial intention. Rather the document engages in a healthy dialogue between the contemporary reality and the biblical reality, and this dialogue transforms the biblical reality into a contemporary one. The Kairos document unapologetically presents a theocentric reality rooted in God, the Creator of all, and in our savior Jesus Christ, who was born in Bethlehem, lived in Palestine, died on the cross in Jerusalem, rose from the dead, and ascended to the right hand of God.

Unlike propositionalism, the Kairos document does not seek to discover what is right and what is wrong. Instead, it depicts our story in which we pursue biblical love and justice. In propositionalism, I come to the Bible to discover what is right and what is wrong. I come to coin a statement that reflects God's mind. Propositionalism does not allow for grey areas, for paradoxes, for living in a maze, or for divine puzzles or surprises. It does not favor polyphonies or inner biblical discussions or

---

7 For further details, see Yohanna Katanacho, *The Land of Christ: A Palestinian Cry!* (Bethlehem: Bethlehem Bible College, 2012), 89–92.

diverse perspectives. It deals with truth in a deadly synchronic pattern that produces death instead of life. Truth is expressed only in propositions, sacrificing or deconstructing the truth of promises, of questions, of myth, and of poetry. It favors truth in black and white, while God's brush is full of colors. Further, the text becomes the powerless oppressed, and God is imprisoned in human logic. The reader becomes God and repeats the sin of Adam. The reader believes the lies of Satan, trying to ascribe to things only two categories: right or wrong. There are no surprises, no adventures, no mysteries, no contemporary miracles; for God is dead and buried in our human categories. There is no romance and no love in propositionalism. Theology becomes a science without art or feeling. The big picture crushes the details in the name of totalizing propositions into a coherent picture.

Unlike the merciless propositionalism, the Kairos document presents the story of a suffering people who insist on loving their enemies without ignoring justice and righteousness. This hermeneutic is neither microscopic, like several historical critical approaches, nor macroscopic, like some academic biblical theologies which show no concern for contemporary realities. Instead, it is stethoscopic, seeking to hear the heartbeats of God embodied in our Palestinian reality. Its propositions are part of God's heartbeats and an aspect of a holistic reality which seeks God's love and righteousness in the midst of a fallen world.

Conclusion

We Palestinians have a Bible and we want to read it. We also have a different pre-understanding and cannot be neutral or objective; at best, we hope to be fair. Consequently, we must nourish and celebrate our diversity, advocating a theology of humility and willingness to listen to each other. We need to present a religious understanding that is not void of mercy, love, or justice. Otherwise, we merely present idols. Hermeneutics cannot be a mere epistemological approach, rather, it is ontological in nature. Interpreting a "sacred text" should lead us not only to a dialogue with the text but also with God who can transform us.

As a Christian, the reader must conform to the image of Christ who expressed God's love even to God's enemies. Love is not an excuse to abandon justice. It is an opportunity to pursue it. The best interpreters are the ones who love. Knowledge without love is arrogance, but with love it is wisdom.

THE OCCUPATION OF THE BIBLE

Nancy Cardoso Pereira

Coming from reading the Bible from a Latin American perspective, I feel at home with Palestinian liberation theology. We are brothers and sisters. We have a common history. The Bible in Latin America is a lot of things at the same time. As a book of a religion, historically imposed, the Bible is part of the Latin American religious polyphony, so conflictive and full of ambiguities. Thus the Bible is everywhere, is all around, important and unimportant, always present. The simplest use might be a common sense slogan of a teacher or a slogan on a car, on the door of a house, the name of a store, in conservative political discourse, in hip-hop made by youth from the periphery, as well as in churches, theological institutions, and academic research done in universities. The challenge for us is how to transform a text imposed by the colonial project into a received text, which is not an easy task. The polyphony of the Biblical text in Brazilian culture is about these different ways to live with or without the Bible.

Let me share some of our learning about why we can say we understand occupation. In the 1960s, liberation theology addressed the problem of a continent exhausted by poverty and oppression. The way liberation theology in Latin America did this was through a network of local communities and pastoral organizations, and it soon became something much more than a church issue. It is about praxis, an intellectual and spiritual expression of a vast social movement, in a complex network of peasants, workers, indigenous people, marginalized people, youth from the periphery, grassroots ecclesiastical communities, and justice and peace commissions. And when I talk about a grassroots reading of the Bible, I'm talking about *these* people reading the Bible. It's not just about a church program. And it *is* about a preferential option for the poor.

From this grassroots perspective, the upsurge of popular revolutions helps us understand the recent history of Latin America. Nicaragua, El Salvador, the struggle for socialism in Chile, the emergence of new worker and peasant movements in Brazil, or the Zapatista uprising in Chiapas in Mexico—in all these experiences, we were brutally interrupted. Any attempt at self-determination of the majorities, poor, and oppressed was fought and destroyed by North American imperialism, with the active participation of Israel in the form of mercenaries, paramilitary training, and arms supply. And as in the case of popular revolution in Mexico and Central America, or the socialist electoral process in South America, or the brave resistance of the Cuba revolution, it doesn't matter; we cannot try. There is no space for us, for *trying*. Many Latin Americans and also Christians, whether clerics or laypeople, paid with their lives for their involvement in the resistance to authoritarian regimes in Latin America, denouncing the torture of martyrs and human rights violations.

Through it all, we feel so close to the situation of the Palestinian people. Yes, we know what occupation is. And if we think about the disgraceful fence on the border of Mexico, and the thousands of deaths every year, we and the Palestinian people are comrades in the search for liberation. In this sense we have a lot to learn from you, the Palestinians.

Land and Bible need struggle. Controlled by a few for so long, land and Bible are the private property of the one who can attest legitimacy given by grace and used for profit. That is what liberation is about: breaking the bourgeois control of land and Bible, confronting power structures with concrete counter-reading. Two major confrontations are needed here. With the fundamentalist occupation of the Bible (we have this in Brazil) and with a postmodern dis-occupation of the Bible, with concrete implications for the people's land struggle in Brazil, in Colombia, in India, in the Philippines, in Mexico, in Palestine.

The first problem, fundamentalism. What is fundamentalism? Fundamentalism is the suspension of the right to decide. Believing in original truth paralyzed the vertigo[8] of interpretation. Interpretation is about vertigo, being surprised. If there are fundamental truths, people expect to observe, memorize, repeat, fulfill, keep, obey, study. This suspension of interpretation is actually the result of an intense interpretative effort that idealizes a sacred past in the form of the text, in the form of authority, in the form of the revealed. Sufficient by itself, in itself, fundamentalism is a politic of no body against a body despite the body, but in the end is one of the most powerful politics for body control. Fundamentalism is a reading of no materialities[9] so it's spiritual. It's a politic of spiritual truth expressed as no land against a land despite a land, but in the end is the most powerful politic of private property of land, denying any attempt or struggle for land as rebellion against God's property, paralyzing the land struggle in Palestine, in the name of the verse in the Bible where God gave the land to Israel. It's to paralyze any struggle for land, paralyzing you here in Palestine and us in Brazil as well. It is the same mechanism. That's why it's so important to confront and overcome the power of Zionist ideology in the occupation of land and Bible.

The second problem is the claim of the postmodern narratives of the globalized world for a growing process of deterritorialization as full comprehension of space-time. It is the eradication of distance and borders. Good-bye, great narratives, good-bye borders; let's be postmodern. It would be the end of history and the end of territory. The planet as a territory for anyone and without borders is at the mercy of the big corporations and interests of states in dispute over access and control of resources. The myth of deterritorialization is thus a strategy of territorial control. These readings, these postmodern readings, can repress and are repressing any attempt by liberationists in terms of the struggle for land sovereignty around the world. Presented as eccentricities

8 Dizziness, qualm, vertigo
9 Matter, substance, materiality, materialities

67

of our old world, a prima donna reaction of backward sectors, here comes the postmodern global village.

Also in theology, in biblical exegesis, we can feel this pressure of the postmodern in the avoidance of issues of territorial dispute, in the weakening of interpretive models that keep the geographical eco-materialities perspective. Postmodernists are avoiding the important and central contents of the structure of the biblical narratives. The Bible is talking about eco-materialities. It's about territory. It's about geography.

The whole discussion on the theoretical borders of the conquest of the land, and the origins of biblical Israel, are under pressure by this postmodern perspective; postmodernists reduced the possibilities of archaeological and literary models. The theology that comes from these postmodernists is the justification of private property, providing a theological basis for the concentration of land, environmental devastation, and military and technological violence by which the system enforces its power. Saying so, or just saying nothing, can be about being passive or active—it doesn't matter. At the end it is a lazy and self-silent theology and exegesis that is not able to let the cry of the world, peoples, and nature be part of the production of knowledge.

The theology of liberation doesn't *explain*—we have nothing to explain. We are here to *un*explain. With no descriptive character, liberation theology is not meant to establish causal connections between this and that, God and the world. The theology of liberation is meant to delay clocks. It attacks permanence and constancy mechanisms, and uninstalls the uninterrupted tick-tock-tick-tock of time. It participates in the creation of the current time, the "kairos," the exact moment where it is possible to intervene, to alter, to destroy, to transform. This is what a Latin American, grassroots reading of the Bible has to offer.

THE BIBLE AND THE OCCUPATION OF PALESTINE

Joakim Wohlfeil

Thank you for the opportunity to share something with you, and I will try to address the issue of the Bible and the occupation, because of my background as a Christian, from a very personal perspective.

However, I would like to bring you back to Stockholm to start my story. At my work at the Swedish NGO Diakonia, I often have to handle telephone calls whenever we say something about the Israeli-Palestinian conflict, when we speak about international law, or when we speak about the situation of the Palestinians. We will often have someone calling us and telling us "how it should be," "what is the truth." And especially since we are an organization that is owned by churches, those telephone calls and letters often have a very religious expression. So I have learned that when my colleagues come with their phones two feet from their ear to protect their ears from somebody screaming in the phone, I know, well, that's probably for me.

One of these calls started with an angry voice presenting himself as representing one of these Christian organizations, saying its task is to advocate for the State of Israel: "Are you real Christians at Diakonia?" And I said, "Well, we are a Christian organization but you don't have to be a Christian to work here. But I'm a Christian."

"Oh, so you are a Christian believer! Do you believe in the Bible?"

"Yes," I said, "I am a Christian. I am a personal Christian. I have been baptized. I believe in the Bible."

"Do you believe in the Word of God and the prophesies?"

"Yes," I said, "I am also a convinced Christian; I believe in the Bible, I believe in the Word of God."

"But then you must put your hope in Israel!"

"Well, no, I'm sorry. I'm a Christian so I put my hope in my savior, Jesus Christ, Lord."

". . . Clearly you seem to be impossible to talk to."

And this brings up, actually, a dilemma that has followed me a lot in my life, even in my own family. For big family gatherings, we don't even have a peace agreement yet. We have a kind of truce—you know this is called a "terror balance." You have a nice family gathering, but if you mention the words *Middle East*, it will turn into turmoil and both sides will be hurt. So I know how to handle these situations and also some of my relatives. But this is so interesting: how do you, as a Christian, explain those ideas that, I would say, clearly are not biblical, but they are still mentioned as a clear part of the Christian faith?

As a young and quite radical Christian, I took part in a lot of campaigns. We were singing and we were preaching in churches but also in the streets, in open spaces, and we spent a lot of time in our "evangelization" teams studying the Bible with our pastors. And in all situations, when there was a question, I remember that the pastor would say, "Go back and study the Bible."

There was one exception, though, because as soon as you brought up the occupation, that was something that had to be *explained*: "You shouldn't read this by yourself." I remember, in other situations, good pastors saying, "Well, as young Christians, it's maybe not a good idea to go by yourself to the Holy Land and meet Palestinian Christians. You know, it's so easy to get confused."

How can you have this attitude in a religion where the general saying is "Study the scripture," and the second saying is "How do you teach?" Even with the evangelists in the Bible, like Luke when he's trying to write about something, he says, "I need to go and look for myself." Or Thomas the Apostle. How can you make knowledge void in a religion where the general, normal ways of teaching are "read the Bible" and "go and see for yourself"?

This might be a little offensive to say, but I've also learned in other experiences that those Christians who very clearly are taking a stand "pro-occupation" because of their belief are very keen on saying, "We read the whole Bible." But I must say that I live near a lot of them, and for some part of my life I was also part of this belief until I realized that I couldn't justify it from reading the Bible. I would say that the people who claim this are not very interested in discussing the Bible as soon as you get beyond five or six phrases that all of them know. Then it seems that the interest in the Bible is over. And I think this is the problem: how can you justify something that is God-less, like occupation, from the book of God? How can you justify killing from a book that says, "Do not kill"? How can you justify stealing in a book that says, "Thou shalt not steal"? And how can you justify cruelty in a book where Jesus himself says that you should treat others as you would like to be treated? Why do we have a teaching in our churches that tries to justify the occupation from the Bible?

I'm trying to understand it myself, but I would say this comes from the way that Christianity, just like other religions, has throughout its existence tried to face its political, intellectual, and moral challenges. For example, the way political powers claim their legality from the Bible. Or it could be the battle between religion and science. Especially problematic is the question of religious relevance, or religious legality, because when you read the Christian Bible or study the history, it is not easy to justify naturalism, natural states, or the establishment of specific states or ethnic groups. If you go to what is considered by many Christians to be the most important question—"What is the mission for you as a Christian?" from the first chapter of Acts—it's actually a very *global* mission, not at all focusing on nation-states. The mission is global but the message is individual. It's very hard to combine this with trying to justify or give a legacy of political power from the Bible.

It's especially interesting if you study the Christian history and the heretics. The heretics, we'd say, were those who were less academic, those whom we Christians burned at the stake in the medieval ages. If you study this, most of the people who were punished as heretics in Christian history did not deny God or the Bible. Though there were exceptions, many "heretics" were actually trying to bring Christianity back to its roots, saying that political power, the king, is not legalized by the Bible itself, the church's worldly power is not endowed by the Bible.

But I think this is a sign of the incompatibility of how you'd like things to be and how they actually are. The same thing occurs when you consider how you treat the challenges of signs, like in the beginning of the nineteenth century when Christians had to cope with the upcoming natural sciences which didn't really mesh with what they read in the Bible. And Christians actually tried to combine the Bible with other nonreligious teachings; this is the beginning of what was called "liberal theology."

I can understand my parents' generation when they, as Christians, would try to analyze what happened after the Second World War, or followed the news from the Middle East, or when they learned that the State of Israel was being created; you of course try to give these events religious meaning. But what is also fascinating to me is that it's difficult, once you have made up an idea by yourself, to climb down from that pole you ascended. When as a teenager I heard ministers say, for example, "Look at Israel; it's the fifth Gospel," all the warning bells should have been ringing loudly. But they weren't because it was a situation where there was incompatibility between how you would like life to be and what the Bible really says. And it's hard to challenge this.

I would like to conclude with a story that I think illustrates this well. Without saying names, there is a person who is very involved in the Christian Zionist movement in Sweden, and is very good friends with my family; we also have this "terror balance" where we try not to challenge each other too much. But whenever she comes back from a trip, she preaches very enthusiastically about what she has seen and God's prophesies coming to life, and she doesn't want to speak about anything else, natural law, etc.

I try to counter this in a nice way, so I say, "Oh, how nice that you've been to the Holy Land. Have you been to any churches?"

As you know, as Christians it's never wrong to ask another Christian if you've been to a church. Of course, this is a little bit mean because I know that if you go to the churches in the Holy Land you will have to answer the question, "Who are the local Christians?"—a painful question. And on one occasion it was even so painful that this woman looked at me and said, "I know, Joakim, that there are a lot of Christians who are Arab, and they have been living there for ages. But you know, my life gets so complicated when I think about it."

This is, of course, not the full answer, but is a very personal angle of how I have experienced the Bible and the occupation, coming from the "inside" and trying to handle these situations. I still think we have the duty to do the moral thing, the legal thing, but also keep up the theological challenge; don't give in when the Bible is brought up as an argument for an occupation.

THE BIBLE AND THE OCCUPATION OF PALESTINE

Deborah Weissman

We mentioned in an earlier panel two things that happened 25 years ago. First of all, we're marking 25 years of Palestinian liberation theology, and my colleague and friend Dr. Yohanna Katanacho talked about his own transforming experience 25 years ago when he became a believing Christian.

So I'd like to mention something else that happened 25 years ago, when I first met Jean Zaru; it was at a World Council of Churches event. (By the way, I think I hold the record for being the Jew who most often attends WCC activities. I just came back from Busan, South Korea, for the WCC Assembly.) Jean and I were on a panel in Toronto at a very special conference that, for me, was a very transformative experience. It really changed my life and moved me in a direction of interreligious dialogue. It was a gathering of women from all over the world, from nine different religions, to talk about religion, politics, and feminism, and we were on a panel about the Middle East. Twenty-five years ago I called for an end to the occupation, and at the time I said that for me a symbol of peace would be when the Hebrew University and Birzeit University would cosponsor a seminar on what really happened here in 1948.

But, I added, for the time being let's not dwell on the past, let's look to the future: we want a better future for our children and grandchildren. What can we do to bring about a better future? And certainly one of the most important things is to end the occupation. I could say the same thing now, except that one of my Jewish colleagues at that conference said, "Don't forget history." I don't think I was forgetting history, but I think that the achievement of peace will involve maybe not recognition or acceptance, but at least an acknowledgement of our different narratives.

I'm going to talk a little bit about our narrative, and again I want to tell you something I said 25 years ago, and I still maintain it: I'm not only a Jew and an Israeli, I'm also an Orthodox Jew and a Zionist. And I believe that Zionism will not be fulfilled until there is a Palestinian state alongside the State of Israel. And I would like to point out there are many types of Zionism. Martin Buber[10], for example, was a Zionist, and I hope that I'm following somehow in his footsteps, and in the footsteps of many other great Zionists who were also humanists or liberals. And whether they were Orthodox or non-Orthodox, they had a kind of spiritual approach to Judaism.

Now, I want to direct your attention to two documents, if you're not already familiar with them. They're on the website of the International Council of Christians and Jews.[11] You can go on this website and look up "Berlin Document: A time for recommitment," and even more specifically, our document about Israel/Palestine that we just issued a few months ago. We took the title from a quotation from Bishop Munib Younan, who is the Lutheran bishop in this region and head of the Lutheran World Federation. Bishop Munib gave us permission to use the quotation as the motto for our document, and it is, "As long as you believe in a living God, you must have hope." And we try in that document to present a nuanced approach.

The reality here is very complex; it's not simple, and I very much resonate with what Father David Neuhaus said about trying to resist the temptation of turning it into a Hollywood film where there are the "good guys" and the "bad guys." I don't see it that way. I think that we need to look at the full picture, which is a much more complex picture.

---

10 Martin Buber (1878-1965) was a Jewish philosopher who wrote about human existence and dialogue.
11 www.iccj.org

Now I want to say something about the Bible. The Bible is a polyphonic book, meaning it has many voices. And I'm only talking about part of the Bible; again Yohanna gave us a very comprehensive definition of Old Testament, New Testament, *Tanakh*, etc. I'm talking about what we call the *Tanakh*, the Hebrew Scriptures. It's a very diverse book that has many points of view, and Jews have never been monolithic in our interpretation. And I would have to say that today as well, some of the political issues within the Jewish community are a reflection of hermeneutical questions: how we interpret our scripture. Someone mentioned the Talmud, but the Talmud is not the Bible, it's a rabbinic compendium. While it is a holy book, it's not considered the word of God. In the Bible, we say: "And the Lord said (such and such)"; in the Talmud: "Rabbi Akiva said—" and "Hillel said—" and "Rabban Gamaliel said—". Human beings involved in a conversation.

Jews today are also involved in a conversation about what our scripture means to us. And I'd like to say that the borders of the land of Israel are given many times in the Bible and they're never the same. So apparently it's not the borders that are holy; there's something about the land that is holy. And we can go into that: why, and how, and what that means. What does "holy land" mean? Maybe it's a land in which people relate to other people in a holy way. But the borders are not holy.

I would maintain that the Bible establishes the initial link between the Jewish people and the land; first we were Hebrews, then Israelites, and later on we became Jews—that's our initial link with the land of Israel. It's not a claim; it's not giving us a right. It's a connection. And the tragedy, of course, is that we have two peoples who represent three religions who have connections to what is largely the same land. And because I respect the Jewish connection, I also respect the Palestinian connection. And what we have to do is figure out a way to share that land.

The Bible talks not only about the land; the Bible talks also about justice. So if I'm going to be a Jew faithful to my biblical heritage, I'm going to try to strive for justice and peace. And I want to conclude with a reference to a work by a contemporary rabbi and commentator whom some of you may know, Rabbi Arthur Waskow of the United States, who is not an Orthodox Jew by any means; he's a religious and political radical who has worked closely with Christians and Muslims. Together with his wife, Rabbi Phyllis Berman, he published a book not long ago called *Freedom Journeys: The Tale of Exodus and Wilderness across Millennia*. There he offers a kind of modern *midrash* (commentary) on an important scene in the book of Joshua. In Joshua 5:13-14, having crossed the Jordan River, Joshua meets a man who has his sword drawn. Joshua asks, "Are you for us, or for our enemies?" The figure, according to Waskow's reading, first replies, "No." And if you have a Hebrew Bible, you will in fact see that the first word is *lo* [Hebrew for 'no']. The Waskow-Berman commentary states, "We hear it to mean, 'I am not here to support either one of you in your war against each other. Nor do I support the conflict itself.'"

Today both the Israelis and the Palestinians see themselves as the victims of the conflict. They seem to be competitors in what I call a "suffering sweepstakes." One of the problems with victimhood is it prevents the victim from assuming responsibility for his or her actions, including the victimization of others. In the Israeli-Palestinian conflict, I believe that both sides are victims and both sides are victimizers. I really think that the least helpful thing people can do, and regrettably many well-meaning people do this, is portray the situation in terms of a zero-sum game, in which if you're pro-Palestinian you must be anti-Israeli, and vice versa. I believe we must be both pro-Palestinian and pro-Israeli because we're pro-people and therefore pro-peace.

THE BIBLE AND THE OCCUPATION OF PALESTINE

Jean Zaru

As I have struggled on my journey to affirm the presence of 12 million Arab Christians in the Middle East and a Palestinian people struggling for justice and freedom in (at least a part of) their homeland, new obstacles and pressures have revealed themselves. For most liberal Christians influenced by Holocaust theology and European history and guilt, I am not, as a Palestinian Christian, a part of their agenda. My very existence disturbs the balance. For fundamentalists, I am not among the chosen; rather I am one of the cursed. As a Palestinian, I stand in the way of the fulfilment of the prophecy of God as they see it. I cannot win, for it seems that I am not part of the theology of many of my brothers and sisters.

Yet my entire life has been affected and encompassed by biblical teachings and interpretations. As a Christian, a Palestinian, a woman, an Arab, and a Quaker, the teachings of Western churches have affected me personally, and my people collectively, in very specific ways.

The use and abuse of the Bible in reflecting on the legitimacy, policies, and conduct of the State of Israel is common, especially but by no means exclusively among conservative American Christians. They see a firm link between biblical and modern Israel. The history of condoning evil through biblical justification is, of course, a long one. Discrimination, oppression, and war have all been justified by references to biblical texts, in most cases taken out of context. In fact, David Ben-Gurion, the founder and first Prime Minister of Israel, called the Bible the "sacrosanct title deed to Palestine" for the Jewish people.

Moreover, an advertisement, paid for by a large group of church people, in the Chicago Tribune newspaper of July 1, 1946, reads: "Because the Jewish people are people of the prophecy, they are the people of the land, and we, knowing Him who made the promise, totally support the people and the land of Israel in her God-given, God-promised, God-ordained right to exist. Any person or group of nations opposed to this right isn't just fighting Israel, but God and time itself."

Alas, when according to so many we are resisting not only the occupation but also God, how can Palestinians claim compassion or justice, let alone rights? It is a worthwhile question to ponder.

Palestinians are traumatized by the daily violence of an armed military occupation which affects both their physical and mental health. And they see the ways in which the Israeli narrative dominates the international discourse on violence. News media outlets headline Palestinian violence and pay almost no attention to the violence—structural and otherwise—which Israel inflicts with impunity. Israeli violence? Clearly, it is not simply a response to Palestinian violence. It is a *policy*. It is a policy of systematic and direct violence that is intended to make life unliveable for Palestinians at all levels.

Chaim Weizmann, who was to become the first president of Israel, remarked long before the establishment of the State of Israel that Zionists would be judged on the way they treated the Arabs of Palestine. It was a wise prediction, but more than 65 years have passed and still the world has made little headway in understanding and nurturing peacemakers.

Why Should Everyone Be Concerned?

In North America and elsewhere, there is still very little awareness of the depth of the violence we Palestinians have suffered in terms of the denial of our rights and self-determination. Despite the courageous advocacy of growing numbers in the international community, and the justice-oriented statements of many Christian denominations, much misinformation remains. And, quite significantly, there is an absence of effective political will on the part of the international community to resolve the Israeli-Palestinian conflict, or even to view the resolution of the conflict as in the best interests of their nations. Yet the situation is becoming more urgent with each passing day.

There are several reasons why I believe everyone should be concerned with this conflict and work towards peace in the Middle East. It is an explosive issue. The Palestinian conflict is at the root of an explosive situation that could become a threat to world peace. It now affects the lives of millions of people in the Middle East; if it widens into regional conflict, it could affect the lives of tens of millions of people elsewhere.

It is an issue in which American and European governments are involved. Several governments, but especially the U.S. government, support Israel militarily, politically, and financially. Each individual has the right, if not the duty, to advocate that his or her government use its influence to promote a peace based on human rights and justice, a peace that ends the occupation, a peace that addresses the right of return and ensures security for all.

It is a major, long-term United Nations issue, and one that tests the credibility and effectiveness of the UN. The "Palestine question" has been on the UN agenda since 1947. Many resolutions have been adopted but not one implemented. Every individual has a responsibility, directly or indirectly, for the action or inaction of his or her own government with regards to the UN.

It is one of the most serious, chronic, human rights issues in the world, and it tests the seriousness of our commitment to human rights. All over the world people struggle for basic human rights, and the issue of basic human rights is central to the Palestinian struggle. If human rights are to mean anything anywhere, they should mean something in this context.

It is a religious issue, with implications for the integrity of people who are Jews, Christians, and Muslims alike. All three traditions stress the dignity of each human being, the justice and the judgment of God, and the importance of peacemaking. The inability of people of these faiths to make serious progress in resolving this issue stands as an indictment of us all.

In our struggle, some people have chosen to accommodate, comply, or manipulate. When we manipulate, we have the illusion of being in control. We can reap some rewards, but in doing so we are accepting the system's terms, its unspoken rules and values, including the often negative values it accords to us. Manipulation does not challenge the low value the system places on us as individuals and as people. When we manipulate the system of Israeli power, we cannot be ourselves, express our true feelings, or share our real perceptions: we mask ourselves. Manipulation may get us some of the system's rewards, but it neither liberates us as individuals nor transforms the structures of domination.

The alternative is to resist. Resistance challenges the system's values and categories. Resistance speaks its own truth to power, and shifts the ground of struggle to its own terrain. Resistance is often thought of as negative, however, resistance is the refusal to be neglected and disregarded. Today, Palestinians find themselves embedded in the structures that neglect and discard their humanity and human rights. Only acts of resistance can transform these structures. I, along with many others, have opted for the path of active nonviolent resistance. To resist is to be human, and yet nonviolent resistance is not easy. It requires constant hard work. Indeed, it is not easy to sustain the path of nonviolent resistance for years and years, over many issues. None of us can resist all the time, in every area of life. We must prioritize our struggles.

Affirmations

Of course, the history of condoning injustice in the name of the Bible or some other religious authority is a long one. But there is a much stronger counter-witness in the Bible and in our religious communities to the bedrock of justice. Justice is mutual and indivisible. Any lasting peace will have to bring forth true justice for all: Palestinians and Israelis, women and men, Christians, Jews, and Muslims. Peace is for everyone, not just for the powerful. We must deal with the present, but we must look to the future of our children and of all humanity. We must build with new materials, with non-combustible materials that will not produce yet more wars.

Power, when shared, is a relationship that enriches everyone. The great rift is not between various human beings and communities, for we all belong together; rather, the great rift is between care and carelessness, justice and injustice, mercy and mercilessness, compassion and indifference. What divides us is not difference but sin, oppression, and injustice. Difference does not destroy creation, rather our sins of allowing oppression and injustice to be perpetrated do.

To create a culture of life, we need more than psychology, spirituality, and community. We need economics, sustainable agriculture, and a politic of liberation capable of healing our world and restoring the earth to life.

THE LAND OF PROMISE

Yohanna Katanacho

The topic of my presentation is "Holy Space in the Gospel of John." I'm going to address how, as a Palestinian, I read the Gospel of John. I have been teaching the Gospel of John for almost 25 years and I'm still fascinated by it. Recently I presented a paper at the Society of Biblical Literature in which I argued that the Gospel of John presents a new world order. John deconstructs major elements of Pharisaic Judaism, presenting them in an Christological, conceptual grid. In the Book of Signs, John starts his first sign with transforming water into wine. It is interesting that water was used for cleansing, and it seems that all the water jars were filled with water, and then all the water was transformed into wine by the Christ who called himself the True Vine. That absence of the cleansing water raised questions about the possibility of cleansing; it paved the way for presenting a disappearing temple, and opened up an important discussion about spirituality and geography.

Before delving into the issue of holy geography in the Gospel of John, it is important to understand the Christo-centric worldview that John is presenting. In my opinion, John is rereading the Old Testament in light of the Christ event. He is restructuring the components of Pharisaic Judaism in relation to Jesus Christ. First, John opens his Gospel in a way that echoes the Book of Genesis and raises our hopes that God's fallen world will be redeemed. Second, unlike the synoptic Gospels, he presents the story of cleansing the temple from its abusers at the beginning of his Gospel. In chapters two and four, holy space is no longer an issue that is limited to Jerusalem or Samaria, for John's spirituality is associated with Christ as the temple and with worshiping God in spirit. Third, in chapter five, John also rereads holy time by insisting that God works on the Sabbath and that God's rest is associated with the work of Christ. Fourth, John rereads the history of Israel, especially the Exodus and the wilderness experience; he argues that the manna, the wilderness rock that produced water, and the pillar of fire which Ancient Israel experienced in the wilderness, must be reread in relation to Jesus Christ. Jesus is the Bread of Life (chapter six), the Source of Water (chapter seven), and the Light of the World (chapter eight). The language has been expanded to include the whole world. Fifth, John opens up the issue of belonging to Abraham, and argues that belonging to Abraham without believing in Jesus Christ is worthless (chapter eight). After leaving the wilderness, Ancient Israel entered the Holy Land. John presents a rereading of the wilderness in chapters six to eight, then he presents a struggle between the Church and the Synagogue in chapter nine. The man who was born blind is forced out of the synagogue and is now a follower of Jesus Christ. Jesus is the way to the Holy Land. John then presents a discussion of the Holy Land in light of a Christocentric worldview. The new world order reaches its climax in John 20.

I focus mainly on holy space, because it will take a lot of time to unpack the worldview about which John is speaking.

The Gospel of John places the cleansing of the temple right after the wedding at Cana in order to continue the theme of a new world order. John informs us that Jesus refers to himself as "the temple" (John 2:21). This statement becomes significant, not only in light of the context that presents new realities centered around Jesus Christ, but also in light of the tradition that associates cleansing the temple with entering into Jerusalem. Unlike the synoptic Gospels that put cleansing the temple at the end of the ministry of Jesus, John presents it between the wedding at Cana and meeting Nicodemus in order to highlight the new world order in which Christ replaces the temple. In chapter three, Jesus is pointing out to Nicodemus that the presence of the Spirit of God is not limited to a specific place (John 3:8). Consequently, the work of the Spirit of God might be everywhere, and those who are born of the Spirit might be everywhere.

The idea is extrapolated and expanded as Jesus is talking to the Samaritan woman. The temple of Jerusalem is no longer needed for worshiping the Father. Jews can no longer have monopoly over the true place of worship. True worshipers do not emphasize the *place* of worship, according to John, but the *nature* of worship. They cannot please God more when they pray on the Temple Mount, for true worship is defined by the true nature of God as revealed in Jesus Christ, not by the place of worship.

Indeed, John has already pointed out this divine reality in John 1:14, which states that Jesus became a tabernacle in our midst. The concept of connecting Jesus to the House of God is further seen in John 1:51, where we are reminded of the ladder of Jacob and the House of God, *Bet El*. Jesus is the true House of God and the true temple. This perception challenges both Judaism and Islam. It also challenges any perception that the Temple Mount, with or without the temple, is the place in which God is found or will be found in the future. In short, the humanity of Jesus is the space of reconciliation with God and human beings; divinity and humanity are fully reconciled in Jesus Christ. The House of God is a human being. God through Christ the temple is accessible to every human being who believes in Jesus Christ. There is no room for ethnic pride.

Now I want to focus on John 10, which I believe, from John's perspective, is actually the Holy Land. In John 10, the Good Pasture parable, Jesus declares that he is the Good Shepherd and the Door. The first expression, the Good Shepherd, is associated with a unique phrase related to going in and out and finding a pasture. It is possible to connect the Good Pasture to the Promised Land. This claim is more meaningful in light of the progression of the argument of the Book of John that we have just discussed.

The connection of John 10 to the Promised Land can also be seen in the similar expressions found in the Book of Numbers, which discusses the topic of entering into the Promised Land and points out that Ancient Israel needs a shepherd. Moses prays, saying, "May the Lord, the God of the spirits of all mankind, appoint a man over this community to go out and come in before them, one who will lead them out, and bring them in, so the Lord's people will not be like sheep without a shepherd" (Num. 27:16-17). The thematic and linguistic similarities suggest reading these texts together in a canonical context. It is interesting that both leaders, Jesus and Joshua, have the same name in Hebrew; Jesus is the New Testament Joshua, who will not kill the local inhabitants of Palestine but will destroy the wolf by offering himself as a sacrifice.

These declarations are discussed in the context of the Feast of Dedication (John 10:22, the only place in the Bible where this feast is mentioned) which highlights the Maccabean revolution and their militant desire to free holy space from their enemies. Jesus is not only interested in the land, but is also interested in the people of the land. Instead of killing the inhabitants of the land, he is willing to die in order to save them. Every human being in this land is a gift from God, whether they are Palestinians or Jews. The identity of Jesus as the savior of the world shapes his behavior toward all the inhabitants of the land. Our identity as light, salt, and yeast of love should also shape our behavior and perception of the land and its inhabitants.

The concept of the Holy Land in John 10 is also related to the concept of the Good Shepherd found throughout the Old Testament. One prominent place that contains several similarities with John 10 is Ezekiel 34. The flow of the text in Ezekiel is extremely important. The literary unit, which starts from Ezekiel 33:21 and ends in Ezekiel 37:28, opens with a clear discussion of Abraham and inheriting the Promised Land. Ezekiel talks about the bad shepherds of Israel, pointing out that God will bring a *new* David who will be the Good Shepherd (Ezekiel 34:23-24). The theme of the New David is also found at the end of the literary unit where we encountered the theme of one people and one shepherd. There will no longer be any division. David will be the one shepherd who will lead them into the Promised Land, according to Ezekiel 34:24-25. This time there will not be another exile. Obviously the book of Ezekiel is not talking about the historical David who died hundreds of years before the time of Ezekiel. Ezekiel is talking about a Davidic figure. This David will be the Good Shepherd, will unify the people of God, will lead them into the Promised Land, and will fulfill the Abrahamic promises. Simply put, Jesus claims that he is this Good Shepherd.

John is rethinking the theme of the Promised Land in a Christo-centric way; no one can truly enter this land without Christ as the door. Exile will not be over by ending geographical exile, but by following the Christ. Christ is not only the Door, he is also the Way. Unless he washes our feet, we cannot be on the way to life and we cannot find the door that leads to life.

Our perception of holy space and the Promised Land should not be divorced from a Christo-centric worldview. Any credible interpretation of the Old Testament must take into consideration the New Testament rereading of Pharisaic Judaism and its major components as they are represented in the Gospel of John. Our perception of the Holy Land needs to be influenced and perhaps redefined by a Christo-centric worldview. Perhaps John's rereading is the best way forward.

People say, "You are a Palestinian, so you are from the cursed Canaanites or Philistines, or whatever." I respond: For the sake of the argument, even though I disagree, even if I am a descendent of the Canaanites, can the cross of Jesus Christ break that curse on me? And my answer is yes. So this is what I present: John rereads the Old Testament to present a Christo-centric worldview. Christ is at the center of the land from John's perspective, as well as mine.

THE LAND OF PROMISE

Nancy Cardoso Pereira

The Holy Land is about tomatoes and potatoes and beans and rice. Holy Land is this holy process of dialogue among us, the sun, water, the seed, the land, and holy food. And we put the world in our mouth and this is holy.

From Palestinian liberation theology, I learned about the Book of Jonah and the critique of an exclusive theology of God, of the people of God, and of the land. The little Book of Jonah proposes prophesy, not as an exercise in confirmation of what we already know, but as an exercise of *otherness*. Prophesy is *the other*, other realities: the role of the foreign people, sailors, people of Nineveh, the whole of all nature, wind, sea, fish, animals, water, is presented as a place of prophesy. Prophetic evidence. It moves from being bounded by ethnocentric, anthropocentric fences to expanding for the inclusiveness of God, of the people of God, and land, holy land.

For us at the Land Pastoral Commission in Brazil, land is more than land. And don't be confused by the simultaneity of the Portuguese word *terra*. For us, *terra* is both "land" and "earth" in English. For instance, my "land" is Brazil, meaning my nation. And "land" is the name of our planet, the planet *Terra*. And "land" is also when we are cultivating, planting seeds. We have the same word for those three dynamics, and can therefore talk about the planet, nation, and agriculture together, all Holy. In the Latin American perspective, the *Pachamama*[12] is the simultaneity of cosmic and ordinary land, and we are living in this extraordinary, ordinary world.

---

12 Refers to the Incan goddess of fertility, planting, and harvesting; also commonly called *Mother Earth*.

That's all I aim for, that I can sow a seed that
will in turn sow a seed
that will sow a seed that...
and so it goes. That's enough.
Paul Myers

Land is a code, an information system. Land is living structures. Land is pathway and trajectory, full of antiquities and maps of the contemporary. Land is key for what we still don't know. Land is material and symbolic structure, organized in orchards, gardens, and plantations; it's a way of dialogue of human groups with nature, with hunger and human labor. Plantations are cultural forms of material and semantic organizations of social relations, and they belong to the body of the world.

Because of this, the occupation of Palestinian land is a tragedy, not only and especially because of the definitive way it hits at the capacity for survival of individuals and social groups, but also because it breaks the material and symbolic access to the vital aspects of life and belonging to the body of the world. The Israeli occupation separates people from land, creates a rupture, and can destroy the ability of Palestinians to solve their most fundamental issue: to live. It is not just the occupation of the land as a political territory, but it is the violent interruption of the living together with nature, in land and with land.

On these stolen lands, Israeli agribusiness is flourishing. Hi-tech capitalist profiteering mixed with colonial conquests exploits Palestinian natural resources and destroys its nature in order to grow genetically modified crops. Israel is ranked sixth in the world in terms of the amount of genetically modified crops it cultivates. Instead of attending to local and traditional agriculture, it engages in mass production and destroys the ecosystem of the West Bank and the hard and semi-arid climate of the Jordan Valley. The intensive agricultural development that the occupation works to implement is made possible only by hi-tech and genetically modified agroindustry. The Jordan River water resource has been drained by two enormous reservoirs. Natural springs have dried up as a result of the deep wells the occupation uses to feed its agribusiness and settlements. The Dead Sea, a unique geological and natural oasis, risks drying out because of the lack of water flowing in the form of the Jordan River. Along with this, the Palestinians are denied the right to bore wells. The occupation has taken the entire Palestinian share of the water, the resource of the Jordan River, and has transferred the water from major West Bank aquifers to meet the demands of Israel and its settlements.

When we talk about "Holy Land," we are talking about a political space. We can talk about a spiritual understanding of the Holy Land, but let's try to think about the real thing: the way that we are organizing our relationship with land, and water, and seed. And let's look for another relationship with land.

Someone asked me what my research into the Bible covered. I responded, "I'm studying pistachios. I'm a doctor in 'Pistache.'" I was never very interested in pistachios, and I actually don't like them, neither pistachio ice cream nor as an appetizer. I always looked at them as one of those unnecessary foods which one normally eats as a snack, until I was faced with Genesis 43 which presents pistachios as part of "the most precious fruit of this land." When asked about returning to Egypt during the famine, Israel responded to his sons, saying, "If it must be so, then do this: take some of the most precious of this land in your bags, and take them as a present to these men [Joseph]. A little honey, balm, and myrrh, pistachio nuts and almonds" (Gen. 43:11, NIV). The text presents an unequal and asymmetrical relationship between the agricultural products from Egypt and the ones from Jacob and his family land. While the production in Egypt is extremely centralized in the storehouses in the general form of grain cereal, the production of Jacob's family group might well be characterized as a collection and transformation of products of the land: balm, honey, resin, myrrh, pistachio, and nuts.

Besides those gifts, the group is also instructed to bring Benjamin, the youngest son, and silver to be used as a guarantee for access to the grain. The centralization of the grain in the imperial storehouse demonstrates the rivalry between the cereal production and the agricultural market as basic mechanisms supporting the empires. Under the control of the state, the grain takes on a monetary value and subordinates the other products of the land, despite its value of unquestionable use in the peasantry's survival, but also as luxury in the palaces as in the case of the pistachio. And the text says, "There was a famine in every land, but throughout the land of Egypt there was bread, and all the land came to Egypt to buy from Joseph because the famine became severe throughout the world." We have on one hand the grain in Egypt, and on the other we have "the most precious of the land." And the relation, the value, the production of value of those items, is so unfair and unequal, connected to money and human slavery. So my study of agriculture in the Bible leads me to think about those very concrete situations, not as a description of what happened, but to describe why people remember and write about those important mediations of being alive. What is the relationship between agriculture—seeds, land, farmers—and empire?

After the Book of Genesis came the Exodus and the promise of the Holy Land, and perhaps we are talking about a nation—"I will give you *terra*, I will give you land as a national border"— but perhaps the text is talking about having a relationship with nature and with land that is sustainable, autonomous, and based on stewardship. We understand the Exodus as a right to access land, a territory for a social-political organization, but also as land to work and land on which to live. In light of this, the Exodus social movement and spirituality becomes an expression of the peasantry way, a movement against the monopoly of the grain, against the forced labor, and an affirmation that the poor will inherit the land. The landless people who experience the Exodus come together with the poor peasantry in Canaan to liberate the land in order to liberate their *relationship* with the land. The

Exodus is the vital experience of the sacred being revealed to the poor, rescuing the land and its hungers, and claiming peace between the grain and the precious products of the land. In the Exodus God reveals God's self not to a nation or an ethnicity, nor to a generation and its geography; God reveals God's self in the struggle of the poor and in the reclaiming of the land and its fruit.

The Exodus is about land as a political territory, but the promise is also about the *access*, the right to establish a stable and creative relationship with land in order to produce life. Perhaps it's not about land in the "national" understanding, but instead about the peasantry way. And I'm so glad that in July 2013 Palestine became a member of the Via Campesina, the "peasantry way." The Via Campesina is the organization of peasants around the world, an international coming together of farmers and those who work the land. In the last assembly of the Via Campesina in Jakarta, we received Palestine as a full member, which is a concrete way to affirm the right for access to land in Palestine, and political autonomy as well, without the exploitation of agriculture, water resources, and so on. Viva La Via Campesina! Viva Palestina en la Via Campesina!

Thank you!

THE LAND OF PROMISE

Pietro Kaswalder

Canaan is the Land of the Promise to Abraham (Gen. 12: 6-7). That is the general and common expression used to present the theme: "Land of Promise." In fact, in very few cases does the Old Testament call the Land of Promise "the Land of Israel" (1 Chron. 22:2 [*eretz yisrael*]; Ez. 37:12 [*admat yisrael*]; possibly Zech. 2:16 [*admat haqqodesh*, the holy land]).

I ask you to take a trip into the history of this interesting biblical theme. In short terms: "From Canaan to the Holy Land," that is, from Gen. 12:6-7 to Zech. 2:16. The word *Canaan* is used many times in the Old Testament but only three times in the New Testament. The word points to the region situated west of the Mesopotamia and northeast of Egypt. We find the name *Canaan* in the inscriptions of the second century B.C.E.

In explaining the name *Canaan*, we see that the scholars have different opinions. I quote only two of them:
a) *Canaan* means simply "the West," the land where the sun has set or the land where the sun goes down. In this case, the name *Canaan* replaces the previous name *Amurru* (West), used in the Mesopotamian texts.
b) *Canaan* is the "land of the purple" (*kinahhu*, in the texts from Nuzi/YorganTepe); from here follows the name of Phoenicia, or Lebanon.

The first epigraphic evidence of the name *Canaan* is found in the inscription of King Idrimi of Alalakh (Tel Achtana, on the river Oronte, Syria, fifteenth century B.C.E.): "I fled to the Land of Kanaan." In the Egyptian historical records, we find the name *Canaan* together with other names, such as Rethenu, Khurru, and Horus; this is true especially for the Letters from El-Amarna, fourteenth century B.C.E.

It is evident that the biblical authors are referring to the Land of the Promise (the Promise to Abraham in Gen. 12:6-7), using the geographical and historical concept of Canaan, borrowed from the Egyptian history.

Here are some examples taken from the biblical texts:

- Num. 13:2: "Send the scouts to explore the Land of Canaan."
- Num. 34:2: "When you'll enter the Land of Canaan, this is the Land of your inheritance, the Land of Canaan."
- Josh. 1:2: "You'll pass over the River Jordan to enter and inherit the land." The Jordan River is the eastern border of the Land of Canaan, as we'll see later.

The Three Levels

In the overall complex of the geographical expressions of the OT, we can find three very different formulations; I prefer to call them levels. The first level: the extension of the Land of Israel based on historical experience, including the Kingdom of David and Solomon, before the division into the two separate kingdoms of Judah and Samaria. The second level: the borders of the biblical land of Canaan, with the concept of Canaan borrowed from the Egyptian experience. The third level: the land of idealistic and utopic extension, elaborated in the post-exilic period.

First Level: The Land of the Historical Israel

With the first level, I propose to talk about the historical experience of Israel in this land: How did it come to be? Through military conquest? Through peaceful occupation? Or nomadic infiltration? We don't know how it happened exactly, but something happened. This fact materialized during the twelfth through tenth centuries B.C.E. We find different formulas and different literary genres in which the biblical authors explain this fact:

- Formula of extension (*from-to*). One biblical formula is very simple and well known: *"From Dan to Beer Sheba"*

(1 Kings 5:4). This formula offers, in great simplicity, the reality of the Land of Israel. (Additional references: Judg. 20:1; 1 Sam. 3:20; 2 Sam. 3:10, 17:11, 24:2, 24:15, etc.)

- Literary narrative (2 Sam. 24:5-7 [the Davidic census])
- Administrative documents (Josh. 13-19 [the territory of the 12 tribes]; 1 Kings 4:7-19 [the Solomonic districts])

We can take for a starting point the text of 1 Kings 4:7-19, the so-called Solomonic districts. In fact, the text is clear: *Solomon has twelve governors over all Israel* (v. 7). The list covers the region under Solomonic administration. In complicated and sometimes difficult ways, the land under Solomonic administration corresponds to the Land of Israel. In fact, it is the historical Land of Israel. In the formula *"from Dan to Beer Sheba,"* we can recognize the united kingdom of David and Solomon before the division that happened after the death of King Solomon.

A second group of texts, the Geographic Document of Josh. 13-19, covers the region in which Israel lives (in geographical terms). The final redaction of this literary complex is made by a Priestly Redactor; we can say that this composition is not very ancient, perhaps from the seventh or late sixth century B.C.E. with special insertions and additions of later periods.

The geographic value of Josh. 13-19 deserves our attention, first because we find the tribes of Judah (Josh. 15) and the tribes of Efraim and Manasseh deriving from the House of Joseph (Josh. 16-17). Their geographical reality is presented in a complete manner: borders, list of cities, sub-regions, etc. Those tribes—Judah and the House of Joseph—made the history of biblical Israel; their regions are the hearts of the two historical kingdoms, the Kingdom of Judah and the Kingdom of Samaria. In different words, we can speak of Southern and Northern Kingdoms.

The other tribes are presented in very loose manner with no complete data. For them, we don't find borders, and in some cases the lists of the cities are incomplete. Take for example the tribe of Simeon (Josh. 19:1-9), the tribe of Dan (Josh. 19:40-48), and the half-tribe of Manasseh in Transjordan (Josh. 13:29-31). Josh. 13:8-32 presents the regions occupied by Israel in Transjordan, outside biblical Canaan: the regions of Mishor, Gilead, and Bashan. The land of the Transjordanian tribes is conquered by order of Moses, and doesn't belong to the Promised Land (Num. 21:21-35; Deut. 2-3).

With the late addition/insertion of Josh. 13:8-32, the final Priestly Redactor offers a picture of "all Israel" or "pan-Israel," something different from historical Israel. The complete picture found in Josh. 13-19 is the result of a combination of the "theology of the Land" of two different classes of Redactors: the Deuteronomistic Redactors and the Priestly Redactors. In fact the literary complex of Josh. 13-19 is inserted into the Deuteronomistic History, but the Priestly Authors add the concept of the sanctity of the Land (Josh. 13:1-7; Josh. 18:1-10). The Priestly Authors offer a different interpretation of the history of Israel: And prepare the way for the future of Israel, without the Land and outside the Land.

Second Level: The Land of Canaan as the Land of Promise

In the second level I suggest the reflection made by the biblical geographers over the historical experience of Israel. When the national identity is formulated, the geography offers a concept already done in the past: the Egyptian Canaan. The historical experience of Canaan ended years ago, but the idea of "Canaan as the Land of Promise" is kept alive.

The text in consideration is Num. 34:1-12; this pericope is the work of a Priestly Redactor. The time of Redaction for Num. 34:1-12 is the post-exilic period, as Ez. 47:15-20, a parallel text. We have sufficient evidence of the presence (power) of Egypt in the region of Canaan.

- El-Amarna Letters, fourteenth century B.C.E. The letter from a king of Babylon to Amenophys IV (Akenathon) deserves special attention: "*Canaan is your land, and their kings are your servants!*"
- The Meremptha Stele (or Israel Stele), thirteenth century B.C.E. Canaan is mentioned together with Israel: "*Canaan is deprived from his iniquity!*"

But as far as the Egyptian inscriptions are concerned, we encounter a big difficulty: the Egyptian records offer only limited evidence of the extension of the region called Canaan.

- In a list of Tuthmosis III (fifteenth century B.C.E.), we read: "*From Yursa to the end of the Land* (i.e. Damascus)." This text is interesting: Yursa is identified with Tell Jemmeh/Tel Gama, situated on the bank of the River Wadi 'Azzeh, or Nahal Besor, of 1 Sam. 30:9-10, 21. This is parallel to a text found in Num. 13:21: "*From the desert of Zin to Leboh Hamat.*"

- The list of cities conquered by Seti I, thirteenth century B.C.E., offers an interesting point of departure: "*Gaza is the city of Canaan.*"

- In Pap. Anas III, time of Ramses II, thirteenth century B.C.E., we read: "*From Sileh to* UPI" (Damascus, or Aram).

With the help of those records coming from Egypt, we are able to identify the southern border of the Land of Canaan: it is the city of Gaza. And to fix the northern border, that is the land of Aram. It means all Lebanon is included in the Egyptian *Canaan*.

The biblical authors and geographers present the borders of the biblical Canaan following the information coming from Egyptian history; in Num. 34:1-12 we read of the borders of the Promised Land starting from the South and ending with the East. To simplify the matter, the southern border starts at the Dead Sea, goes on to Ma'ale Aqrabbim, reaches Qadesh Barnea and the Brook of Egypt (v. 5), and ends at the Mediterranean Sea.

Following a long tradition initiated by the translation of the Old Testament into Greek (the Septuagint, LXX), and consolidated in post-biblical times (the Madaba Mosaic Map), the Brook of Egypt is identified as the Wadi el-Arish. But if we made a comparison between Num. 34:5 and Josh. 15:4, 47, where we again find the name *the Brook of Egypt*, we reach a different picture. For Josh 15:4 and 47, the border of the territory of the tribe of Judah is the Nahal Besor or Wadi 'Azzeh (1 Sam. 30:9, 10, 21).

In this explanation, I follow the Israeli scholar N. Na'aman of Tel Aviv University. Nahal Besor/Wadi 'Azzeh is the border of the arable land; in historical times, the Assyrian conquest toward Egypt added a lot of land reaching to the Wadi el-Arish. It is an expansion of about 85 kilometers of land.

On the northern border we find one name of great interest: Leboh Hamat, identified with Ein Libweh, in the Lebanese Beqaa' Valley. The eastern border is delineated from Mount Hermon to the Kinneret Lake, to the Dead Sea; that means that the Jordan River is the eastern border of biblical Canaan. In fact, following the Egyptian records, the Transjordan lands are not included in the kingdom of the Pharaohs. For that reason Israel has to pass the Jordan River in entering the Land of Canaan in Josh. 1:2.

Third Level: The Utopic Land of Israel

At the third level belong the biblical expressions in which an idealistic or utopic "Land of Israel" is presented. The most celebrated text is Gen 15:18: "*From the River of Egypt, to the great River, the Euphrates.*" Similar expressions are found in Ex. 23:31, Num. 22:5, Deut. 1:7, Deut. 11:24, and Josh. 1:4. This geographic formula reproduces the Assyrian province of "Beyond the River" (*abar nari*, King Asharradon, seventh century B.C.E.). Or later, the Fifth Satrapy of the Achemenid empire (Neh.2:7-9; Ezra 3:7, 4:10-20, 5:3,6, 6:6,13, 8:36). In those texts we read the equivalent in Hebrew or in Aramaic: *abar hannahar* and *abar naharah*, respectively.

In the biblical formula of Gen. 15:18, the River of Egypt (*nahar mizraym*) is obviously the River Nile. But this physical element has never been a border. It is different from the previous mentioned "Brook of Egypt", or *nahal mizraym*, an impressive border itself!

I quote the interpretation of a second Israeli scholar, Z. Kallai: Gen. 15:18 is a metaphor for the Promised Land, and was never realized in history.

Later Interpretations: The Post-Exilic "Land of Judah"

In the history of biblical Israel, there are two definite dates; in both cases, catastrophes are followed by the loss of the Land: the end of the Northern Kingdom (eighth century B.C.E.) and the end of the Kingdom of Judah (sixth century B.C.E.). It is true for the geography as for the theology of the Bible.

The above geographical expressions are concerned with the Land of Israel. In the post-exilic expressions, the concern shifts to the small province of Judah, called *YEHUD*. The time referred to is the Persian (or Achemenid) period. This province of Judah is confined to the territory around Jerusalem, from Jericho to Azeqa; from Mizpah (Bethel) to Beth Zur (Neh. 3:7-17), where the five districts are mentioned: Jerusalem, Beth Hakkerem, Mizpa, Beth Zur, and Qeila.

The Exile changes the data of the geographical problem. Israel in the post-exilic period doesn't think to occupy "all the Land of Israel" (Canaan), but limits itself to free the region of Judah. The dimensions of the "Land of Judah" are not comparable with the "Land of Israel" of the pre-exilic times. It is true that in the following periods, the Asmonean and the Herodian expansions reached the dimensions of a new Kingdom of Judah. But this is out of my present discussion.

During the post-exilic times, some new reflections are inserted into the oldest geographical expressions. One of them is the notion of the "unconquered land" or the "land that remains." Quotations are Josh. 13:1-7, Judg. 1:1-28, Judg. 3:1-6. In fact, it explains that Lebanon (in the north) and the Philistia (in the south) are not part of the Land of Israel. We can take this notion of the "land that remains" as a severe critique of the concept of the "conquered land," especially the one found in the Book of Joshua. It is a plain contradiction of the concepts of Canaan, Egyptian or biblical. Is it also a critique of the idea of a Promised Land?

So why do I say at the beginning: a trip from Gen. 12:6-7 to Zech. 2:16? The loss of the land has produced a New Israel, more dedicated to service in the Temple, or exclusively interested in the Torah. In post-exilic times, "the Land of Promise" is confined around Jerusalem and clearly points to the Sanctuary. In addition, in the later prophetic writings, the attention shifts more and more onto Jerusalem and the Sanctuary:

- Zech. 2:16: "Yahweh will take possession of Judah, his portion in the Holy Land [*admat haqqodesh, the holy land*], and again make Jerusalem his choice!"
- Ben Sirach (Apocrypha), *Wisdom* speaks in Ecclus. 24:10: "In the holy tent I ministered before him, and thus became established in Zion. In the beloved city he has given me rest, and in Jerusalem I wield my authority."

The prophet Isaiah, in the third part of the book, tells us about the future of the Holy City and of the Holy Land:

- Isa. 66:18: "I am coming to gather every nation and every language. They will come to witness my glory."
- Isa. 56:6-7: "As for the foreigners . . . these I shall lead to my holy mountain and make them joyful in my house of prayer."

The universalistic vision of the Late Prophecy of the Old Testament is prepared by the loss of the Land and is open to all nations. The glory of God is no more confined to a region, nor limited to a single people.

DOES THE BIBLE HAVE A FUTURE?

Peter Du Brul

I have been asked to answer the question: Does the Bible have a future? Here are a few thoughts I have been collecting for the past month and a half for this talk. For convenience sake, the thoughts can be assembled as "Three Cs."

First of all, C is for "challenge." I said in one of my notes: Does the Bible have a future? Does the Matterhorn have a future? Does Dostoyevsky's *The Brothers Karamazov* have a future? They will have a future as long as those works, the earth's works, God's work, Dostoyevsky's works, challenge us. And they do challenge us. You don't climb the Matterhorn in a helicopter. The challenge of the climb draws the best out of a climber, but it's best to climb in a group. And this is the same with the Bible.

The Bible will have a future as long as people can respond to the challenge of the Bible, and the challenge of the Bible is to get to the top. But the top is different for different people; they are climbing for different reasons, but they might never get to the top before they say they've had enough. Like a Belarusian journalist I met some years ago, sort of a man's man who had lots of buddies in Belarus who'd disappeared, fellow journalists. I said, "Have you been in the country long?"

"About three or four days," he replied.

"Have you been to the holy places?"

"I don't have much time," he said.

"Have you been to Bethlehem?"

"No."

"Maybe tomorrow before your plane I could pick you up and take you there. You could see the cave for a few minutes, and then I could take you back…"

He said, "No, I don't need to go to Bethlehem."

"Jerusalem? Did you have a bit of time in Jerusalem?"

"I had an hour."

And I'm not imitating the tone I'd like to, but he said, "And that was *enough*." And he said "enough" as if, you know, "I've had *enough* of the souvenir stores."

He came and spoke much about the disappearance and torture of fellow journalists in Belarus, but when he said that, I said, "Oh my God, I bet people spend weeks, years, here and don't get what he got in an hour." And that's getting to the top. I don't even know if he got to the Holy Sepulchre. But he got to some top inside of himself. This is the future of the Bible. I think that as long as people can respond to such a challenge, the Bible has a future.

True, which "face" of the Bible are you going to go up? The Hebrew Bible? In Hebrew? Or at least the Hebrew Bible in some other language you can read more easily? The Septuagint—call it the Greek Bible? Again, translated? Which face do you want to go up? Try to read Isaiah and do nothing else but read Isaiah for a couple days. Not just a couple hours. Or Jeremiah. Or the Song of Songs. And try to get it to read you. To read it so deeply that it pulls you, me, us, out of ourselves. That's why, without being against anything, I say to myself, "Beware of getting obsessed with some kind of theme, even the land, even suppression, even the Palestinians, even the Jews, even liberation theology, or historical critical theology, or psychoanalytic theology, or spiritual theology, any theology." Read the book. Let the book read you. Let the book focus us. That's the future of the Bible, that there are still unperceived angles to go up, unperceived angles to look down at the world, unperceived things in ourselves, resources in ourselves we have to call on to go farther into the Bible. Let the Bible go farther into us.

My first C is challenge. My second C—I'm not too happy with the word—is "completion." To complete the Bible, in my opinion, is to get into the presence of God. And to get into the absence of God. And to feel him tugging at us like we're a fish on a line, and he's pulling us; he's pulling us to him, to his heart. He might be playing with us, and for years, we may have doubts. And, as Hind Khoury said, "There are difficult places in the Bible." Thank God, there are still difficult places in the Bible. Life is not long enough to answer all the questions that the Bible poses. We will die before we have all the answers. Yet we learn that the very search itself has changed us. This is the point: where does the Bible begin and where does it end for us? One place where I like to begin with my students is to look for the smallest little piece that I think has everything in it, and that is Psalm 117. This is the shortest Psalm in the Bible, where all people of all nations and translations are invited to come to praise the Lord for his truth and for his love. But this is a small little place where I begin to give my students what I call a kind of a ladder, which we can perceive right down to St. Paul and right down to the Apocalypse.

Which brings me to: where do we end? We end with apocalypse. Recently it has been reemphasized that the present situation calls out more than ever for a prophetic voice, speaking out to the Palestinian people and others, especially to the youth, so that they are not stopped by certain difficult texts in the Bible, by troubling aspects of God, by violence, by texts that are being used by Christian or Jewish Zionists to justify suppression, marginalization, and disempowerment. But in our opinion, a prophetic voice is not enough. You cannot come to the end, that is, the purpose of the Bible, without going through and beyond prophecy and wisdom, with its Siamese twin of foolishness. You come to the end of the Bible without reaching apocalypse. Beyond the prophetic lies the apocalyptic.

And so completion means getting to the apocalyptic, which is getting to the future. The future of the Bible is apocalyptic. Where does the Bible talk about the future? It's in Joel, of course in Daniel, and in Zachariah. It's sketching out the future, especially in the books written in the time of the Maccabees. The Israelites got out of Egypt and into the promised land, but they lose it by their own mistakes and are taken to exile first in Assyria and then to Babylon. Hardly do they return with Persian patronage and they are at war with the Greeks, and then at war with their former allies, the Romans. The apocalyptic literature and the apocalyptic spirit behind it show that as the pressure builds up, the time of release approaches. Apocalypse is setting a clock. It's not just saying, "Oh, there are the end days. Death, judgment, Heaven, Hell." It's more like a bus station where it's been announced that there's a bomb in one of the lockers and we've been told that it's going to go off at 9:15. *Uh oh. Clear people out.* The aspect of apocalypse is urgency. There's only so much time to find the bomb and dismantle it, or to get out of the station. I think that we're living in such an urgent situation.

The city of David, the settlements, the verbal wars in the press, in the satellites, in the blogs. Words, words, words, until you've just had enough. I don't even want to listen to the radio anymore. But how does it complete? Think of our beloved starting points—each of you has his/her own beloved starting points in the Bible—but then there are the end points, which are apocalyptic, which are the unknown. And there, I think, the structure—and I know there's more than one structure of the Bible—is law, prophets, and wisdom books. But without being just structured in parts of books, apocalypse comes up as early as Deuteronomy, if not earlier, with Moses telling the people, "*Now*, choose between life and death, between goodness and evil." *Now.* That refrain of "now" keeps coming up as Moses stands on Mount Nebo shortly before his death, and he's getting that generation that's come up again 40 years later, after the generation that failed to obey God's words in detail. He wants them to make a second covenant, and they do. But there's an apocalypse there.

But the thing with the apocalypse is that there is the law, and the prophets keep that law on target. They come up—Jeremiah, Isaiah, Micah—to keep the law centered. And the wisdom books are this wonderful literary genre of the people—the Psalms, the Proverbs, the Canticle, Ecclesiastes, and then Job.

You are changed. This is completion. The completion is not just the beginning and the end; it's the middle, where that book turns us inside-out, as all the classics do in their own way. It might be a film, it might be a poem—one little poem can be enough. But this book is trying to make us come alive, trying to make us live and to live with God's life, down in what they call the Image of God. You get ahold of the structures: you've got the law, you've got the prophets. You're beginning to see how they work together through the wisdom books. But with the apocalypse: you don't know what it's going to hit. That's what the Bible is doing: it's leading us up to this "now" of Moses. *Now* do it. Like St. Augustine in the garden outside of Milan, hearing the children saying, "Take and read. Take and read. Take and read." He goes back to the little kiosk in the garden and he opens the book of Romans, and he puts his finger blindly on the verse: chapter 13, verse 13. That's easy to remember. "Change your life. *Now*." Wow! We don't know what it's going to hit, and that's the whole idea. Where's it going to hit? I don't know!

There's an excitement in the Bible and if we don't find that, we're not reading the Bible! There's going to be someplace in *The Brothers Karamazov* where your memories start linking up with one or the other of the brothers or these magnificent women in the book. This is completion. It's the turnabout, turning inside-out.

And lastly is the C for "community." The Bible's not a book—I mean, not *just* a book. It came out of community and it's for community and it builds community. It's not *just* in community, it's in liturgy. We pray the Bible. We talk to God through the Bible. From different voices: the way Jeremiah talks is not the way the Canticles talk, etc.

So it not only builds community and liturgy, it's *meant* for liturgy; but it's leading us beyond the Bible. We've got to get out of the Bible. We've got to go to the Qur'an. We've got to start reading the Qur'an in the way we read the Bible. Find a place where you can get into it and where it starts to pull you in, and then be faithful to reading. Maybe it'll take you more than a year to read the Qur'an, maybe you'll never finish it. But after a while, just as with this, you catch on. There are structures in the Qur'an, and there are some very interesting books that are coming out by Christians. I can mention Michel Cuypers, a Little Brother of Jesus, who has written a great work on the Fifth Sura of the Qur'an ("The Banquet"), as well as Ernst Benz from North Carolina, and Neil Robinson too. I believe they're all, if not Christians, at least "open" researchers in religious studies who are working with their students on how to read the Qur'an, how to get into it, how to get it into you. Into us.

But we've got to go farther than the Qur'an. What about secularism? Do we, does anybody, read Nietzsche anymore? I mean really read him? Or spend some hours with Kierkegaard? These are the major sources; they're not secret names. But take the works of Nietzsche and beyond, reread Frantz Fanon's *The Wretched of the Earth*. There are hundreds such books in the whole corner of liberation, and of suppression, around the world. But read them, deeply, at that level where we come to the peak, to the "I am." We might remember that level when, as adolescents, we read *Wuthering Heights,* when Cathy says, "I am Heathcliff."

The point is what? Reaching that level of "I am" which stuns us, like in John's Gospel, where Jesus says it, and he's at a peak of himself, which is going to cost him his life. And that life comes to us again through John's Gospel, where, as in the first letter of St. John, we acknowledge once again that we're sinners. *He who says he has fellowship with God and lives in the dark is lying to himself. And he's not doing the truth. He who says he's not a sinner, again, he's lying to others. And he who says that he's never sinned is lying to God.* So where's the truth? Where's the truth that's going to get us out of the lies that we're in? The future has its lies, our past has its lies. But perhaps together, in the presence of God, in the presence of those peak experiences, we can not only confess our sinfulness to one another, but also confess that we're on the same rope climbing this mountain into the presence of God. There's the future. And there's no future forward if God doesn't keep drawing us; no one comes to the Father unless the Father draws him. So my prayer is that God may draw us to Himself through one another and beyond one another. Now.

We all know what the future tense is: "I shall, you will, he/she/it will…" The future perfect is more rarely used: "By next June, I will have completed my studies." So I think that these "three Cs" of mine—these three thoughts about challenge, completion, and community—trace a future perfect. In the future, the community that responds to its challenge of the Bible, and occasionally reaches a part of its completion, will not only have endured, it will have prevailed. And to telescope the message of these "three Cs," I would say that the Bible will have prevailed, not only then, but now.

DOES THE BIBLE HAVE A FUTURE?

Gary Burge

When I first read the title of this session, it seemed to me that there was some conclusion predisposed in it. It seemed to imply that the Bible should not, or could not, have a future because of all the harm that has been done through it. In fact, someone sent me an email, saying, "My goodness, the Bible has been the source of theft, murder, war, genocide, forced conversion, and environmental degradation." I wanted to add that it probably contributed to the economic collapse of 2008. You might think in light of these problems that if we got rid of the Bible we would achieve some nirvana, world peace, or economic prosperity, but nevertheless, there are detractors. I will offer five thoughts that will give us some guidance on how we think about the Bible.

I want to begin by acknowledging that the Bible has been misused. I want to acknowledge that interpreters and users of the Bible misuse it grievously. You can be a liberal theologian in the United Kingdom, you can be Pentecostal in Nigeria, you can even be an Evangelical from Chicago, but everyone has misused the Bible, and we have asked it to serve our own interests. We elevate themes which we think are important and we say, "This is what the Bible teaches." I have even heard Rush Limbaugh, a prominent conservative radio talk host in the United States, do this. Making the Bible serve our own interests is an old art form.

One of my favorite unused passages in the New Testament is 2 Peter 3:15-16, where Peter summarizes Paul's wisdom in his letters, and then he helpfully adds, "There are some things in Paul that you just can't understand." Peter then says, "But there are ignorant and unstable people who twist Paul's words as they do the other Scriptures." Even in the first century, people misused the

Bible everywhere. In our context here, I think about the promise to Abraham for children and land in Genesis 12. This promise has been readily appropriated in our own day, but little is mentioned of the third aspect of this promise, which is that Abraham is to be a blessing to all nations, not just Israel. Israel enjoyed the first two elements of that promise, but ignored the third. The Bible has suffered the indignity of misuse for two thousand years, and misuse continues today.

In my classes at the College, we assign our freshmen to read a book called *Divided by Faith*, which is a Christian book about race relations in the United States. It demonstrates in its first two chapters how the Bible was used to defend slavery. For our students, this is an important and eye-opening experience. In this context, I think of another conversation I have had. I was with someone discussing a small, Muslim village just to the north of Hebron called Halhul, which has had a lot of conflict with the Israelis. You would think Halhul could be left to itself, but I give my students a thought experiment. I ask them to imagine if a group of New York settlers came to Halhul and said, "Thank you very much, ladies and gentlemen, for preserving Halhul for us for two thousand years, but it's time for you to go. Its true residents have arrived, and we are taking over. We will call ourselves Kiryat Halhul." They produce Joshua 15:58, in which Halhul is actually mentioned on the city list for Judah. Can you take Joshua 15:58, see the reference to Halhul, transport it three thousand years, and use it for modern politics? The Bible has been misused, and we need to be honest about that.

My second point is that there has been a lot of exaggeration concerning the misuse of the Bible. I wonder if the claims of misuse are not actually misplaced themselves. It reminds me of how we sometimes view our governments: we love to decry the abuses of power in our governments, but the truth is 99 percent of our public servants are doing good public service and advancing the common good. We like to identify those politicians who truly are corrupting the public processes, and we say, "Aha! We cannot trust the government." Even if there is misuse of the biblical tradition, remarkably that tradition is self-correcting. In other words, in the Scriptures, the entitlement and privilege we see in Old Testament Israel abruptly meets the Old Testament prophets. There is self-correction here, and this capacity to be self-critical, to be prophetic, is one of the legacies of the Church as well.

As a contemporary example: an unfortunate fifteenth century for the Catholic Church led to the Reformation, which in turn to the Counter Reformation. Before you know it, we have experiences like I had at 6:15 this morning at the Church of the Holy Sepulchre. Since my sleep is not quite adjusted yet, I walked to the Holy Sepulchre, to a place where I like to sit and read the Scriptures where tourists do not tend to go. As I entered, there was a large group of Polish Catholics coming in to have Mass in front of the Anastasis, the tomb of Jesus. They all put on white robes as they stood before the tomb, and I asked a person next to me who spoke English, "What are you doing?" He responded, "We have been baptized as children, but we are a renewal movement and we are rededicating our lives to Christ today for the first time. In front of the tomb of Jesus, we are having Mass. Would you like to worship with us?" I thought to myself, "My goodness, what happened to the fifteenth and sixteenth centuries?" I was there, a Protestant from Chicago, before the Anastasis, with Polish Catholics, praising Christ. There is something about the self-correction of the Church as well, in which we can actually get things right, and that is encouraging.

Some who despair of the Bible sometimes look to other sources of authority to give us promise or urgency. Some of us look to the government; some look to science; some look to international treaties; some look to the progress of civilization. I hope our knowledge of history is sufficient to put those notions away permanently. I do not look for hope in those places.

My third idea for consideration is what I call the legacy of the Bible. Despite the Bible mischief-makers, the Bible has provided us with a legacy we often forget. I think, for instance, of a wonderful book written in 2011 by an Indian man named Vishal Mangalwadi, *The Book that Made Your World: How the*

Bible Created the Soul of Western Civilization. He writes from an Indian university in a Hindu context, and looking at Western civilization he says, "Do you folks realize what you have that we don't?" He is an intellectual who wants us to see that inside the biblical tradition there is a legacy that has shaped us, but we take it for granted.

About a year ago, I was working with one of my student interns outside of New Delhi on my first trip to India, and we traveled up to the foothills of the Himalayas. We stayed in a village where he was serving in a nonprofit organization. I was befriended by a wonderful Hindu man who spoke perfect English, and while I was there, he took me on walks every day in the foothills of the Himalayas. He told me, "We'll do this on one condition. On the way up I will explain to you Hinduism, and on the way back you explain Christianity to me." I thought, "This is a moment! The Himalayas on one side and a Hindu man next to me."

Coming down the foothills, I asked him: "There is a very poor man digging through the garbage. Tell me why I should feed him. Should I help him? Should I even care about him?"

"Yes, you should, so that he does not become a monkey or worse in the next life," he responded. "Why would *you* care about him?"

"Because my God calls me to love him as my neighbor," to which he responded, "We have different worldviews."

The Bible has given us the credibility of moral codes. The Bible has given us charity. One of the earliest legacies of the Christian Church in the Roman Empire was charity. The Bible has given us accountability of the state before God, the idea that there is truth, and the idea that there is public social critique. Of course we have had our lapses with every one of these, but we regain our footing and we come round right.

I think, for instance, of the super-typhoon in the Philippines this month [November 2013], which I thought about as I was flying to Palestine. I also thought about my community at Wheaton College—about 2,600 undergraduates, 500 graduate students, and 250 faculty. Just before I flew here, we said to our entire community, "We need to act. We do not know who these people are. We've done research; let's choose World Relief together." We told every student on our campus not to send food or clothes, but to send cash because World Relief is tied with the Philippine Relief and Development Service (PHILRADS) which is active on the ground and knows what to do. I thought to myself, "This is incredible. Thirty-five hundred Christians, mobilizing together, saying we are going to act out of charity toward people we don't even know." As my wife and I were online giving our $200 to World Relief, I thought, "This is a wonderful experience!" And I thought of Matthew 22:39, "Love the Lord, your God, and love your neighbor as yourself." The legacy of the Bible has given us something, and we do not want to step away from that.

My fourth point is that theologians call this legacy the self-validating character of the Bible. This is an idea as old as the Psalms. Psalm 1 says, "Blessed is the person who is planted by streams of living water." This idea is repeated, not only by medieval Catholic mystics. It was especially important to John Calvin, and you will also hear it in modern authors. Something happens when we read the Scripture joined to faith and in the presence of the Holy Spirit. Scripture becomes Scripture when it sings. Scripture is not like finding a sheet of Mozart's music, an original perhaps, and saying to yourself, "Aha, now I have Mozart!" Mozart never intended to produce *sheets of music*; Mozart intended to create *symphonies*. It is what is lifted off that page that brings me what Mozart intended. Likewise, when the Scriptures are read, not simply as an instrument of scholarship, but in the company of the Spirit, music appears.

This has always been the testimony of the Church and its faithful. The Bible presents what it promises. In cooperation with the Spirit, it has always been an instrument of life and transformation. Stories abound, and my favorite is how Aleksandr Solzhenitsyn's[13] life was preserved, how the Scriptures saved it.

---

13 Aleksandr Solzhenitsyn (1918-2008) was a prominent Russian author known for his criticism of Russian communism and his theological works stemming from his imprisonment and exile in Siberia.

My fifth and final point is what I call the problem of perspective. The deepest problem we have with the Bible, and what puts its future in jeopardy for some communities, is how we view where we stand when we read it. We see ourselves as privileged, as entitled, as the elect, the chosen. We see ourselves as exceptional. Simply look at the history of the interpretation of the parable of the great banquet. Remember how the banquet host sends out invitations and excuses come back to him. The history of the interpretation of that parable has always been used for evangelism. In other words, we are at the banquet and we are listening to all those people who have rejected the invitation. They should respond. In fact, however, the cutting edge of that parable is that we hear that *we* are the recipients of the invitation, and therefore *we* should be chastened for rejecting it.

We, therefore, have to rediscover the central themes of the Bible and live them: repentance, redemption, renewal, the kingdom of God. Not simply do individuals have to rediscover these themes, but whole societies must as well. The message of the Bible is the reconstituting of creation, of setting it right. We can read the Bible with our friends in the majority world, and I think this is essential. But when I read the Bible with Latin Americans, Africans, and Asian Christians, my peculiar personal interpretations are chastened and I am humbled. We should read the Bible not asking how we can cull from it what we want, but instead how it can change the way we look at the world.

Does the Bible have a future? I would say absolutely. It not only delivers to us the Word of God, but it *is* a word of truth. In the estimate of the Church for twenty centuries, it is the Word of God *written*. In our frailty and with repentance on our lips, we need to learn how to use it rightly. When we do use it rightly, not as a guarantee of privilege, not as something reinforcing my entitlement, but honoring it, studying it, and listening carefully to it, it will always be a constant supply of hope and promise.

DOES THE BIBLE HAVE A FUTURE?

Gregory Jenks

This panel discussion arises out of the following critical awareness:

Since the Bible has been used to support highly destructive moments of human history such as theft, slavery, murder, assassination, war, genocide, population transfers, forced conversions, and environmental degradation, perhaps the Bible is too dangerous for the masses. Maybe we should take it away from the laity and only allow it to be read and interpreted by professionals. Yet neither political leaders nor the Church's anointed have been free of biblically justified atrocities. Perhaps the Bible should be counterbalanced by other authorities such as scientific findings and the UN's Universal Declaration of Human Rights. Can the Bible be redeemed and used as a source for human advancement, and if so, how?

This panel has the theme, "Does the Bible have a future?" This is a very different kind of topic, and it plays into my own research and writing about the "once and future Bible." It could be a theological diversion from the challenges of justice and peace, but perhaps it is also about asking what ways we might imagine the Bible contributing to justice and peace, rather than promoting and endorsing violence and oppression.

Let me begin by noting a simple but significant error in the title of our panel and of our conference. The title refers to *the* Bible, but there is not *one* Bible. Rather there are *many* Bibles, as Yohanna Katanacho reminded us. There is more than one form of the Bible and one expects there always will be, just as there is more than one expression of Church. This diversity of Bibles extends beyond the formal differences of content among Anglican, Armenian, Catholic, Ethiopian, Jewish, Orthodox, Protestant, and Syrian

Bibles, since—even when we have the same set of books in our Bible—we may choose to read some parts while ignoring others.

So much of the power talk around the Christian Scriptures speaks as if the Bible was a single thing that exists in one agreed form and through which God speaks with one voice. I suggest this is simply not so. The Bible is diverse and God speaks through the Bible in many different voices.

Yet, so often our language about the Bible reflects an assumption that the Protestant Bible, as it emerged in Northwest Europe at the time of the Reformation, is "the Bible." That particular form of the Bible is the Bible most of us know, but it is not the Bible of the Catholic Church nor of the Eastern rite churches. It is the Bible of the North Atlantic theological organisation, but it is not the only Bible. It is not the ancient Bible. And it is not the best Bible.

I suggest, with as much humility and grace as I can muster, that the first thing about the future of the Bible we need to embrace is that the Bible has always existed in multiple forms and will continue to do so. Our desire for certainty seduces us into thinking of the Bible as a single thing that speaks with one voice, and that plays into theological power games which—as we see in this and other lands—can have unjust outcomes for the people of the land, the *am-haaretz*, the little ones of God.

So I have no doubt that the Bible has a future, even if I find it hard to predict just what the future of the Bible may be like.

A further response to this topic would be to ask why we are discussing this theological topic rather than a real topic? My own response to this comment is that—in my view—an authentic Christian response to occupation, dispossession and violence must be derived from our understanding of Jesus, and for that I need the Bible. Not because I will ever take the Bible literally, but because I must always take it seriously.

So let me be clear at the outset that I have no doubt that the Bible has a future. Indeed, I am sure that the Bible *does* have a future, but I do wonder whether it will be a future that serves the powers that be or a future in which the Bible functions as a prophetic text, calling us all to repentance, renewal and action.

Let me also say that how this future takes shape rests with the communities of faith for which the Bible serves as sacred text. Academics will not determine the future of the Bible. The future of the Bible will be determined by the people of God, in all their diversity.

While I am sure that the Bible has a future, I am not sure whether the future of the Bible will be toxic for humanity or a good thing for us all. For sure, I suggest the toxicity of the Bible rises in direct correlation to its integration with the powers that be, whether those powers be inside the Church or outside the Church.

Not every reading of the Bible is healthy and good for us. I wish I could promise that the future of the Bible is one characterised by life-affirming readings, but I fear this will not be the case. People of power will always find it expedient to co-opt and exploit the Bible for their own ends, while evading its prophetic claim upon our lives. In this respect, I have found the contributions of Nancy Cardoso Pereira to be challenging and transformative for me.

As we reflect on this further, I would affirm that the Bible, in its diverse forms and with its diverse voices, is a key text for both victims and perpetrators, and will continue to be so unless we can change the ways in which people read the Bible. This suggests at least two different futures for the Bible: one that assists victims to use it more effectively, and another that disarms the Bible so that it cannot be used as a weapon of fear and hate. The trick is not to change or domesticate the Bible, but to change and empower the readers.

So I invite you to think about the two sides of the coin for the future of the Bible: how to make it work better for the little people, and how to make it work not so well for (and even against) the powerful people. Some of the strategies will contribute to both outcomes, so they are high value options. These would include:

- Improving biblical literacy within the churches and in the wider community
- Accessing contemporary critical biblical scholarship
- Recognizing diversity within the Bible and attending to the minority voices

- Acknowledging the dark side of the Bible
- Celebrating the positive side of the Bible

One key element will be reading the Bible contextually:

- In its ancient historical contexts
- Through its history of interpretation across the centuries
- In our own contexts now
- In the context of scientific insights and human rights values
- In our multi-faith context (as one religion among many, not as the *only true religion*)

If we can make progress across these issues, then the Bible will not only have a future but it will be a future that brings healing and hope to all people.

BIBLE STUDY

"Land of Promise"
How do we understand the promise of the land?

Naim Ateek

One of the major problems facing Christians in the twenty-first century has to do with the way people understand, interpret, and use the Bible. This is a cause of great concern for us, Palestinian Christians, due to the abuse of the Bible which we observe especially as it relates to the Israel-Palestine conflict. We believe that the Bible is meant to be an instrument for liberation and redemption, but our experience today is that it is being used as an instrument of enslavement and oppression. There were times when the Bible was used to justify slavery, war, the silencing of women, and many other evils. One of the latest abuses of the Bible, especially after the creation of the State of Israel, is the way it has been used to justify the oppression and the ethnic cleansing of the Palestinians.

In my theological writings, I have often emphasized two words: exclusive and inclusive. I believe that the movement in the Bible story is from exclusive thinking and beliefs about God, people, and land to more inclusive concepts. In other words, the story moves from a tribal way of thinking about God and people to a more inclusive theology. In this Bible study, I would like to present the land promise as recorded in the books of the Torah, then show how religious thinking developed after the Exile, continuing into the New Testament writers' interpretation in light of the coming of Christ. I will conclude with a discussion of how contemporary Christian thinkers continue to interpret the promise.

Pat Robertson, one of today's prominent Evangelical fundamentalist voices, represents an exclusive perspective of the land promise. He pulls out several verses that, he believes, attest to the land promise to Abraham, including Genesis 13:15 (*For all the land that you see I will give to you and to your offspring forever*) and 2 Chronicles 20:7 (*Did you not, O our God, drive out the inhabitants of this land before your people Israel, and give it forever to the descendants of your friend Abraham?*) and notes that there are "literally dozens" of verses that "prove" God gave the land of Israel to Abraham. In discussing these verses, Robertson says,

> This is a permanent possession given by God to Abraham, and all of this territory is the land of Israel. There is no such thing as a Palestine state, nor has there ever been. . . . If we ally ourselves with the enemies of Israel, we will be standing against God Almighty.[14]

Robertson believes that Christians need to support Israel because God gave the land of Canaan/Palestine to the Jewish people.

As Robertson mentions, there are a number of texts in the Bible, especially in the Old Testament, that seem to support this understanding of the land promise. Genesis 12:7 is one of the first texts to mention the promise:

> Then the Lord appeared to Abram, and said, "To your offspring I will give this land." So he built there an altar to the Lord, who had appeared to him.

This promise is repeated in various ways. Genesis 15:18-21 describes the boundaries of the land:

> On that day the Lord made a covenant with Abram, saying, "To your descendants I give this land, from the river of Egypt to the great river, the river Euphrates, the

---

14 The 700 Club. "Pat Robertson Warns against Dividing Jerusalem." www.cbn.com.

land of the Kenites, the Kenizzites, the Kadmonites, the Hittites, the Perizzites, the Rephaim, the Amorites, the Canaanites, the Girgashites, and the Jebusites."

Genesis 17:4-8 reiterates the covenant in connection to the land of Canaan:

As for me, this is my covenant with you: You shall be the ancestor of a multitude of nations. No longer shall your name be Abram, but your name shall be Abraham; for I have made you the ancestor of a multitude of nations. I will make you exceedingly fruitful; and I will make nations of you, and kings shall come from you. I will establish my covenant between me and you, and your offspring after you throughout their generations, for an everlasting covenant, to be God to you and to your offspring after you. And I will give to you, and to your offspring after you, the land where you are now an alien, all the land of Canaan, for a perpetual holding; and I will be their God.

It took many years of biblical study before I became aware that God made similar land promises to other people. In Deuteronomy 2:4-5, God is quoted to have said to Moses,

You are about to pass through the territory of your kindred the descendants of Esau, who lives in Seir. They will be afraid of you, so be very careful not to engage in battle with them, for I will not give you so much as a foot's length of [the Edomites'] land, since I have given Mount Seir to Esau as a possession.

In Deuteronomy 2:9, a similar promise is repeated about the land of the Moabites:

The Lord said to me (Moses): "Do not harass Moab or engage them in battle, for I will not give you any of its land as a possession, since I have given it as a possession to the descendants of Lot."

The same promise appears in relation to the Ammonites (Deut. 2:19):

> When you approach the frontier of the Ammonites, do not harass them or engage them in battle, for I will not give the land of the Ammonites to you as a possession, because I have given it to the descendants of Lot.

These texts reveal the tribal structure of these primitive societies. Tribal societies were built on three important pillars, namely, the people of the tribe or tribes, the god or gods of the tribe, and the land or territory they inhabited. Their belief system was quite exclusive: their god belonged solely to them, they possessed great loyalty to their tribe, and the land was exclusively theirs because they believed it was given to them by their god. In my study of the Bible, this tribal belief that reflects a very exclusive understanding of God, land, and people is quite prevalent. These texts reflect an historical period characterized by exclusivity; although the texts were written, finalized, or edited hundreds of years later—around the time of the Exile—they reflect some traditions, folklore, and legends of earlier times.

Numbers 33:50-53 exemplifies the tribal, exclusive understanding of God common in these early texts:

> In the plains of Moab by the Jordan at Jericho, the Lord spoke to Moses, saying: Speak to the Israelites, and say to them: When you cross over the Jordan into the land of Canaan, **you shall drive out all the inhabitants of the land from before you,** destroy all their figured stones, destroy all their cast images, and demolish all their high places. You shall take possession of the land and settle in it, for I have given you the land to possess. (emphasis added)

In this text, God and the land are seen to belong exclusively to the Israelites, and the people previously living in the land must be driven out and their sacred places destroyed.

In Deuteronomy 20:16-18, the tribal mentality is again clear, and the author records an even stronger position than in the Numbers passage:

> But as for the towns of these peoples that the Lord your God is giving you as an inheritance, you must not let anything that breathes remain alive. **You shall annihilate them**—the Hittites and the Amorites, the Canaanites and the Perizzites, the Hivites and the Jebusites—just as the Lord your God has commanded, so that they may not teach you to do all the abhorrent things that they do for their gods, and you thus sin against the Lord your God. (emphasis added)

In Palestine and Israel today, extremist settlers use these texts to justify the driving out or the annihilation of the Palestinians on the basis of a biblical mandate.[15],[16]

After the Exile, however, we begin to see a critique of that kind of an exclusive theology. The tribal, ethnic, and exclusive have been challenged and contested. Ezekiel is basically calling for a new inclusive theology of God and land. He attributes his words to "the Lord God." This means that Yahweh is prescribing a new theology of God, people, and land. God, through Ezekiel, does not say, "Drive the people out" or "annihilate them," as we saw previously; instead:

> You shall divide the land among you according to the tribes of Israel. You shall allot it as an inheritance for yourselves and for the aliens who reside among you. They shall be to you as citizens of Israel; with you they shall be allotted an inheritance among the tribes of Israel. In whatever tribes aliens reside, there you shall assign them their inheritance, says the Lord God. (Ez. 47:21-23)

---

15 Shragai, N. (26 March 2008). "An Amalek in our time?" *Ha'aretz*. Accessed 18 June 2014. <http://www.haaretz.com/print-edition/features/an-amalek-in-our-times-1.242717>.

16 Rosen, Y. (22 June 2006). "Morality requires: Hurt hostile population." *Ynet News*. Accessed 18 June 2014. < http://www.ynetnews.com/articles/0,7340,L-3266113,00.html>.

The word "aliens" in the text is problematic for Palestinians since they do not consider themselves aliens in or newcomers to the land. They are the natives and the indigenous people of the land. The word "alien" must be understood in its historical context. The essence of this amazing text, however, is in its inclusive nature when compared with the above exclusive texts. Ezekiel is critiquing the earlier exclusive texts that negated the rights and even the very presence of the indigenous inhabitants of the land. By doing so, he reflects a more inclusive theology of God, people, and land. Ezekiel is simply saying to the returning exiles, "Live with the people and inherit the land equally together."

Similarly, Isaiah writing after the Exile presents another example of this shifting theology of God and land. He writes,

> I (God) will pour water on the thirsty land, and
> streams on the dry ground; I will pour my spirit upon
> your descendants, and my blessing on your offspring.
> They shall spring up like a green tamarisk, like willows
> by flowing streams. (Isa. 44:3-4)

In 1989, I commented on this text in my book *Justice and Only Justice*:

> Isaiah's great theological breakthrough lies in his
> realization that God's promise of [the] outpouring
> [of] the Spirit of God on the people is essentially
> more important than the possession of the land. The
> relationship with God did not depend on being in
> the land. God without the land is infinitely more
> important than the land without God. With God's
> Spirit poured on the people, they can be the carriers
> of God's blessing and become God's witnesses
> everywhere.[17]

It becomes clear in the Hebrew Scriptures that the Israelites and Jewish people move from a tribal and exclusive theology to a more inclusive theology; the later writers critique the tribal and

---

17 Ateek, Naim. (1989). *Justice and only justice.* Maryknoll, New York: Orbis Books. p.111.

embrace the inclusive. While the prophets still vacillate between exclusive and inclusive, the inclusive grows stronger throughout the biblical narrative.

In 1942, Rabbi Samuel Goldenson preached a sermon about Zionism in which he said,

> Judaism does not fare well at the hands of Zionism. For in order to find support in Judaism for its nationalist philosophy, Zionism necessarily tends to stress the racial, tribal, and folkish elements of Jewish history and thought. Such elements are admittedly found in our literature, a literature which covers thousands of years. All historical religions are composites. In the passage of time men [and women] and events contribute to such religions many and diverse elements. Some of these elements are crude, primitive, temporal and local. Some are advanced, transcendent, eternal, and universal, as in the teachings of the great Prophets of Israel. It is in the high visions of our Prophets and in the all-encompassing truths enunciated by them that Israel has found the urge to live on, despite the loss of its land, and to live everywhere as a religious community, bearing witness to the Living God.
>
> The danger to Judaism in the Zionist doctrines is in its emphasis upon the earlier and narrower features of our heritage, the features that lead to separatism and exclusiveness. Such tribal ways of thinking lie behind the very ideologies that are now causing us Jews and the world at large the greatest suffering. How much agony the world would have been spared during these tragic days, if men [and women] of every creed had learned to take counsel of the higher and nobler teachings of their own faiths![18]

---

18 Naim Ateek, from a copy given by Rabbi Samuel Goldenson's grandson, David Glick.

As Christians, we must continue in this trajectory and consider the promise from the perspective of the New Testament. Unfortunately most Christian Zionists, who are dealing with the promise the way it is written in the Genesis account, do not realize the revolution set in motion by the coming of Jesus Christ. In his letter to the Galatians, the Apostle Paul reinterprets the promise through the lens of Christ's coming:

> Now the promises were made to Abraham and to his offspring; it does not say, "And to offsprings," as of many; but it says, "And to your offspring," that is, to one person, who is Christ. . . . for in Christ Jesus you are all children of God through faith. (Gal. 3:16, 26)

This is the revolution: Since Christ is the true offspring of Abraham, he is the true inheritor of the promise and the land belongs to him. And since by faith we too have been baptized into Christ, we have become children of God, and therefore, we too are Abraham's offspring.

Paul continues in expounding his theology of God, people, and land:

> As many of you as were baptized into Christ have clothed yourselves with Christ. There is no longer Jew or Greek, there is no longer slave or free, there is no longer male and female; for all of you are one in Christ Jesus. And if you belong to Christ, then you are Abraham's offspring, heirs according to the promise. (Gal. 3:26-29)

Paul takes another bold step forward when he writes to the Romans:

> For the promise that he [Abraham] would inherit the world [cosmos] did not come to Abraham or to his descendants through the law but through the righteousness of faith. For this reason it depends on faith. (Romans 4:13, 16;17a)

Interestingly, nowhere in Genesis does God tell Abraham that he is to inherit the *cosmos*, the world. Abraham is told he will inherit the *land*. In the letter to the Romans, Paul reinterprets the promise to Abraham in light of the coming of Jesus the Messiah (Christ), saying that Abraham is to inherit the world. In Paul's interpretation, the coming of Christ transforms the exclusive theology of land and turns it into an inclusive theology that includes all the people of God and the world beyond the territorial borders of the initial Genesis promise.

Furthermore, in Paul's theology, if he interpreted the offspring of Abraham as being Jesus Christ and that God's promise to Abraham was that he would inherit the world (*cosmos*), then it stands to reason that for Paul the promise of the land was fulfilled in the coming of Jesus Christ; in Jesus Christ, all the people of the earth would be blessed or in Jesus Christ the people of the earth will bless themselves. (Genesis 12:3c: *"And in you all the families of the earth shall be blessed."* In another translation: *"By you all the families of the earth shall bless themselves."*)

Theologically speaking, the gift of the land was provisional until the time in which the purposes of God would be fully realized in the coming of Christ. Similarly, using such a biblical and theological logic, the Law of Moses was also provisional and temporary until the coming of grace. *"The law indeed was given through Moses; grace and truth came through Jesus Christ"* (John 1:17).

In Mark 1:14-15, the author writes:

> *Jesus came to Galilee, proclaiming the good news of God, and saying, "The time is fulfilled, and the kingdom of God has come near; repent, and believe in the good news."*

In the New Testament, the focus is no more on the land, as we see in the Old Testament. The focus shifts to the kingdom of God. God's kingdom is an inclusive and universal concept. God's kingdom is where God is sovereign and where God reigns. This means that one can live in God's kingdom anywhere in the world and live his/her life of faith and fidelity to God and in service of others. The theology of land is transformed.

Even among every-day Christians, theology of land vacillates between the exclusive and inclusive. Christian Zionists continue to focus on the Genesis texts about the promise; I call them Old Testament Christians because they fail to interpret the promise from the perspective of the New Testament. But even my own church, the Anglican Church, is hesitant in articulating a theology of land that is based on justice and inclusiveness. In an Anglican report titled *Land of Promise?*[19], the role of the modern State of Israel is discussed. The following quotes help illustrate some problematic interpretations of the promise, with my comments included in bold:

- "The particular place which the land of Israel and city of Jerusalem hold for Jewish people must be taken seriously by Christians." (2.6, 2.15, 7.11) **What about the Palestinian people? What is their claim to the land and Jerusalem?**
- "Israel as a people has been chosen by God to serve his mission." (1.1-3) **From a theological and a Christian perspective, all of us have been chosen to serve God's mission.**
- "The Jewish people have a continuing role within the purposes of God." (6.52) **All people have a role within the purposes of God.**

It seems that the theology of those who prepared this report was more focused on the Old Testament than the New Testament, more exclusive than inclusive in its theology of God and land.

Other Christian groups, however, have made great progress in developing an inclusive theology of land, and I would like to end by using several quotes that reflect the growing movement toward an inclusive theology of land.

---

19 Anglican Consultative Council. (2012). *Land of promise? An Anglican exploration of Christian attitudes to the Holy Land, with special reference to 'Christian Zionism.'*

The first document was produced by Friends of Sabeel Netherlands in 2012 under the title *The Walls have been Broken Down*. It states:

> Since God's love is for all people, [God's] people can spread from Israel across the whole earth, and in this way the promise of the land can encompass the whole earth. Paul already saw this universal scope in the promise to Abraham, when he wrote in Romans 4:13 that Abraham and his descendants were promised that they 'would inherit the world.' This universalization of the promise of the land is not a spiritualization either, because it concerns real people on this real earth. Moreover, this universalization means that all people have been granted a place on this earth where they can live in safety, freedom, and peace.[20]

The Church of Scotland published a wonderful document, titled *The Inheritance of Abraham? A Report on the 'Promised Land'* (May 2013). It states:

> To Christians in the twenty-first century, promises about the land of Israel shouldn't be intended to be taken literally, or as applying to a defined geographical territory; they are a way of speaking about how to live under God so that justice and peace reign, the weak and poor are protected, the stranger is included, and all have a share in the community and a contribution to make to it. The 'promised land' in the Bible is not a place so much as a metaphor of how things ought to be among the people of God. This 'promised land' can be found— or built—anywhere.[21]

---

20 Kairos Palestine Netherlands and FOS Netherlands. (2012). *The walls have been broken down*. p.14

21 Church and Society Council of the Church of Scotland. (2013). *The inheritance of Abraham? A report on the 'promised land'*. p. 9

These groups are developing powerful arguments for an inclusive understanding of land, continuing the liberative theology that Sabeel has been developing for the last 25 years:

"The land that God has chosen at one particular time in history for one particular people is now perceived as a paradigm, a model, for God's concern for every people and every land. As God commanded the Israelites to obey God's laws in their life in the land, so God demands the same from all peoples in their lands. God's unequivocal demand that the Israelis not defile or pollute the land with injustice, lest the land thrust them out, becomes a warning to all governments and to the peoples of every land. God requires every human being to live according to the divine standard of righteousness.

The particular has become universal. The blessing of God's concern for one people is universalized to encompass every people and every land. Consequently, every nation can say about its own country, "This is God's land, God's country, this is part of God's world. This is the Lord's land and the Lord demands a life of righteousness and justice in our land."

Such a blessing obviously does not exclude the Jews or the modern State of Israel. Neither does it justify their invoking an ancient promise—one that betrays a very exclusive and limited knowledge of God in one stage of human development—in order to justify their uprooting an entire people and expropriating their land in the twentieth century. To cling only to the understanding of God in those limited and exclusive passages is to be untrue to the overall biblical heritage.

The tragedy of many Zionists today is that they have locked themselves into this nationalist concept of God. They are trapped in it and they will be freed only if they discard their primitive image of God for a more universal one.[22]

A final challenge from the Kairos Palestine Document:
Our task is to safeguard the Word of God as a source of life and not of death, so that "the Good News" remains what it is: "Good News" for us and for all. In the face of those who use the Bible to threaten our existence as Christian and Muslim Palestinians, we renew our faith in God because we know that the word of God cannot be the source of our destruction. Therefore, we declare that any use of the Bible to legitimize or support political options and positions that are based upon injustice, imposed by one person on another, or by one people on another, transform religion into human ideology and strip the word of God of its holiness, its universality and truth.[23]

---

22 Ateek, Naim. (1989). *Justice and only justice.* Maryknoll, New York: Orbis Books. p.108-109
23 Kairos Palestine. (2009). *A moment of truth.* 2.3-2.4.

PART II
REALITIES ON THE GROUND

"The Status Quo in Israel and Palestine"

Mustafa Barghouti

I thought I would use this moment to present the reality of the situation and the political context of what's happening in Palestine. I will also try to touch on the ongoing processes and how things can change. At the same time, I will try to show you what the Palestinian people go through and how much effort it takes to survive in these difficult circumstances.

Two-State Solution

Today, the so-called peace process, where people are talking about a two-state solution, is nothing new; the whole principle of a two-state solution was developed back in 1947. Before that, Palestinians wanted to have one democratic state where Palestinian Muslims and Christians could live in peace, side-by-side with Jewish people, and with equal rights and equal duties. It was the United Nations in 1947 that decided on the creation of the two-state solution, according to which Israel would be in 56 percent of the land and Palestinians would be in about 44 percent of the land. This didn't happen: Israel was created during and after the war in 1948 on 78 percent; what remained was the West Bank and Gaza Strip, which constitute less than 22 percent of the land of historic Palestine.

In 1988, under tremendous international pressure and with great efforts from the international community, the Palestinian Liberation Organization (PLO) decided to accept a compromise. The compromise was to have a two-state solution: a Palestinian state in the West Bank and Gaza, on only 22 percent of the land, which is less than half of what had been decided by the United

Nations. This is important to remember. And this compromise was the basis for the signing of the Oslo Agreement in 1993.

Even after agreeing to this compromise, the Palestinians at Camp David in 2000 were offered a very different state: a state without Jerusalem, a state without the Jordan Valley, without borders, and without the many areas occupied by illegal Israeli settlements. Later, the Israeli government started to talk about taking not only the *borders* of the Jordan Valley but the *whole* of the Jordan Valley and wide areas around Jerusalem. So while peace talks have been happening during the last twenty years, while peace talks are happening today, the same process is going on: the process of land appropriation, land confiscation, building settlements, and shrinking the space and the land for the Palestinian people. It's very important to understand that today the existing peace process is used as a cover for Israeli actions of land appropriation and land annexation. Probably the biggest mistake the Palestinian Authority committed, as well as the international community and the United States, was to accept new negotiations without first insisting on a total and complete stop of all settlement activity.

Looking at a map of the West Bank, you can see the Green Line, the 1967 borders. And the main Palestinian population centers are designated Area A, where the Palestinian Authority exists. But even when you hear "Palestinian Authority," don't take it for granted that this is a sovereign authority. In reality the Israeli army can invade any of these places and arrest people, regardless of the presence of the Palestinian Authority. Then we have Area B, where the Palestinian Authority has some kind of functional authority, which means it could be in charge of some sanitary facilities, garbage disposal, health and education services, but no military or security authority. And the rest is Area C, which constitutes 61 percent of the land of the West Bank. In this 61 percent, Palestinians cannot build a house, a school, a clinic, or even have a water supply without Israeli permission, which is either rarely or never granted.

The whole plan today is to force the people who live in Area C off their land, to repeat what happened to the majority of Palestinians in 1948. In a way, what is happening to the Palestinians in the Jordan Valley and in the area of Jerusalem today is no different from what happened to the people of Nazareth, the Galilee, Akka, or Haifa during the *Nakba*. And this is happening according to a plan. The plan was put in place in 1967 by the Deputy Prime Minister of Israel, Yigal Allon, who designed this plan to deal with the fact that not all Palestinians left when the Israeli army occupied the West Bank. Many of the people decided they would not go through the humiliation of becoming refugees again, and decided to stay even if that meant they could be killed. Because of that, the Palestinians created what the Israelis call the "demographic factor," and Israel's way of dealing with the demographic factor was to create large settlements in the Jordan Valley, around Jerusalem, and in the north and south, with one aim: to transform the Palestinian West Bank, with Palestinian citizens in it, into a situation where Palestinian communities become clusters of foreign bodies, besieged and surrounded by settlements that are spreading everywhere.

Why do I say the peace process is meaningless when Israeli settlements continue to grow? Mainly because the growth of settlements does nothing but enhance the cancer that is eating the possibility of the two-state solution. If you look at maps of Jerusalem, you will see how many new settlement units were built inside the settlement blocs around Jerusalem alone during the last two years. We are talking about 13,000 new units in a settlement called Giv'at Yael, 8,000 units in Har Homa, etc. Thousands and thousands of new units, in order to change the demographic reality.

The map of the West Bank today is an example of how impossible it is to build a state if these Israeli processes are allowed to continue. The first thing the Israeli government does is to expand the settlements using settlement master plans. These master plans give the settlements, which are not more than two percent of the size of the land they occupy, 6.5 percent of the land, and then later give them a space of almost 42 percent of the West Bank. Then the Israelis create settlement outposts, closed military areas which Palestinians are forbidden from entering, Israeli military bases, the segregation wall (which has taken a big part of the land and basically annexed it to Israel), declared state land which Palestinians cannot use, and Israeli by-pass roads which are exclusive for Jewish Israelis or Israeli settlers. This is followed by settlement and outpost expansion, the uprooting of Palestinian trees, demolishing of Palestinian houses, etc. How can we build a state in such a map?

If everybody says they agree that there should be a two-state solution, and everybody agrees there should be a Palestinian state, then for God's sake, how can these processes be allowed to continue?

The only other map that looks similar is the map of the South African apartheid system. There were large Bantustans, some bigger than the whole West Bank, and some with their own governments. In one of these, there was even a king. But that meant nothing, because all these Bantustans were under the auspices and full control of the apartheid system in South Africa.

Let me give you an example of what Israel did to the birthplace of Jesus Christ in Bethlehem. There are three towns in the Bethlehem area: Beit Sahour, Beit Jala, and Bethlehem. In 1967, Israel illegally annexed East Jerusalem and made it part of Israel, and with it annexed 17 percent of the land of Beit Sahour, 8 percent of the land of Bethlehem, and 22 percent of the land of Beit Jala. And later they built the wall, which further annexed 10 percent of Beit Sahour, one percent of Bethlehem, and 24 percent of the land of Beit Jala. So we are talking about 44 percent of one town's land being annexed to Israel, and then to add insult to injury, Israel built new settlements in the same area. And I am sure, sooner or later, Israel will start to expand the segregation wall to annex more land.

Now many people ask the question: Why does the Israeli community turn to selecting and electing racist and extremist parties, like the Jewish Home party, or Likud, or the party of

Avigdor Lieberman? And the simple answer is clear: Many Israeli people are benefiting from occupation and benefiting from land appropriation. The size, the amount, the cost of the land that was confiscated in the Bethlehem area alone is worth $30 billion, and it is used in construction and investment. So the state and the people are making a profit from occupation, and unless we make this occupation and this system of discrimination costly, they will not change their course.

Many Israelis object to the use of the word apartheid, and I don't blame them because I don't think there's anything more shameful today than being called an apartheid state. But then I ask these Israelis to give me an alternative word to describe the situation at hand, where you have, on average, a Palestinian allowed to use no more than 50 cubic meters of water while an illegal Israeli settler is allowed to use up to 2,400 cubic meters. How do you describe the situation when the GDP per capita in Israel is $32,000 while it is only $1,400 for Palestinians? Yet the Palestinians are obliged to buy products at Israeli market price because of the imposed market union, tax union, and control of borders. How do you describe a situation where Palestinians, making 22 times less than Israelis, are obliged to pay double the price for water and electricity?

And on top of that, Palestinians lose much of their land to the so-called segregation roads which are exclusively for Israelis, and if a Palestinian is caught walking or driving on them, he or she can be sentenced to six months in jail. Not even in the South African apartheid system nor in the worst time of segregation in the United States was there a situation where roads were segregated. There were segregated buses, segregated towns, but not roads. This is unprecedented in human history. And if you take a look at the growth of settlements in Jerusalem, you can see how large they've become. And this is the proof that the biggest mistake of Oslo, as well as the biggest mistake of today's negotiations, was to conduct peace talks while Israeli settlements continued to expand.

Israel has segregated and separated Jerusalem from the rest of the Palestinian territories since 1992, especially since the signing of the Oslo Agreement in 1993. There are checkpoints built around Jerusalem to block the roads and prevent people from reaching the city, and that's why 99 percent of the Palestinians in the West Bank and Gaza, like me, are forbidden from reaching Jerusalem. I was born in Jerusalem. I worked in a hospital in Jerusalem for 15 years. But since 2005, when I ran for president, I've been forbidden from coming to Jerusalem.

To come and speak at this conference, I wanted to be polite and test one more time. I received an invitation from the Norwegian embassy, and I presented a request for permission to come and speak, but was rejected. So what do I do? I must speak at the conference, so I simply violated their decision. I don't recognize their law; their law is a violation of every basic human right. I know I might leave the room and they could arrest me—which they've done several times—but I think we cannot accept their indoctrination and we cannot accept what they are trying to force on us. If we do, we will be accepting injustice.

House Demolitions

House demolitions are a very big problem in the case of Jerusalem. The reality is that people are not given permits to build. Families grow and people need houses, so they are faced with one of two options. They can leave Jerusalem (East Jerusalem) and go build somewhere outside the municipality, but they would then lose their Jerusalem residency ID, they would lose their right to be in Jerusalem, they would be forbidden from coming to Jerusalem, and they would lose their health insurance and social security.

The second option is to build without permits. Today there are 10,000 houses in Jerusalem that are threatened with demolition; every week, some houses are demolished. The Israeli army comes to the Palestinian home and says, "Either we demolish your house at a very high cost, or you can demolish it yourself." And frequently you find families who spent all their savings building a house now having to demolish it by themselves because it's cheaper than having the Israelis demolish it. There's nothing more humiliating and insulting than what they are doing to the people.

I'll give you an example. In Silwan, which is just outside the Old City of Jerusalem, the Israelis have confiscated much land and built settlement units. Now they are planning to demolish 120 houses in the neighborhood so that the illegal settlers can have a park.

Gaza

I cannot speak to you without mentioning Gaza, because Gaza, contrary to what many people think, is still under occupation. It's a different kind of occupation. The Israelis are besieging this little piece of land from all sides, even though it is no more than 140 square miles with 1.7 million people living in it, one of the most densely populated areas in the world. The Israeli ships are blocking the sea, so fisherman will be shot if they go more than six nautical miles into the sea, and the airspace is controlled by Israeli planes that can shoot and kill any time they want. Today the people of Gaza suffer from the worst siege and blockade. My colleagues in medical relief spoke to me, telling me they are having great difficulty providing healthcare because they don't have electricity for more than five hours a day. Hospitals, clinics, schools, facilities, houses—no one has more than five hours of electricity every day. As a result, they have to rely on generators which pollute the environment, and they have to spend a lot of money to find fuel.

Separation Wall

When we speak about the wall I am always surprised that it is described in American media as "the fence." When you say "the fence," that implies a mild structure that exists between nice neighbors. In reality this wall is a huge structure, three-times the length and twice the height of the Berlin Wall. This wall is destroying and has destroyed many people's lives. A woman's house in the Bethlehem area is surrounded by the wall in three different directions. A couple of years ago she was told she cannot go to the roof of her own building because she would represent a threat to the wall.

The road I used to go to work between Ramallah and Jerusalem is gone, cut into two pieces by the wall. And 85 percent of the time, the wall is not separating Palestinians from Israelis, but Palestinians from Palestinians. Farms, houses and markets have been completely destroyed by the building of the wall.

Qalqilya, a city with 46,000 people, is besieged completely by the wall, leaving only one little passage, this little tiny road which is eight meters wide, and a gate. Israeli soldiers hold the key to the gate and they can shut off the city any time they want. About 150,000 people are besieged behind the wall today; they cannot cross in and out except by these gates. But if they want to cross, to go to school or university or hospital, they need military permits. And even if they have permits, they cannot cross except at times assigned by the Israeli army: from 7:40 to 8:00 in the morning, from 2:00 to 2:15 p.m., and from 6:45 to 7:00 p.m.

People suffer a lot at checkpoints, but the depth of violations of human rights in the occupied Palestinian territories is missed in the international media. There are many videos which reveal how grave these violations are. One taken in the Bethlehem area, in a village called Abediya, shows the Israeli army searching for somebody. They searched by bombarding the house, making a hole in it, scanning the house with gunshots, and then using dogs. An innocent woman who happened to be in the area at that time was attacked by the dog.

Nonviolent Resistance

We are encountering this terrible occupation and oppression with a very noble movement. We call it the movement of nonviolent resistance; we started it 10 years ago and it's growing. Nonviolent resistance is deeply rooted in our history, but there is a new stage of nonviolent resistance where people are determined to break down the system of oppression. We organize demonstrations, joined by a number of Israelis and Jewish people who, though still a minority, believe in Palestinian rights and participate with us. There are communities like Bil'in and Ni'lin that have been demonstrating every Friday for the past nine years. Even when there's a wedding, the groom and the bride go out to the demonstration and peacefully demand the end of the occupation and the terrible apartheid wall.

We are met with severe violence; the army uses tear gas bombs in huge quantities. Israel has machines that can throw 40 tear gas bombs at once at one spot, which can be very dangerous because it creates what we call a "closed-room effect," and people can suffocate. That's what happened to a young woman, Jawaher Abu Rahmeh, 32 years old, who suffocated to death because of tear gas.

The army also uses other methods; they use high-velocity bullets. A young boy, Ahmad Hassan Yousef, was shot in the head during a peaceful demonstration and was killed. They use what they call rubber bullets which are nothing but metal bullets covered with a very thin layer of rubber, which can be fatal if they hit the head or the eye.

And sometimes they do even more horrible things. There is video of a young man who was demonstrating with us, peacefully carrying a flag, and he was arrested. The Israeli army blindfolded him, handcuffed him, forced him to sit on the ground for two and a half hours, and while he was blindfolded and handcuffed, the soldiers shot him from a distance of one and a half meters.

You would expect that after such an incident, the Israeli Defense Minister would resign or the officers would be taken to court or the Prime Minister of Israel would apologize. The only person who was punished after this was the 16-year-old girl, a school girl, who took the pictures from the window of her house. She was interrogated five times, her father was detained for 10 days, and her brother was shot in the thigh when their home was invaded.

Even some international supporters who have come and demonstrated with us have been severely punished. In one case a protest was held against the closure and segregation of the road, and there were a number of young people, Palestinians and internationals, cycling on the road to protest the segregation. And the army attacked a young Danish man, who was 21 years old, just because he was demonstrating with us.

So frequently you hear about Palestinian violence and terrorism, but no one is speaking about this horrible Israeli violence that is practiced against the people. But we are not giving up. The resilience and determination is powerful. Another example: in the village of Wallajeh, near Bethlehem, near the Cremisan Church, the army has put up a huge military checkpoint. And people, including church people, have been demonstrating against the checkpoint for two years because it separates the church from its land, separates the village from all its land, and stops people from reaching Bethlehem or Beit Jala. And for two years, the Israeli army did not care; nobody cared. You know what we did last month? We went there with young people, and with our bare hands removed the checkpoint and threw it down the bank. By the time the Israeli army knew about it we were already in Abu Dis, demonstrating in another place.

The Palestinians are not victims. Of course we suffer, but we're not trying to victimize ourselves and emphasize that. I want you to see Palestinians as people who are determined to live and determined to succeed, regardless of all this suffering. But you cannot accept—and nobody can accept—the claim that in this struggle we are the oppressors and that the Israelis are the victims. This is not true.

Here is an example of how beautiful the work of people is. A young man named Mustafa was born in Aboud, a village near Birzeit, and he suffers from muscular dystrophy. He became paralyzed and can only move his head. He could have died, but our wonderful young volunteers who work with Medical Relief in the community-based rehabilitation program helped him. They helped his family. Then they worked with the school to integrate him, and he was integrated into a normal school. And he did well and reached the tenth grade. We thought he would go into the humanities branch because it's easier, but he said, "No, I want to go into the science branch," and he was helped to do so. He reached the final state exam and while he couldn't write, we spoke with the Minister of Education who sent two teachers to help him write his exams. He passed the exam, got 87 percent, and then said, "I want to study physics." Today he is in his third year studying physics at Birzeit University. Of course, if you ask him he tells you his role model is Professor Stephen Hawking and he wants to be like him.

So we want, as Palestinians, to be like everyone else: we want to succeed, we want to be achievers. We want things all other people have achieved, like freedom, independence, and equality. Sometimes I say we want to achieve a situation where we sometimes will have the luxury of being bored, like everybody else.

Recently the Deputy Prime Minister, Yair Lapid, spoke to the Washington Institute for Near East Policy (WINEP). Lapid is not considered the most extreme politically; he's sort of in the middle. But listen to what he said at WINEP. He said, "If you support Palestinians, you are supporting terrorists." He also said, "The problem is not about land, it's not about settlements, it's not about Jerusalem. The problem is psychological. Palestinians need the help of psychiatrists to get over the hatred that they have." And he said this is not David versus Goliath, this is "al-Qaeda versus the U.S.A." We the Palestinians are *al-Qaeda,* and Israel is the U.S.A.

A few years ago, a wonderful leader who became the icon of freedom in this world, Nelson Mandela, said two things that I am very proud of. He said that "the Palestinian issue is the greatest moral issue of our time," and he also said, "We will not be completely free until Palestinians are free." So it's not *al-Qaeda* versus the U.S.A.; it's Lapid versus Mandela. Please remember that.

Thank you very much.

"Perspectives from Gaza"

Mads Fredrik Gilbert

I will try to share with you some perspectives from Gaza, occupied State of Palestine, which is the correct term since October 2012. I warn you that I will take you to the realities on the ground in this talk, to the grim realities of the Palestinian people.

I'm a medical doctor and I was in Gaza during the Israeli attacks named "Operation Cast Lead" (2008-9) and also last November (2012) during "Operation Pillar of Defense." I've been working in Gaza for the last 15 years as a medical doctor with various medical solidarity projects. My first engagement with the Palestinian people was in Beirut in 1981 and 1982 during the Israeli army siege and bombing of West Beirut.

I'll start with a photo from Jabaliya camp, one of the many refugee camps in Gaza, taken November 2012. It shows a funeral procession and was taken by a very brave Swedish photographer named Paul Hansen, whom I stayed with in Gaza during the Israeli onslaught, November 2012. I had told him about a severely wounded woman that we treated in a respirator in the ICU in Al-Shifa Hospital and about her husband and two children who had been killed. We were just discussing among ourselves, the doctors, when was the right time to inform the woman about the loss of her husband and two children. Paul was very touched by the story and went to Jabaliya where he happened to enter into the funeral procession. The picture he took shows the two killed children and their father, the woman's husband, behind. Paul actually won the award of "Photo of the Year" from World Press Photo, the most prestigious prize in photojournalism.

Here is the backstory: On the 19th of November, at 7:30 in the morning, an Israeli rocket struck the house of the family Hijazi in Jabaliya, a small two-story building. Ten family members inside. No escape. Fouad, the father of the family, a janitor at the local school, was killed instantly, and so were Mohamed (4), and Sohaib (2). Amna, the mother I talked about in the ICU, was severely wounded, and so were three of her other children. So this is the reality. And this picture shows their funeral. Mohamed was named after his bigger brother who was killed in January 2009, during Operation Cast Lead.

How did Israel react to this award-winning picture? Well, they accused the photographer of having manipulated the picture.

So whenever I come back from Gaza, and when I am there, my main question is: what can we learn from them, the Palestinians? They can manage, they're good. They're doctors and high-level nurses, and paramedics; they don't need my medical skills. They need my solidarity and they need my voice. Actually, this lecture should have, of course, been given by a Palestinian and not by me, because it's their narrative. But they need our voices; they are voiceless and the occupation forces them to be voiceless.

So I relearn, every time, about Palestinian resistance and dignity. The moral imperative is on the Palestinians' side, and that gives them dignity. We have been discussing the *Nakba*, 1948, the tents. But it's reoccurring. It's coming back and coming back. When I went back to Gaza half a year after "Operation Cast Lead," I went to Zeitoun [a poor neighborhood outside Gaza City] where I met the Samouni children. They were back in the tents because their whole habitat, the family's houses, had been completely destroyed by the Israeli massacre in the Samouni family village in Zeitoun in January 2009. Back in the tents, like in '48.

There is an endless, ongoing *Nakba* in Gaza: "Operation Summer Rain" in the summer of 2006, "Cast Lead" (2008-9), then "Pillar of Defense" last November (2012), just to mention a few recent attacks. And on top of this, there is the merciless siege and the economic sanctions from 2006 followed by the blockade of Gaza from 2007, with malnutrition as a direct consequence.

Israeli impunity

In my opinion, one of the most important and challenging moral, political, and medical issues of today is Israeli impunity. That the global community actually accepts these ongoing, systematic, preplanned, exactly executed attacks on the Palestinian civilian population in Gaza and the West Bank, and also the plights of those in the Diaspora in Syria, in Lebanon, and in Jordan.

The issue of legal responsibility for the Israeli killing fields in Gaza received a small notice in *The Guardian* in August 2013; a very small notice indeed. The article states that *one* Israeli soldier had been convicted of a crime committed during "Operation Cast Lead." He is the sole person convicted. Fourteen hundred and fifty Palestinians were killed, 5,300 wounded, the majority civilians. This one Israeli soldier was convicted because he shot two Palestinian women, Majda Abu Hajaj, and her mother Raya. The women came out of a house that was being bombarded by the Israeli forces, and they were waving a white flag. The soldier shot them at point-blank range, and he was sentenced to 45 days in prison. *That means 22.5 days per Palestinian life.* It's less than you get for drunk driving in Norway. And I think these numbers—one convicted and 22.5 days for a Palestinian life—tell you everything about the Israeli apartheid system.

Israeli weapons

What are the weapons the Israelis are using against Gaza? Well, first of all, the siege. No escape, no safe place, no warning systems, no bomb shelters, nothing like that. Then the blockade: the blockade of food, of water, of anything you need for daily life. Utensils for the kitchen, cooking gas, and building materials (window panes, tiles); all you need to rebuild after the bombing. The bombing is done with Israeli F-16s, Apache helicopters, and drones. Then the ground invasion, the huge Merkava tanks and their deadly artillery will come and the soldiers go in with their sophisticated hand-held weapons—very deadly.

And do not forget the Israeli propaganda machine: flyers being dropped from airplanes, phone calls all the time—"Get out, we're going to bomb your house"—and "knocks on roofs" when the drones are hitting the roofs of apartment buildings with small rockets, indicating that this house will be heavily bombed within four minutes. And then in terms of the families, the children, and the elders who are in this situation due to the blackout: they face the cold, the hunger, the insecurity, the fear, the uncertainty about what is going to happen next, and the repetitious Israeli collective punishment of the civilian population, which is highly illegal according to international law.

The sanctions and siege started in 2006-07 and are ongoing. As you know, Gaza is a very, very small piece of land, only a marathon long—45 kilometers from the border with Egypt up to the border with Israel, and 5-12 km wide. There are only two entrances, either through Israel at Erez or through Egypt at Rafah. The whole Strip is completely fenced in on all sides: on the ground, in the air, and on the sea. Gaza City is in the north with 660,000 inhabitants. A beautiful place and one of the oldest cities in the world. Al-Shifa Hospital, where I worked, could have been a university hospital: six operating rooms, all specialties, 500 doctors capable of performing excellent, modern medicine, also open heart surgery. But the hospital is under so much strain from the siege, lack of spare parts and materials. "One and a half million Palestinians are imprisoned in Gaza," said John Ging, the brave UNRWA Head of Mission, in January 2009. Today, 1.8 million Palestinians are still imprisoned in Gaza. Don't forget that this is a child population; the average age in Gaza is 17.6 years old. Sixty percent are 18 or below, so more than one million children and young people are imprisoned in Gaza.

Medical effects

As a consequence of a lack of sufficient and varied food, there is endemic nutritional anemia, protein malnutrition, stunting (the children are more than two standard deviations shorter than they should have been at that age), and hypothermia due to lack of heating. All are *man-made* medical consequences, leading to ill-being for the people.

The Israeli, and now also the Egyptian, siege causes lack of all daily needs: food, water, power and energy, waste disposal at the municipality level, and lack of the materials you need to rebuild your habitat following the bombing. Seventy-four percent of the bombed buildings have not been repaired due to lack of material. The Israelis bombed 28 schools and none of them have been fully restored. And there is, of course, no human security and no export, so the economy is totally wrecked. Gaza is a civilian society that has been systematically forced on its knees by the Israeli siege and blockade. Then, on top of that comes the bombing; the occupier attacks and starts bombing, again and again.

No doubt there is a humanitarian crisis in Gaza. It's man-made, one hundred percent. Only 10 percent of the water is drinkable. Seventy-five to eighty percent of the families are food insecure, meaning they don't know in the morning what to eat for breakfast or lunch or dinner. Three out of four families are totally aid-dependent because of the breakdown of the local economy. That's the situation.

And as we are speaking, having our coffee and tea, and enjoying our flush toilets, most of the people of Gaza have none of this. The weekly reports from the UN[24] are very accurate; for example, they stated in their report the third week of November that the Gaza power plant shut down, and Israel imposed a total ban on transfer of construction materials, which continued for a period of several weeks. The reason for the Gaza power plant shutdown was that the Egyptians closed all the tunnels, which, following the Israeli siege beginning in 2007, had become the lifeline, the umbilicus of Palestinian civilian life. Now, this has also been completely shut off. Influx of building material was stopped from October 13, 2013, so that even UN rebuilding projects are fully stopped.

Gaza is being choked as we speak.

This is just a brief sum-up from the same report, pointing to the fact that all aspects of civilian life, including schooling, primary healthcare, and all provisions that you need for daily life

---

24 For more information, see: http://www.ochaopt.org/

in a community, are being stopped, obstructed, or destroyed by the siege; and the hospitals are facing even more hardship through the lack of spare parts and spare materials.

The day before I left for Jerusalem and this conference, I got a letter from the mayor of Gaza with an urgent appeal; in this letter he urged the mayor of my home city (we are a twin city with Gaza) to come to Gaza's aid because the people were drowning in sewage. Added to this letter was a panel of pictures showing how the sewage was flooding the streets of Gaza. Why? Because they cannot get hold of the 4,000 liters of diesel they need per day to operate the sewage pumping system. So not only are they bombed and starved and denied free access to the world, they are being drowned in their own sewage. And again, this is a one hundred percent *man-made* disaster, made by the State of Israel, supported by the government of the United States.

The Israeli occupation is the key determinant

This is the reality as we are speaking, my friends. There is no human security for the Palestinians. Professor Rita Giacaman, the brilliant Palestinian researcher at Birzeit University, says, "Palestinians are people who were never safe, even before the 1967 Israeli occupation." I totally subscribe to that. In a paper in *The Lancet*, Rita states that "all qualitative measures of health, suffering, fear, humiliation and exposure to violence are increasing." That is a strong statement, but it is documented with extensive scientific evidence. And if you want to know about the relation between the Israeli occupation and health, you should get the issue of *The Lancet* which came out in March 2009, called "Health in the Occupied Palestinian Territory." It's a collection of scientific articles with high standards from a number of scientists.

Summed up, their conclusion is that "hope for improving the health and quality of life of Palestinians will exist only once people recognize that the structural and political conditions that they endured in the occupied State of Palestine are the key determinants of population health."

It is the occupation that is the core problem; so don't send more bandages, don't send doctors, don't send field hospitals. Lift the siege and stop the bombing, and people will be fine.

One of the studies published in *The Lancet* is a whole scale study where they ask more than a thousand Palestinian families two questions: What is causing you most insecurity, fear, and threats? The top four answers:

1) The siege (92%)
2) The occupation (90%)
3) The last war (85%)
4) Internal Palestinian fighting (83%)

And they were asked: What is the most important thing for you now? What you need? And they didn't talk about human rights or voicing their problems to the world:

1) A source of livelihood (75%)
2) To get their homes repaired (58%)
3) Some utilities: water, electricity, and cooking gas (56%)

Why can't the Palestinians in Gaza have that? How come the President of the United States, Barack Hussein Obama, is allowing the government of Israel to starve the people of Gaza in this way?

I shot video in November 2012 in Gaza City, driving through the city on our way to a meeting. What strikes you is the number of children. Everywhere children. And this was just days after the ceasefire, following the attacks in November 2012.

You realize how quickly the Palestinian communities are recoiling after bombardment. They have a formidable *resilience* and the children are getting back to school and they try to get back to normality as quickly as possible. As quickly as possible. There is garbage floating in the streets because the garbage cars are being destroyed by the bombing, and the Israelis don't allow spare parts to be imported, nor the gifts (garbage trucks from Japan, for example, are sitting on the Israeli side). But this is Gaza alive.

Obviously these videos which show children in the streets and the bombings will give you an idea why such large numbers of wounded and killed are civilians. Following each bombing, we wait in Shifa Hospital for the civilians to come in, just like in January 2009. Hanadi Abu Zoor, 10 years old, was admitted to the ICU after she was almost killed when the Israelis bombed her family's house at four o'clock in the morning while they were sleeping. The Israelis were polite enough to "knock on the roof" with a rocket, but the family didn't manage to get up in four minutes and get out of the house.

Pillar of Defense

During the week-long "Pillar of Defense," the Israeli forces killed 190 Palestinians with 1,490 wounded, while six Israelis were killed and 224 wounded. No Israelis or Palestinians should be killed, but the Israeli people and the Israeli government have to understand that living as an occupying state will not give them peace. The only way you can have peace is to have justice for both people. Leave the apartheid system and have justice for the Palestinian people. A just, political solution is the only thing that can stop these killings and the suffering on both sides.

Among the 1,400 injured, 34 percent were children, i.e. 504 were children. And among the 504 children, 39 percent were younger than five years old; so you had 195 children under five injured in one week. The other Abu Zoor children, the boys who were injured and a girl, were not fatally wounded. One needed life-saving surgery and survived.

The physical destruction was immense. The Israeli armed forces have developed a military doctrine called the "Dahiya Doctrine." "Dahiya" in Arabic means suburb, and it refers to the suburb in Beirut where Hezbollah has its stronghold. The Israeli army developed this strategy in 2006 when invading Lebanon and continues to use it in Gaza. These buildings in central Gaza City were completely destroyed by Israeli bombing in January 2009. A quote from Major Yoav Galant, who was the commander of the Israeli southern command, the day after the Cast Lead began, illustrates the "Dahiya Doctrine." Galant says that the aim of the Israeli attack should be *"to send Gaza decades into the past"* while at the same time *"attaining the maximum number of enemy casualties and keeping IDF casualties at a minimum.*" In more simple words: to destroy as much as possible of the infrastructure and to intimidate the inhabitants by inflicting on them large losses of human life in order to break their resistance. This is to intimidate and scare the population. This is collective punishment, and as such, is forbidden according to the Geneva Convention. And they also state in the "Dahiya Doctrine" that they should make the reconstruction as long and painful as possible. That's why they don't let Gazans import building materials.

Just look up pictures of the aftermath following the fierce Israeli bombing. I took a tour in Zeitoun three days after the ceasefire in 2012, and you can see the immense destruction in this residential area.

The house of the Abu Zoor family, where Hanadi lived, was completely destroyed. In this house, she was sleeping with her family and four people were killed: Mohammed (4), Zahar (29), Nisma (20), and Iyad (26). And the five children who survived were severely wounded and all were taken to Shifa Hospital for life-saving treatment: Mahmoud (8), Mohammad (12), Fatima (12), Foad (5), and Hanadi (10). I name them because these are human beings, not numbers. These are humans of flesh and blood, like you and me, like your children, like your grandchildren, like my children. They are not numbers or statistics. They deserve the same respect, dignity, and security as we do.

Terrorism
Terrorism is defined as "the systematic use of terror, often violent, especially as a means of coercion." If what the State of Israel is doing against the Palestinian people in Gaza is not state terrorism, I don't know what is. This is systematic intimidation, carefully planned attacks, executed in order to scare the population.

The picture I have of Mohammad Abu Zoor (12), just coming off the ventilator in the Shifa Hospital ICU, reminds me of the pain which results from such human atrocities. Pre-planned, premeditated, executed by one of the strongest military powers in the world: Israel.

The key sponsor of Israeli state terrorism is the United States. Times are changing, however, and there are currently a number of very important initiatives from the United States to stop the military support to Israel. There is a postcard campaign: "Yes, we can end military aid to Israel." And on the backside it says: "I urge you to hold Israel accountable for its violation of U.S. laws and cut off military aid rather than increase it." *I urge you to hold Israel accountable.* Now those of you from the United States, my brothers and sisters, you have the key. You are the most important solidarity workers in the world if we are to stop this state terrorism against Palestine, because you can pressure your government and that is the most important precondition for the Israel atrocities. The current upsurge of the BDS-movement across the U.S. is indeed promising.

Let me take you back to "Operation Cast Lead." A political cartoon of rockets firing into a prison labeled "Gaza" said that it was like "bombing a besieged child prison." It really was. In both Cast Lead and Pillar of Defense, nobody gets out. Nobody can escape. Not like the pictures from other wars we see on the TV: long lines of people on bicycles, cars or donkey carts with their piles of some utensils, families flying into the jungle or a neighboring state to escape the bombardment. You can't escape from Gaza. You're locked in. You're in a cage. The Israelis are bombing a caged people. Can it be more cowardly than that? To bomb a population who cannot fly away or have any safe haven?

The numbers from Cast Lead: 13 Israelis killed, 10 of whom were soldiers, five of whom were killed by their own. Fourteen hundred and thirty Palestinians killed. The ratio of killed Israelis to killed Palestinians is 1 to 100; injured 1 to 10. This is also in contravention of international law. Fighting forces are obliged to use *proportional* military force. The Israelis are not using proportional force; they are using overwhelmingly brutal, disproportional force. That's why you get these proportions of people killed.

The children come running into the emergency room in Shifa, scared, injured, looking for their parents. What do they see? What do they hear? Smell? Understand? Fear?

Do they remember? And do *we*, at least, remember *them*?

Another child, just from the ICU, survived though he had a severe head injury. During the three weeks in December and January 2008-2009, Israeli forces killed more than 400 children (18 years old and younger) and injured more than 1,800 in Gaza.

Now, do the acid test. What would the world have said if the Palestinians had killed 400 Israeli children and injured 1,800 Israeli children? What would the government of the United States have said? What would my government have said?

They sat idle, and they accepted these numbers of killed children in 2009.

This was also the first really extensive Israeli drone war. These unmanned airplanes that can carry six rockets, are equipped with very strong cameras, and can be airborne for up to 72 hours. The U.S. uses them extensively in Afghanistan and Pakistan, and the Israeli governmental army uses them in Gaza. When I am in Gaza, I hear them all the time. The drone pilots sit safely in a bunker somewhere in Israel. They see everything on the ground through these very sharp cameras, and fire the rockets with a little joystick. They see everything on the ground. They can tell the difference between an adult and a child, a man and a woman. They video-record every hit. They know exactly what they're doing, what they hit.

And this is what we get into the hospital. Children with extensive shrapnel wounds, like Mahmoud Masharawi (11). We tried to resuscitate him. He had been hit while playing on the rooftop of the family's house in central Gaza City, together with his cousin Ahmed (16). Ahmed was completely torn apart and killed on the spot. Mahmoud died in my hands from all these inlets from the drone rocket, the so-called small diametric bomb.

More than 1,400 were killed during Operation Cast Lead, and, I warn you, there are pictures you do not want to see. Ahmed (12) came in following a drone attack; we took him straight to the operating room while trying to resuscitate him. Unfortunately he died. He came from al-Montar, a neighborhood in the outskirts of Gaza City. Both his legs had been completely cut off by the drone explosive. He had extensive burns, and when we turned him to the side his buttocks were completely sliced off from the pelvis, opened into the abdomen.

Ahmed should have played, gone to school, traveled, attended college and have a girlfriend; done all the things other children do.

Was this a "successful campaign" seen from the Israeli side? Yes, it was. This is what the President of Israel, Shimon Peres, said two days before the Israeli troops withdrew: *"Implementation of the current operation has gone 90 percent according to plan."*

Nobody has been held accountable or taken to the International Criminal Court for the killing of Ahmed or the more than 400 other Palestinian children. This is the rest of president Peres' statement he gave during a meeting in Jerusalem on the 14th of January, 2009, when he spoke to a group from the Israeli lobby organization AIPAC:

"Israel's goal was to provide a strong blow to the people of Gaza so that they would lose their appetite for shooting at Israel. That's all."

That's precisely the Dahiya Doctrine, made public. It is collective punishment, and as such is illegal.

If you want to learn more, read our book *Eyes in Gaza*. It's available in Arabic and it just recently came out in the second English edition with a sharp foreword by Noam Chomsky.

To conclude, let me share with you the story of nine-month-old Jumana. She came to Shifa Hospital on January 5, 2009, following the massacre of the Samuni family in Zeitoun. We had to amputate most of her left hand because it was completely crushed. Her mother was gone, and we heard that her father and her grandparents had been killed next to her. The Samuni family (more than a hundred of them) were forcefully collected by the Israeli invading ground troops, in a warehouse overnight, and in the morning bombed by Israeli forces. Between 20 and 30 were instantly killed, around 50 injured, among them Jumana. She survived and her mother finally came about, but her father was killed next to her.

I went back to Gaza in August 2009, half a year after the attack, to see Jumana. She was now 15 months old, sitting comfortably on the arm of Maysa, her mother, who was only 18 when she was widowed during the attack. Maysa was concerned and asked if I could take a picture of Jumana's little hand with the two remaining fingers, and I said of course I can. But I asked the mother, "Why do you want me to take this picture?"

"Maybe you can take it to Norway and maybe we can do some operations to put back the three lost fingers," she answered.

"Of course I will do that," I said.

To me, this little child hand has come to symbolize the plight of the Palestinian people. Who has been held responsible for this mutilation?

I went back again January 2012. Now Maysa was 21, and Jumana 3 years and 9 months. Gaza was still under siege, poor, gray, but clean. Jumana had grown, and was still very confident. Maysa had started at university. We had a beautiful afternoon.

I asked Grandfather, a servant in the local mosque, "What am I going to tell the American people next time I go there to lecture about Gaza and the occupation of Palestine?"

He responded quickly: "Tell them this one thing. Tell the people of the United States: Your tax money is killing us. The U.S. is subsidizing Israel $2,500 USD per capita per year, with taxpayers' money. Tell them that. They have a responsibility."

I went back to see the family again in November 2012, after the Pillar of Defense attack. Jumana is a lovely and nice little girl. The entire family is strong, dignified, friendly, and show me great hospitality. They tell me, like all the other Palestinians I know: life has to go on.

Gaza is survival, Gaza is resistance, and Gaza is courage and dignity.

We owe them our solidarity.

Here's my take-home message:

- The main factor for Palestinian ill-health is the Israeli occupation of Palestine.
- The second factor for this ill-health is Israeli impunity.
- The third factor is the international acceptance of the Israeli apartheid, not stopping them, sanctioning them, or doing more to impose the legal, nonviolent political tools of boycott, divestment and sanctions.

So I conclude with this image, back in Zeitoun in November 2012.

I visited the Abu Zoor's family house and their neighbors, the Azzam family. They had arranged for a banner to be suspended between the ruins of the two family houses. The text reads (in Arabic): *"We stand steadfast despite occupation, siege, and bombing. The Family Azzam."*

They don't give up, and we should not give up. *Al-Sumud*, steadfastness, is part of Palestinian culture and resistance. I talked to the young boy Ahmad Azzam (9), whose house had been bombed, and asked him "What do you want to do with your future?"

The boy looked at me with his very calm eyes, and said in broken English, "Dr. Mads, I want to be a doctor."

He doesn't want to be a terrorist. He just wants justice, freedom, and a dignified life, like all of us do.

One day, *insha'allah*, Jumana and the other children will disarm the Israeli occupation forces. And maybe one day, *insha'allah*, both people will have peace.

But there will be no peace without justice and there will not be peace with the ongoing Israeli occupation of Palestine. Endure and resist, my friends. *Shukran jazeelan*. Thank you very much.

"Perspectives from Israel"

Hala Khoury-Bisharat

I want to give you an overview of the socio-political, legal, and human rights situations of the Palestinian citizens of Israel. I will demonstrate that the human rights of Palestinians inside the State of Israel have deteriorated in the past couple of years in several areas, focusing on three topics. My first topic is the Prawer-Begin Plan (also known as the Prawer Plan), concerning the evictions and displacement of Bedouin citizens from "unrecognized villages" in the south of Israel. My second topic addresses the racist, anti-democratic, and discriminatory cluster of bills that have been proposed in the Israeli Knesset. And my final topic is the ban on family reunification in Israel between Palestinian citizens of Israel and Palestinians from the Occupied Palestinian Territories (OPT).

The Bedouins are indigenous Palestinians who are citizens of Israel who live in the *Naqab* (Negev) desert, and have predominantly agricultural livelihoods. The Prawer Plan, which was accepted as an Israeli governmental plan two years ago, aims to displace up to 70,000 Bedouins living in so-called "unrecognized villages." Many of these indigenous Bedouins were first displaced in 1948, and in the 1950s the Israeli military government ordered their displacement yet again, sending them to where they currently live today. Israel has been practicing displacement against these Bedouins since 1948, and it continues the process with the Prawer Plan. The Prawer Plan aims to initiate another mass displacement of the Bedouin citizens.

But what do we mean when we talk about "unrecognized" villages? They are called "unrecognized" because the State of

Israel, in refusing to recognize the villages, does not connect them to any state infrastructure. These villages have no electricity, no running water, no sewage, no healthcare, no education, and no roads. Why is the State of Israel doing this? It is doing this in order to force these people to leave their ancestral lands and move to other places, specifically very impoverished towns. The aim is to confine them into one specific area, and to get rid of the legal mechanisms that these Bedouins have been using for years to defend their rights on their lands.

Umm al-Hieran and the Prawer Plan

I will give you an example of the village of Umm al-Hieran. On 10 November 2013, the Israeli government announced that it plans to accelerate the eviction of all the Bedouins living in Umm al-Hieran. We are talking about 150 families, around 1,000 people. The government wants to demolish the village, and on the ruins of the village, it wants to establish a new Jewish settlement. For 10 years, Umm al-Hieran has been trying through many mechanisms, especially legal mechanisms (such as Israeli courts and planning committees), to fight the demolition orders against them, but it is not helping. On 20 November 2013, there was a Supreme Court hearing about the Umm al-Hieran eviction, not long after the Israeli government announced that it wants to demolish the village as soon as possible. On 19 March 2014, the Supreme Court denied the appeal against the demolition order, allowing the demolition to continue. These legal avenues that have been used by Bedouin citizens to prevent the state from carrying out its plans have led the Israeli government to say, "We cannot handle every time one of these villages goes through the legal mechanisms when we file the demolition orders. We have to stop this. We have to wipe them away with one stroke. What is the best way to do this? Through the Prawer Plan."

The Prawer Plan aims to demolish all 35 unrecognized villages in the Negev, displacing almost 70,000 people. On 20 November 2013, for example, the unrecognized village of Al-Araqib was demolished for the 61st time. But the residents rebuild their village again and again, and continue to struggle to stay on their land. The government wants to confine them into a very impoverished Bedouin town called Hura. The same story goes with Umm al-Hieran, which will be demolished and the families moved to Hura. Hura suffers from a very poor socioeconomic situation with high poverty and crime rates. Imagine people living in the same houses with their herds in the backyard, with the horrible smell, because of the overcrowded conditions of the town. When the State of Israel talks about its "offer" to the Bedouin people, it is only offering to evict these people from their ancestral lands into impoverished areas.

If we look at the history of the village of Umm al-Hieran, in 1948, the people were not just living in Umm al-Hieran but also other territory beside it. But after the establishment of the State of Israel and the *Nakba*, the Bedouins were forced to leave their lands and move to another area. Then again, in 1956, the Israeli military government evicted the families to the place where Umm al-Hieran stands today. So imagine, after more than 50 years of cultivating the lands and living there, the state now wants to demolish the houses and evict them once again.

When we look at this case legally, we are talking about the infringement of constitutional rights of these Bedouin citizens. We are talking about the right to equality, the right to dignity, the right to fair housing, the right to choose your own housing. All these rights are part of international treaties that are considered part of international human rights law. The State of Israel is bound by these treaties because, since 1966, the state has been a party to the International Covenant on Civil and Political Rights, which refers to the freedom to choose your own place of living, to equality, and to dignity. Israel has been violating these rights of the indigenous Palestinian people of the Negev.

The Prawer Plan is a discriminatory policy. If we think about it, what is the government doing? It is entrenching an historic injustice against these Bedouins by evicting them and establishing Jewish towns over their lands. They did not even say to the Bedouins, "Maybe some of you would like to stay in this place and be part of Hiran, the Jewish settlement that will be established." The case of Umm al-Hieran thus exemplifies the essence of the Prawer Plan.

The international community has, of course, called upon Israel to stop this discriminatory policy and to stop the Prawer Plan from being implemented. But the Plan is happening *now*. We have demolition orders against many villages, and in June 2013 the government approved the first reading of the bill that will turn the Prawer Plan into law. It is now being prepared for the second and third readings, even while it is already being implemented on the ground.

The international community, including United Nations human rights bodies, has repeatedly expressed its opposition to the Prawer Plan and called upon Israel to stop the Plan, but nothing is helping. In March 2012, the UN Committee on the Elimination of Racial Discrimination called on Israel to withdraw the proposed implementation of legislation of the Prawer Plan on the grounds that it was discriminatory. In July 2012, the European Parliament passed an historic resolution calling on Israel to stop the Prawer Plan and its policies of displacement, eviction, and dispossession against Palestinians.

In 2013, the UN High Commissioner for Human Rights, Navi Pillay, issued a statement in which she called on Israel to reconsider the Prawer Plan, stating, "I'm alarmed that this bill, which seeks to legitimize forcible displacement and dispossession of indigenous Bedouin communities in the Negev, is being pushed through the Knesset." She continued, saying, "If this bill becomes law, it will accelerate the demolition of entire Bedouin communities, forcing them to give up their homes, denying them their rights to land ownership, and decimating their traditional, cultural, and social life in the name of development. The government of Israel must recognize and respect the specific rights of its Bedouin communities, including its recognition of Bedouin land ownership claims."

Discriminatory bills in the Israeli Knesset

My second topic covers the cluster of racist, discriminatory and anti-democratic legislation that has been proposed by members of the 19th Knesset. The human rights of Palestinians in Israel and Palestinians in the OPT are the targets of this legislation. What is amazing about these bills is that they affect both Palestinian citizens of Israel and Palestinians from the OPT, so we always see the connection. For example, if you think about the Prawer Plan, we are talking about the same kind of displacement that occurs in the OPT: establishing Jewish settlements and confiscating land from Palestinians. This is happening on both sides of the Green Line.

The Prawer Plan is only one of these new discriminatory bills. A second one is the Contributors to the State Bill, which gives preferential treatment to discharged soldiers in employment, rent, purchasing of land for housing, civil service jobs, university admission, student housing, and other areas. The bill, which effectively excludes most Palestinian citizens of Israel, also states that these additional benefits will not be regarded as constituting unlawful discrimination. Another bill is the Basic Law: Israel as the Nation-State of the Jewish People Bill, which seeks to change the Jewish and democratic definition of the state by subordinating the democratic component to the Jewish component.

Another one is the Counterterrorism Bill, which would entrench many emergency regulations currently in effect into Israeli law; it is a move that will significantly undermine the rights of Palestinian security detainees. A fifth bill, the Jenin-Jenin Bill, allows Israeli soldiers to file class-action lawsuits against a film director, journalist, or any other individual for defamation regarding criticism of their conduct during military operations in the OPT. Another example, a bill to raise the electoral threshold from 2 percent to 3.25 percent, threatens to squeeze the Arab political parties out of the Knesset without creating safeguards for minority representation in the country's law-making body. My final example on this issue is a new amendment to Israel's compensation law, which would further restrict Palestinians from the OPT who were injured or whose family members were killed by the Israeli military from filing damage claims before Israeli courts.

These bills give you an idea of what is going on in the Knesset, not even considering what is happening in daily life. For example, there is increasing incitement and racism against the Palestinian minority in Israel, which we see in hate speech from both Israeli officials and from the public, including incitement to physical violence. We see destruction of property, we see hate graffiti, etc. This is what is happening now in Israel.

The ban on family reunification

My third topic also affects Palestinians from the OPT. The ban on family reunification is the clearest example of the connection that Israel is drawing between Palestinian citizens of Israel and Palestinians from the OPT.

Each one of us begins by saying that every human being has a right to decide to whom they wish to get married. We have the right and the freedom to choose our spouses and with whom we want to spend our lives. Not so in Israel. In April 2013, the Knesset extended a law that bans family reunification of Palestinian citizens of Israel with their spouses from the OPT, including Gaza, and from any other countries which are deemed "enemy countries" by Israel. According to this law, a Palestinian cannot get married to somebody from their national group— another Palestinian from the OPT—and live together inside Israel.

This is a racist law that has no parallel in any democratic country in the world. There are laws in other countries that decide who may enter a country, but you do not have a law that specifically states that "Palestinians are banned from..." They are named: *Palestinians* are banned from family reunification under the Citizenship and Entry into Israel Law. This law was originally passed in 2003 as a temporary order for only one year, but the government has extended the law again and again. As a result, the ban on family reunification for thousands of Palestinian citizens of Israel with other Palestinians has now been going on for a decade. This infringes upon and violates their human rights, their constitutional rights to citizenship, their freedom to choose their partner in life, their right to dignity, and their right to equality. The law not only infringes on constitutional rights, but also constitutes racial discrimination. Remember that Israel is a party to the International Convention on the Elimination of All Forms of Racial Discrimination, so by maintaining this amendment to the Citizenship Law, Israel is violating its duties under international law.

I want to again stress why this is racial discrimination: the law bars individuals from family reunification solely on the basis of their national and ethnic belonging. If this is not racial discrimination, what is? So what does the state claim as a reason for this law? The state alleges that the purpose behind this ban is to protect Israel from threats to its security. However, if we look at the numbers involving family reunification applicants and those convicted for security-related offenses, the law is totally disproportionate.

What is the true agenda behind this law? It is about the right of return for the Palestinian people. The government does not want Palestinians entering the country; it is frightened, and it is making efforts to maintain a Jewish demographic majority inside Israel. That is the aim of this law, and nothing else.

The state calls Palestinians "threats to security," but where is the threat to security if Palestinians from the OPT are allowed to enter Israel to work on a daily basis? We are talking about thousands of people who are able to get permits to enter Israel. Where is the security threat? Security is not the real reason for the law. Adalah, the Legal Center for Arab Minority Rights in Israel, has tried with other Israeli human rights organizations to fight this law through legal mechanisms, namely the Supreme Court, but again and again, the petitions are denied. We filed petitions in 2003, in 2006, and 2007. We have to remember that this law, as I mentioned before, was supposed to last only one year. But it turns out the law was widely promoted by the government in order to keep extending it. None of the petitions succeeded in striking down the law.

The growing incitement and wave of racist legislation in Israel are all a continuation of the same idea. The Supreme Court could not give us solutions to our petitions, and the ban on family reunification continues. Because Palestinians remain a "threat" to the country, racism and hate towards them are nourished. The fact that the Supreme Court would not strike down the ban on family reunification effectively gave the Knesset the right to introduce the cluster of racist bills we are witnessing in Israel today.

What did the international community do about this? In July 2013, the UN Committee on the Elimination of Racial Discrimination joined with other human rights treaty bodies and called upon Israel to revoke the law, expressing their concern "that thousands of Palestinian children are deprived of their right to live and grow up in a family environment with both of their parents or with their siblings, and that thousands live under the fear of being separated because of the severe restrictions on family reunification under the Citizenship and Entry into Israel Law."

To sum up, the citizenship of the Palestinians inside Israel is a second-class citizenship. This is what the state is telling us on a daily basis: you are a second-class citizen, and we will determine the laws that affect you. We will determine to whom you can get married. If you want to marry a Palestinian from the OPT, or from any other Arab country, you will not live here in Israel together. If you want to be together, leave. Leave and go to another place. You will not live together in Israel.

"Breaking a Generation"

Gerard Horton

There is something that I would like you to think about as you climb into bed tonight and turn off the light. About 20 kilometers from Jerusalem is a refugee camp called Al 'Arrub. Al 'Arrub is located on the main highway between Bethlehem and Hebron, and as you turn off your light tonight, the residents of Al 'Arrub will be turning off theirs.

But that is probably where the similarities end. You see, Al 'Arrub is situated at one of the friction points in the West Bank. Some friction points occur where an Israeli settlement is built close to a Palestinian village or refugee camp. Other points of friction can be found where roads used by the Israeli military and settlers pass close to a Palestinian centre of population. And it is at these friction points that many children and adults are arrested.

Most children are arrested for throwing stones, either at the military or at settlers at these friction points. To put it into perspective: according to U.N. figures, since June 1967—when martial law was imposed on the West Bank—between 750,000 and 800,000 men, women and children have been arrested and prosecuted in Israeli military courts. Each year this works out to between 500 and 700 children. The minimum age of criminal responsibility in these military courts is 12 years old.

I would now like you to consider this from the military's perspective. What is it that the military is trying to achieve? Why is it arresting so many adults and children? Essentially, this occurs because the role of the military in the West Bank is to protect the settlers, and if you allow 560,000 civilians to live in occupied territory, you are going to cause friction. Consider it this way for a moment: Imagine if the U.S. or its allies had tried to relocate half a million American civilians to Afghanistan or Iraq, and they built towns and villages, roads, hospitals and schools. Can you imagine the security implications this would have and how difficult it would be for a military to guarantee their safety? You might find that most military commanders would tell their political masters that the task is impossible and cannot be done. And yet this is precisely what has been going on for the past 46 years in the West Bank.

I think it is interesting to consider how this has been achieved. How is it possible that so many civilians have been encouraged to live in occupied territory? And how is it possible, according to the U.S. State Department, that not a single settler was killed in 2012? This is extraordinary. In 2013, four settlers were killed; again, an extraordinary state of affairs given the circumstances.

So the question remains, how has this been achieved? As mentioned, the military's task is to guarantee protection for the settlers. The problem for the military is what to do when stones are thrown at these friction points, at places like Al ʿArrub. If an Israeli military convoy enters some place like Al ʿArrub, the young Palestinian men and boys are likely to throw stones, and from time to time, stones will also be thrown at settlers. The problem for the military commander is what to do when, in many cases, you cannot positively identify the stone throwers. I think there is a choice. You can ignore the incident, but if you do you will probably find more people throwing stones the next day, and pretty soon you will have lost control of the West Bank. So from the military's perspective, ignoring stone throwing is not a viable option.

So what is to be done? After reviewing over 700 testimonies and talking with many people, including former Israeli soldiers, the response seems to be simple and effective: once a stone throwing incident has been reported, but the perpetrator has not been identified, the local military commander makes a number of assumptions. First, he assumes the stone throwers came from the nearest Palestinian village, which is quite possibly correct. Secondly, he assumes that the stone throwers are young men or boys. Again, quite possibly correct. The next thing the commander considers is who has previously been arrested from the village. As in other places, when in doubt, authorities have been known to simply round up the "usual suspects." With at least 750,000 men, women and children detained since 1967, chances are there will be plenty of "usual suspects" in the village from which to choose.

In addition to the "usual suspects" option, informants from the village are contacted for information. After 46 years of military occupation, the system is well developed. Children frequently report that attempts are made to recruit them during interrogation; interrogators offer small inducements or make threats to press the children to confess against other children, or to encourage them to provide information on an on-going basis. Of course, it is difficult to collect accurate information about this type of recruitment because no one readily admits to providing information. But bear in mind that some children are no more than 12 years old and the interrogations are often coercive. This has always been a useful form of intelligence for any army of occupation.

From these sources a list is compiled, and several nights later, after the lights have been switched off, there is every possibility that a military convoy will enter that village intent on arrest. The intelligence is usually excellent, so the army knows precisely where the people they've come to arrest live. The first thing the family or any of the children know about this is banging on the front door, with yelling in Hebrew or Arabic. Once the family has been gathered together, the officer in charge compares identity cards with the names on his list. Once identified, a person on the list is separated from the rest of the family, even children as young as 12, although the most common ages are 15 to 17. The child's hands are usually then tied behind his back with a plastic zip tie, ties that can be tightened but not loosened. From the young soldier's perspective, he has been told that this village is a dangerous place. He will want to get in and out of the village as quickly as possible. So, the ties are put on quickly, but the problem is, when you put these zip ties on quickly, it's very easy to overtighten them. The more the person struggles, the tighter they get. The tighter they get, the less blood flows to the wrists. The hands then swell up, and on it goes. The child is also blindfolded in most cases, and then led out of the house.

A particularly disturbing aspect of the system is that very rarely will the soldiers come with any form of documentation for the family. Rarely is an arrest warrant produced. The family will be pleading with the soldiers, asking why the child is being taken, and frequently the soldiers do not respond. Sometimes the commander tells the family that the child is being taken for a few hours for questioning and will then be returned later that morning. But the child is never returned after a few hours. The reason the commander says this is to calm the situation down so he can get his men out of the village as quickly as possible without provoking a riot.

The child is then taken out of the house. Often the mother and the father follow the soldiers, seeking information, but are soon forced back into the house at gunpoint. The child is placed in the back of a military transport. After the soldiers get into the transport, the vehicle drives off into the night. The child is then taken to an interrogation centre and handed over to Israeli police for questioning. These interrogation centres are in or near a settlement; in the case of Al 'Arrub, the interrogation centre is near the settlement bloc of Gush Etzion, just south of Bethlehem. In the North, most interrogations occur in the police station in Ariel settlement.

The journey to the interrogation centre can take 20 minutes or many hours; meanwhile the child is tied and blindfolded. At this time the child is generally not given anything to eat or drink, and is not allowed to use the toilet. A number of children wet themselves, either through fear or because they haven't been allowed to use the toilet. In over one-third of cases, the children are transported on the metal floor of the vehicle, simply because there are not enough seats for everybody. If there is a spare seat, the child is put on the spare seat. Naturally, transport on the floor causes further injury and stress to the child.

When the child eventually arrives at the interrogation centre, he is usually led straight to interrogation. The child will not, generally, see a lawyer before he is interrogated. Under military law, he is supposed to be told that he has the right to consult with a lawyer, although the law does not say when the consultation should take place. In practice, very few children ever get to see a lawyer until they are inside the military court days later. Under Israeli military law, the child is supposed to have the right to silence, but rarely does anybody tell the child about his rights. The child is also not accompanied by a parent during interrogation. One point worth remembering is that if an Israeli child living in a settlement—perhaps only 500 metres away from the Palestinian child—is arrested, he will be dealt with under civilian law and will generally be accompanied by a parent. This is important because a child is less likely to be mistreated if accompanied by a parent.

By the time the child is interrogated, he is usually sleep deprived and in pain from the hand ties. Most likely he is also thirsty, hungry, bruised and fearful. He probably still does not know why he has been arrested or what is going to happen to him. He is put on a chair, the blindfold removed but his hands frequently remain tied. The interrogator then does what is necessary to get a confession out of the child. This usually begins with a general allegation, nothing specific. The allegation may be: "Why do you throw stones at Israelis?" The child invariably denies that he throws stones, whether or not this is true, and the interrogator then approaches the child, bringing his face close to the child's and yells threats and abuse. Frequently reported threats include: "You'll be subject to physical violence if you don't confess." "You'll go to prison for a very long time if you don't confess." "We will hand you over to the Shin Bet for interrogation if you don't confess." The interrogator will also know if the child's father has a permit to work inside Israel. If yes, the threat might be: "We will revoke your father's work permit if you don't confess."

If the threats do not work, the interrogation may become physical. The interrogator might slap the child or push him off his chair. In a much smaller number of cases, the violence is more severe. For example, a few months ago we documented a case where the child alleged that he was tasered during an interrogation. But generally, threatening a sleep-deprived child is sufficient. Extraordinarily, in at least one-third of cases, children report being shown documents written in Hebrew which they sometimes sign. Frequently the child does not know what this document contains and must rely on what the interrogator tells him.

Within a couple of days of the interrogation, the child is taken to a military court where he meets his lawyer for the first time. And there's not a great deal a lawyer can do at that stage if the child has provided a confession. In most cases, the child is denied bail, and this is a big problem. Although under the rules of evidence that apply, confessions have to be given voluntarily, this is very rarely challenged because to do so often results in longer jail time. If a child pleads guilty to throwing stones, he is given, on average, two to three months in prison, depending on the circumstances. If, on the other hand, the child decides to challenge the case, perhaps because he alleges he was mistreated, bail will most likely be denied, and he remains in detention. The child's case would probably not come for a final hearing for four to six months. In other words, the quickest way to get out of this system, whether innocent or not, is to plead guilty, and this is what most people do. And, indeed, according to the latest statistics issued by the military courts, the conviction rate is a staggering 99.74 percent.

As far as imprisonment is concerned, in over 50 percent of the cases, children are transferred to prisons inside Israel, in violation of Article 76 of the Fourth Geneva Convention. Under this Article, all prisoners must remain in the occupied territory. In the case of adult Palestinian prisoners, the proportion held in violation of the Fourth Geneva Convention exceeds 80 percent.

To be frank with you, I'm not sure the military could control the West Bank in any other way. That is the inherent problem with prolonged occupation. So, even though what is happening may not be legal, it is very effective. When the children are released, most have some level of post-traumatic stress disorder. They may not tell you as much but their mothers will. The mothers of these children frequently describe how their boys wet their beds, have nightmares, drop out of school, and become isolated. Many boys will often say that they never want to see another soldier again and they want to stay as far from a friction point as possible. And that, from the military's perspective, must be considered as a success.

And so, returning to our starting point: how does an army protect 560,000 civilians living in occupied territory? Through intimidation on a grand scale, which helps to explain why 750,000 people have been detained. The population generally avoids confrontation and shuts itself away. This form of psychological control is far more efficient and cheaper than placing a large number of soldiers on the ground.

It is unrealistic to expect major changes without a just political solution. There is no nice way of maintaining a military occupation whilst at the same time constructing settlements. However, there are six core recommendations that, if effectively implemented, would make a difference.

1. Children should only be arrested during daylight hours except in rare and exceptional circumstances. This can be safely and practically achieved through the issue of summonses.
2. All children and their legal guardians should be provided with a written statement in Arabic informing them of their full legal rights in custody. This statement must be provided at the time of arrest or as soon as possible, but prior to questioning.
3. All children must be given the opportunity to consult with a lawyer of their choice prior to questioning.
4. All children must be accompanied by a family member throughout their questioning.
5. Every interrogation must be audio and visually recorded and a copy of the tape given to the defence lawyer prior to the first hearing.
6. A breach of any of the above recommendations should result in the discontinuation of the prosecution and the child's immediate release.

"Negev Report"

Gordon Matthews

On Saturday, during the Sabeel conference, I joined an excursion to the Negev. Three coach-loads of conference participants travelled from Jerusalem to visit Bedouin villages in the semi-arid southern part of Israel.

After a brief stop at a service station on the way, the coach that I was on stopped first at a village—rather, the remains of a village—north of Be'er Sheva, one of the largest cities in Israel and almost exclusively Jewish. The village, Al Arakib, was home to 573 Bedouin villagers when it was first destroyed in 2010. The village was "unrecognised," and so was not provided with water or electricity by the Israeli authorities. In spite of this, the houses of these semi-nomadic people had both water and electricity. And everyone had work.

In 1999, and again a couple of years later, the whole area around Al Arakib was sprayed with defoliant, causing serious damage to olive trees and other crops. In 2010, the 63 houses in the village were demolished and 4,000 olive trees uprooted. Where several hundred Bedouin villagers had been practising sustainable agriculture, the Jewish National Fund has planted thousands of trees, including eucalyptus, which require much more water than is provided by the scanty winter rainfall. Israel is mining the aquifers of Palestine for water.

After the destruction of their village in 2010, the Bedouin rebuilt it as best they could. But then it was demolished again, rebuilt again, demolished again, until now it has been demolished more than 60 times. Some villagers have sought refuge in nearby towns. They are mostly unemployed. A few remain with their animals in tents beside the cemetery.

The sheikh, the head of the village, who is now 65 years old, had recently been arrested for building illegally. When he appeared in court, the judge was using his mobile phone throughout the proceedings.

Our next stop was al-Surra, a village to the east of Be'er Sheva on the way to Arad, a small town near the southern end of the Dead Sea. In 1948, around 11,000 Bedouin were transferred to a roughly triangular area between Be'er Sheva, Arad, and Dimona to the south. They were all that was left of a total Bedouin population of 90,000. The rest became refugees.

There are now 70,000 Bedouin living in unrecognised villages in this area. They face displacement once again, this time to two towns and five recognised villages.

Many of the 500 villagers in al-Surra are already unemployed, because much of their grazing land has been confiscated. We could see a large military base which was constructed in 1982. Some villagers still herd animals while some commute to work further afield.

We were welcomed at the entrance to the village by Khalil and his delightful four-year-old daughter. Khalil pointed out a mosque and told us that there are two day care centres for young children in the village. Older children go to a school in a recognised village 15 kilometres away.

Khalil showed us some solar panels which he has been installing since 2003 to replace noisy and costly generators. He keeps 15 chickens to provide eggs, and he uses waste water to irrigate a few olive trees. One of the trees beside his house turned out to be a mulberry tree.

We sat around tables on the veranda at the front of the house and were treated to a delicious and substantial lunch.

Our coach then took us back past the growing town of Hura to Rahat, a large Bedouin town north of Be'er Sheva. We were joined by the other two coach-loads of conference participants to listen to a Jewish volunteer with the Regional Council of Unrecognised

Villages telling us about the Prawer Plan being debated in the Knesset. If the Prawer Plan is approved, 30,000 Bedouin living in 35 unrecognised villages will be transferred to two towns and five recognised villages. Their claims to the land that was allocated to them in 1948 will be terminated. Jewish settlements are already being built in the area.

We were all encouraged to write to our MPs or representatives in Congress and to the Israeli Ambassadors in our home countries to call for cancellation of the Prawer Plan.

PART III
INTERNATIONAL LAW

INTERNATIONAL LAW AND RELIGION

Jonathan Kuttab

As I think about the role of international law as it pertains to the Israel-Palestine question, I have to go back and remind myself of something that has really been central for Sabeel. Sabeel is first and foremost a *Christian* Palestinian organization. As such, our faith needs to be at the center of what we do. Many people on the outside look at what we do and see the political aspects—the advocacy, the human rights—and they think about us as a political organization. We are not! We are first and foremost a group of Christian Palestinians who are trying to understand for ourselves what Christ teaches and what he would have us do in this particular situation. And if that happens to be political activism, if that happens to be taking a prophetic stance that may or may not be popular, that may or may not be in accordance with our national interests, that's fine. We have to start with our faith and see where that leads us.

With that in mind, Rev. Naim Ateek has asked me to speak about the biblical basis for what we are doing in the area of law and international law.

What does the Bible say about law generally? I know that as Christians we tend to contrast law with grace. Law is the Old Testament, grace is the New Testament. And we tend to forget what a huge blessing and what a radical concept the concept of law was in Old Testament times. Because law—even laws which are not very good—is a blessing from God when we contrast it with anarchy, chaos, with the strong oppressing the weak, and with every individual doing what they damn-well please. The Bible, particularly in the Old Testament, introduced from God, the blessing of Law as a gift to humankind. There *are* rules; you can't do what you damn-well please.

Now, this is really the essence of law: it is a formal restriction on what we can and cannot do. Why is that a blessing? It's a blessing because, by its very nature, law is universal. Law means nothing if it doesn't apply to everyone, otherwise it's no longer a law. By being universal, it doesn't distinguish between rich and poor, strong and weak, people belonging to a particular tribe or tribes. It also should not distinguish between male and female, between one ethnicity and another. So, law is good. By its very nature it is universal. And the minute we hear anybody or any government claiming exceptionalism—"We're different, this doesn't apply to us. It applies to everyone else but not to me."—we should be alert. People are trying to avoid the God-given requirements of law being applicable to everyone.

For us, this is very important. We often hear of U.S. exceptionalism and we hear the State of Israel claiming it is somehow different and should not be held to the same standards as everyone else. Immediately, that should alert us, should be a red flag. John Locke explains that law is a form of social contract whereby each of us gives up part of our absolute liberty and allows the government to control our behavior, and without that social contract we cannot have society. Society requires law and requires laws.

This brings us to international law, because international law is just an extension from our starting point. During the last century, especially the second half of the last century, we saw an explosion in the understanding of international law. When it began, international law meant to reduce wars by regulating and governing behavior between countries. Each country, sovereign, considered itself free to do whatever it wanted in the international arena, not to mention to its own citizenry. During the past century, people realized that you can't have every country do whatever it pleases. There have to be some rules and regulations, otherwise we'd kill each other. The destructiveness of modern warfare became so oppressive that people realized that we need international law, and we need international law not just to govern the behavior of states during times of war. Eventually we saw that even during times of peace we cannot tolerate a particular state acting in a totally lawless manner towards its own population, since this could spill out and affect international peace as well.

So the concept of human rights came into the picture. There is something very religious and very biblical about the concept of human rights. In point of fact, much of the concept of human rights has biblical roots, and some of the original authors of the Universal Declaration of Human Rights were Christians, including the Lebanese diplomat and philosopher Charles Malik. But it is also true that in the end, the concepts and instruments of human rights were presented as universal concepts without specific reference to any one religion. So, yes, these are secular concepts and I fully respect and accept that, but they are deeply rooted in a biblical view of humanity. We are born in the Image of God, and by virtue of this fact we are entitled to certain rights and respect, whether we are poor or weak, educated or uneducated, male, female, of this ethnicity or that ethnicity, of this tribe or that tribe, of this country or that country. Such differences are irrelevant. We are entitled to certain rights endowed to us by God.

There has been movement in the direction of organizing those rights, of understanding them, of expanding them, of having institutions like the United Nations, the World Health Organization, the International Labor Organization, and others. Increasingly, there is greater and greater international cooperation and understanding of the role of law in international affairs: how it can be used, not only to keep the peace and prevent total destruction, but also to safeguard the rights of individuals and promote the interests of humanity.

You might say, "But wait a minute. How do you enforce law?" Well, obviously, within the national context there needs to be a government, there need to be courts of law that will find out if someone is violating laws or not. There needs to be a police force, and maybe jails. There needs to be sanctions. There needs to be a way of enforcing law on those individuals who violate the law.

Without that, we're back into anarchy. The law means nothing if there are no ways to enforce it.

Just as after the fall, we have sinful people, we also have sinful organizations and sinful countries that prefer not to be under any law: God's or Man's. They prefer to go their own way. At the United Nations, they came up with the concept of a Security Council that governs international law, which alone should have the power to impose sanctions under Chapter VII of the United Nations Charter. But the five permanent members said, "We're afraid you would use this against us and restrict *our* sovereign right to do as we please." So they invented the concept of the veto. They said that in order to impose real sanctions you need to have not only a majority in the Security Council, but each of the permanent members has the power to use the veto to deny you the ability to impose sanctions or pass resolutions. This is a very serious problem which we need to find ways to go beyond.

While sanctions are an essential part of any legal system, they are not the only part and, perhaps, not the most important part. What really makes people follow the law is its moral power and the legitimacy it carries. You drive on the correct side of the road because it's in everyone's interest to do it. Not because there's a policeman standing at every kilometer of every street ready to give you a ticket if you drive on the wrong side of the road. There is a certain moral power and legitimacy to law. Law, in fact, provides a self-enforcing mechanism. Now, people still violate the law, particularly those who are powerful enough to do it, but this is where the prophets come in. A prophet is not a person who has the military power to sanction the king or to sanction society. He or she is a person who reminds everybody of the law and points out that violation of the law is going to bring pain, suffering and destruction on their society.

Perhaps this is what is happening with international law these days. Perhaps the prophetic voice of the Christian community, when it seeks to speak truth to power, is precisely based on this concept of the moral power of the law. A reminder, particularly to the powerful, that there is a law, there is a God, and there is a community that expects proper behavior. If you do not follow proper behavior, there will be dire consequences. We will not allow you to get away with violations of the law.

At the international level, to go back to our particular situation, that's the whole point of the Boycott Divestment Sanctions (BDS) movement. People talk about boycotts which shame and ostracize the violator of law. People talk about divestment, which is to keep ourselves morally pure and not allow ourselves and our investments to support the oppression of others. But there are also sanctions, the ability to hold accountable those who egregiously violate international law.

The good news is that the powerful have not been able to block the progress of international law. Towards the end of the last century, as we were moving into a new millennium, there was a slowing down, a reduction in this process of increasing, improving and developing international law. The United States and Israel have been instrumental in trying to dampen the enthusiasm for international law, and particularly for putting any teeth in its enforcement. But they have not been totally successful. There has been progress in a number of fields that makes clear that international law can and will be used.

One of the most important and interesting developments has been the creation of the International Criminal Court (ICC) through the Rome Treaty, which allows for the criminal prosecution of individuals who carry out war crimes and crimes against humanity. The United States tried very hard to prevent the development of this treaty, and when it realized that it could not escape the creation of the ICC the U.S. resorted to a large number of bilateral treaties with different countries supported by U.S. foreign aid and made them agree that they will not bring cases against it and its soldiers. So, the U.S. obtained a sort of exemption in that it got different countries to promise in advance that they would not sue the U.S. in international criminal courts.

Israel is not as fortunate. Israeli leaders today are subject to possible prosecution before the ICC even though Israel, together with the U.S. and four other countries, have refused to accede and join the ICC. It is still subject to it and can, in fact, be prosecuted under that treaty. So, sanctions are an influential tactic.

But before I get into the mechanics of this, I want to add one last theological point about law. I said that by its nature, law is universal. It applies to everyone across the board and that's one thing that makes it good. The other good aspect is that law, at its very core, contains the concept of justice. Now, it doesn't necessarily follow because not every law is just and not every country passes just laws and sometimes laws are passed that are unjust, like apartheid laws, racist laws, laws that blatantly discriminate against one particular population. The beauty is that these laws are easier to attack and to challenge. Even in a place like Israel, which doesn't have a constitution, the concept of constitutionalism, the idea of an overarching framework or context under which the laws themselves can be judged, is very much prevalent and relevant.

Biblically we've seen it. Biblically the word for "justice" is the same as the word for "righteousness," and when the Bible speaks of righteousness it is also speaking about justice. Throughout the Old Testament there was a very clear message that God expects, requires, the ruler to be just. That justice also includes doing justice to the weak and the vulnerable in society, to the stranger in your midst, to the orphans, to the widows, to the poor, to those who have no power on their own. God looks out for their rights, and we, as Christians, are called to play that prophetic role and be advocates for justice: to call the nations of the world to justice, both in terms of their laws and in terms of their day-to-day behavior.

This framework, theologically, directs us as we go about our work. What we have to do, the actual practical work that remains, is to find out what the substance of the law is: what does the law require? Then we decide how to properly document the injustice to prove it in a court of law. Finally, we discuss the process of enforcing the law, bringing it to justice, and becoming actors and instruments of justice in international law.

As a lawyer, much of this combines my faith and belief with my law practice. Now, of course, I cannot use the Bible as a substitute for international law, because the actors and players in international law are not Christian and do not accept the authority of the Bible, as I do. It is therefore wrong, and perhaps counterproductive to try and use the Bible as a substitute for international law when speaking to those who are not Christian, but who, nonetheless understand and accept the universality principle embodied in international law.

But it's important for us to know that we all live under God's law. We can all be agents of God's justice and we all can benefit from the wonderful blessing of law and international law. Law is not just an academic concept, it is not just irrelevant idealistic thinking, it is not just something the United Nations cannot impose because of the veto. No, law is the essence of how our beliefs become relevant to what happens around us and what we do.

INTERNATIONAL LAW AND RELIGION

Diana Buttu

When I was first asked to speak about this, it was a little difficult to try to think of what to say that I haven't said before or, quite frankly, that you haven't already heard before. And I thought of giving a very technical international law lecture as I sometimes do, and I found myself getting very bored with it. Yes, I put myself to sleep sometimes. I started to look closely at the topic of today's theme, the idea of transitioning to international law, and something went off in my mind. It was interesting that the words "international law" were the words that were chosen, and not the word "justice," because what it implies is that there is somehow a distinction between law and justice, and this is exactly what I want to speak about today.

The problem with much of law, as the lawyers here know very well, is that it becomes a very user-*un*friendly topic for people who haven't studied it. Who here really knows what a "tort" is? Or what is the "law of perpetuities?" And the reason that I say this is that we, as lawyers, end up spending a great number of years in the practice of law learning a type of jargon, getting very deep into the text of things; but what ends up becoming eviscerated and ignored for the most part is the concept of justice. We go very deep into the specifics of law, but the bigger concept of justice, of what is just, of what is right, of what is correct, seems to often be obscured by what is "legal." We have to start moving away from the concept of what is legal. And not because I'm afraid of international law. I'm an international lawyer; I believe that the law is on my side. But I think that we need to start focusing on this concept of justice.

I say this because if you look at the Palestinian context, and if you look at the way that law is both used and abused, the concept of justice is something that is completely ignored. For example, I want to give you two scenarios that actually do exist in the Palestinian context, and then I want to tell you what the legal response has been to both of these contexts. They're both real cases. The first is a small community, not too far away from here, of about 500 people called Khan al-Ahmar. Khan al-Ahmar is a very small Bedouin community on the way from Jerusalem to Jericho. The people there have been living in shacks, tents, unsuitable housing for a great number of years. These are people who are living in what is called Area C, without electricity, without running water, without the day-to-day amenities of life that we take for granted on a daily basis. A few years ago, in 2009, the community decided that they were going to build a school for their kids instead of having their kids walk more than seven kilometers each way to get to school. The community decided, using tires and mud to build a school, a tiny little school with just one room in order to be able to educate the children there. Because this was built without an Israeli permit, and therefore is illegal, the school has a demolition order pending on it. Since 2009, Israel has been trying to demolish this school, built out of tires and mud, and has since extended this order of demolition beyond the school of tires and mud to the very community itself. All of this is being done under the pretext that none of the construction was done "legally." So you see the difference between law and justice.

Now, after a great number of petitions to the Israeli courts and the Israeli government, the army has still not demolished this school. It still hasn't demolished the community, but the community lives under the daily threat that one day the community *will* be demolished. The kids live under the daily threat that one day their school will be demolished.

I contrast that with my own upbringing in Canada. When I was a child going to school, I never once had to worry about my school being demolished, my community being demolished. These are things that are absolutely absurd.

Now, I want to discuss another example, Al Arakib. This is a similar community, but this time it is inside Israel, not in what's considered to be the West Bank (not in Area C). Yet, Al Arakib is another community facing the exact same conditions—no electricity, no running water, no schools. But this time, unlike the community of Khan al-Ahmar, which has not been demolished, the community of Al Arakib, the *entire community*, has been demolished not once, not twice, not three times, but 61 times as of November 20, 2013. These two communities are not too far apart from one another. I bring up these examples because I want to show you what the international legal response is in both situations.

For Khan al-Ahmar there are arguments that "this is illegal," "illegal under international law," "this is a protected community" and so on. For Al Arakib, what is the response? This community is subject to Israeli law, and Israel is allowed to continue to do whatever it wants because there are Israeli laws, not international law, that are imposed and applicable. So you see the absurdity of the situation facing these communities, one people in similar circumstances. Depending which side of the Green Line you're on, one case is considered illegal and one case is considered legal because it's under Israeli law. The problem with using this framework, with using the international legal framework, is that it's obscured the very problem. The problem is not just that Khan al-Ahmar, the community in Area C, is facing demolition. The problem is that we are *all* facing demolition, not just based on one border, not just based on whether you're in the West Bank or in the Gaza Strip or in East Jerusalem. There is a consistent Israeli policy vis-a-vis the Palestinians, and therefore our response should not be just to look at international law to determine whether these actions violate the rule against perpetuities or whether it's a tort, etc. We must focus on the concept of justice. And in focusing on the concept of justice rather than just on international law you see that what is being done in Khan al-Ahmar, the community not too far away from here, close to Jericho, is exactly the same as what is being done in Al Arakib, further down to the south.

This isn't to say that international law isn't useful. It is a very useful tool. It's a tool that I have used and that Jonathan Kuttab has used, and many lawyers have used to try to promote our rights, but I don't think it is the only tool, and I certainly don't think that it should stop there. The problem with using international law is that we end up caught in the jargon of international law. We start looking at whether this is really considered "displacement," whether it really fits into the concept that international law has outlined for us, the square peg. What it doesn't really look at is whether this is actually *correct* and *just*, and whether we are doing the *right* thing. This is why we need to start using international law as *one* tool, but not the *only* tool to be able to advance our rights.

The reason I say that we have to use international law only as one tool rather than simply *the* tool is because law, as I'm sure you know, is infused or developed by power. There's a reason why white-collar crimes get shorter sentences than other crimes do all around the world, even though they affect more people. And this is because law, at its very core, is built and founded on the idea of power. Power. And so, by focusing on the concept of justice, we move away from the concept of power, we start looking power in the face, and, as the phraseology goes, we speak justice to power. That's why I think it's really important that we start looking at this situation not just in the context of international law but in the bigger framework in which Israel operates.

I'd like to give another example. Since the 1967 occupation began, the number one thing that Israel has been doing is building settlements; within two weeks of the start of the 1967 occupation, Israel began to build settlements. And the settlement construction has not stopped. If you look at the statements on the part of the U.S. officials and European officials, there's been a consistent theme when it comes to the issue of settlements. Right? We see that it's consistent? No. I say this because, if you look at the Nixon administration, what did the Nixon administration come out and say? "Settlements are illegal." What are settlements today, according to the Obama administration? "Unhelpful." "An obstacle to peace." But not all settlements. Let me break it down a little further: "*Continued* settlement activity." So where does the "continued" begin? At what point did building stop for them to "continue?" Do you see what I mean?

The problem with international law is that, because it is based on power, it is constantly being eroded. Today settlements are no longer considered "illegal" by the United States and those who are going to impact and carry out international law; now *continued* settlement activity is *unhelpful*, not *illegal*. This feeds very nicely into what we are experiencing today in the peace process. Today, even as negotiations are ongoing, we don't see anybody coming forward and saying to the Israelis, "Not only do you have to *stop* the settlement activity, but you have to reverse it now. There has to be a complete decolonization process." What we see instead, because law is based on power, is that there's pressure on the Palestinian side to accept the large settlement blocs that exist. In other words, because international law is based on power, or founded on state activity and only implemented through power, what we end up seeing is that what was once illegal is no longer illegal. The demand is not for perpetrators of illegal activity to stop, or those who are carrying out illegal activity to be held to account, but that those who are victims of the illegal activity somehow accommodate that illegal activity. This is where the dangerous trends are now flowing. And this is why, I believe, that instead of simply focusing on international law, we need to start focusing on the concept of justice.

So what does justice demand? Justice says to us that we don't have to go to courts, we don't have to get lawyers, we don't have to go to the police, we don't have to do this or that. Justice says that we ourselves can recognize what is just and what is unjust, and that we ourselves have the ability to carry out and ensure that justice is implemented. Now Jonathan spoke very eloquently about how to do that, and the first and foremost thing is to recognize that this whole system is unjust. It's not just unjust when it comes to the Palestinians in the West Bank, Gaza Strip, and East Jerusalem. It's been unjust for *all* the Palestinians, whether they are living in Nazareth, like my parents, or whether they're living in East Jerusalem, the Gaza Strip, the West Bank, or outside the state's boundaries. Israel's actions toward the Palestinians are unjust, and therefore we have to start focusing on the Palestinian community as a whole, demanding justice for Palestinians as a whole. Not just selective Palestinians.

We have the ability to be able to implement justice ourselves by focusing on boycotts, by demanding sanctions on Israel, and by insuring that our money is no longer being invested in Israel (i.e. divestment): BDS. This is the way that we as individuals can start addressing the injustice infused in Israel, and not simply selectively focusing on issues.

The third thing is that I'm so happy so many people attended this conference, because what I firmly believe is that once you leave from visits to Palestine and conferences like Sabeel's, that this isn't only going to affect you. You are then going to spread the message to everyone else: to your neighbors, to your friends, to everybody that you know, and start demanding justice for Palestinians. I don't believe that we really need to bog ourselves down by odd terminology and jargon in order to understand and recognize that what Israel is doing is unjust; we all see that. What we really need to do now is start working to ensure that the injustice is remedied.

"INTERNATIONAL LAW AND THE PALESTINE-ISRAEL CONFLICT"

John Quigley

To talk about the international law issues related to the Israel-Palestine conflict is a bit daunting because there are so many individual issues. Natural resources in the West Bank are only one. You have the law of belligerent occupation that governs the situation of the West Bank and Gaza, and that body of law requires the occupant, in this case Israel, to act in the best interests of the population. Taking out natural resources for an occupant's own use is inconsistent with that obligation. There are some major issues currently where one finds Israel taking resources—mining in quarries in the West Bank, and extracting water from the aquifers under the West Bank.

Thus, one way in which international law is relevant is that it imposes obligations on Israel under the law of belligerent occupation. One other way is that international law consists of institutions that protect states and their peoples in various ways, and there are different individual ways that international law institutions and procedures can be used. Take the example of Palestine's affiliation with the United Nations Educational, Scientific and Cultural Organization (UNESCO). One of UNESCO's functions is to designate certain sites in the world as "World Heritage Sites," meaning they become internationally protected because of their significance to the world at large. In 2012, at the request of the Government of Palestine, the Church of the Nativity in Bethlehem was designated by UNESCO as a World Heritage Site. Only a state may request such a designation, but UNESCO has admitted Palestine as a member state, a status increasingly accepted in the world community.

One factor that makes it difficult to deal with issues of international law on Palestine is that "facts on the ground" have moved so far from what is required under international law that it becomes hard to find an adequate remedy. Generally in international law we talk about "wrongs" and "remedies," and the goal is to restore the status quo. But can you restore the status quo of 1948? Very difficult. Can you restore the status quo of 1917? Even more difficult. You see all along the way violations of international law that have adversely affected the Palestinian people.

And I didn't pick 1917 by accident: that was the year the Balfour Declaration was issued by Britain. That document said there should be a Jewish national home in the historic area of Palestine. Whatever that formulation may have meant, the implementation of the Balfour Declaration led to immigration that eventually resulted in the dispossession of the population of Palestine in a manner inconsistent with the rights of that population. It was issued by the British Government for reasons having nothing to do with the welfare of the Jewish people or the Arab people, but instead as a tactic that the British Government thought would help it defeat Germany in World War I. It had nothing to do with this part of the world, but everything to do with Europe. In fact, after the Balfour Declaration was issued, the British Government had it translated into Yiddish and British pilots dropped thousands of copies over central Europe, hoping to convince Jewish soldiers fighting in the German army to defect.

Rather quickly the British Government realized that the Declaration was going to lead to no good. When Britain had a change of government in 1923 it undertook a reassessment of the Balfour Declaration, the documents of which were only declassified many years later. The Cabinet examined the implementation of the Balfour Declaration up to 1923 and concluded that the continuing migration of Jewish people from Europe would lead to a very severe conflict with the existing population of Palestine. Further, the Cabinet concluded that they had no way around that dire eventuality, which was at odds with what they were telling the world publicly. In their reports to the League of Nations, the British Government was proclaiming that the situation between Arabs and Jews could be worked out peacefully. But behind the scenes, when they spoke internally, within the Cabinet, they acknowledged that they saw no good way to resolve a conflict that would get worse over time.

Nonetheless, the British Government decided to continue the policy of promoting migration into Palestine, partly because the British Government wanted to have troops near the Suez Canal, its route to India. Britain, moreover, at that point held a mandate from the League of Nations over Palestine. When it sought that mandate, Britain had told the League of Nations that a Jewish national home would be promoted. The Cabinet feared that reneging on this statement might prompt the League of Nations to revoke the mandate. Thus, the reasons for continuing to implement the Balfour Declaration had nothing to do with the welfare of the populations in Palestine, Jewish or Arab, but everything to do with the interests of the British Government.

Now skip forward to the time of the United Nations, and again the rights of the existing population of Palestine took a back seat to other interests. The United Nations made a fundamental error in the way it approached the situation in Palestine in 1947. Unable to resolve the conflict between the two populations, Britain withdrew from Palestine at this juncture; the United Nations' error was to decide to deal not only with that issue—what should happen to Palestine coming out of the mandate—but also with the question of displaced Jewish persons in Europe. That is, the two issues were considered together. Palestine and the issue of displaced Jewish persons should have been dealt with separately. But at the time the major powers were not willing to accept displaced Jewish persons in their territories, even though most of the displaced Jews at the time desired to come to the West. Additionally, the Zionist movement saw an opportunity to force these people to settle in Palestine.

So the two issues were taken up at the United Nations as a package, and that is why in the resolution adopted by the General

Assembly in November of 1947, usually referred to as the Partition Resolution, the partition was done in a way that would give the bulk of the land, and the better land, to the state that would be designated a Jewish state. Less than half of the land was projected to constitute an Arab state, even though at the time the Arab population made up two-thirds of the population of the country. And that imbalance led to the rejection of the Partition Resolution by the Arab community of Palestine, and the subsequent forcing out of the Arab population: the *Nakba*.

The United Nations did, of course, address that dire situation. The UN General Assembly said that Israel was required under international law to repatriate those displaced people, but the United Nations took no action to *compel* Israel to repatriate. Under Chapter VII of the Charter of the United Nations, the Security Council is supposed to deal with threats to the peace, and certainly the refusal to repatriate those persons constituted a threat to the peace. But the United Nations, and the Security Council in particular, never dealt with it in a serious way.

The next major historical event involving international law and the situation of the Arabs of Palestine was the war of 1967, during which Israel occupied the Gaza Strip and the West Bank of the Jordan River. And again we see a lack of action by the United Nations. In the Charter of the United Nations, one finds the proposition that territory is not to be taken by force: Article II of the UN Charter prohibits aggression. And Chapter VII requires the Security Council to deal with aggression or with any breach of the international peace.

When the war broke out in June of 1967, the Security Council did understand that peace had been broken, and it went immediately into session. Abba Eban, representing Israel, explained to the Security Council Israel's version of what was occurring. Eban said that on the morning of the 5th of June, 1967, the Egyptian army had launched mortar shells into three villages in southern Israel, stating the village names. He said that this shelling prompted Israel to respond with force; hence by his account, Israel was acting in self-defense against an actual

Egyptian attack that had taken place that morning. The major caveat was that Eban's account was fiction. There had been no Egyptian attack that morning. The story's falseness, however, was not immediately apparent; most members of the Security Council did not know whether it was true. Nonetheless, Eban's account was sufficiently plausible that the Security Council did not accept Egypt's account—an accurate account—that Israel had acted aggressively.

Egypt's President Gamal Abdel Nasser, perhaps without sufficient thought, had put Egypt's troops in a vulnerable position on the Israeli border. The leadership of the Israel Defense Force (IDF) saw the Egyptian troops drawn up to the border and concluded, correctly, that they were stretched far from sources of supplies in Egypt, and that they were already short on re-supply. The generals in the IDF saw a chance to destroy the Egyptian army, and that's precisely what they did. On the morning of June 5, 1967, they attacked by land and by air. The IDF generals knew that Egypt was not about to attack Israel, so the Israeli attack on Egypt constituted aggression.

The United States Government knew that Eban's account was fiction, because for two or three weeks prior to June 5, Israel and the United States engaged in a rather remarkable dialogue that involved Eban trying to convince the United States that Egypt was going to attack, and therefore that Israel should strike first. Israel feared that if it attacked, the United States might condemn it, as, indeed, the United States had done in 1956 when Israel invaded Egypt. But U.S. President Lyndon Johnson was not buying Eban's pitch and repeatedly told Israeli officials that Egypt was not about to attack Israel. The Central Intelligence Agency (CIA) was supplying Johnson with reports almost daily, saying that while Egypt had drawn troops up to the Israeli border, it had done so because Israel was threatening to invade Syria. Syria had in fact complained to the United Nations over Israel's threats. In this context, Egypt drew troops up to the Israeli border to deter an attack by Israel against Syria. The CIA did not see Egypt as potentially initiating a military attack against Israel.

This resulted in a situation of aggression that should have been dealt with by the UN Security Council, but when Eban recited his fictional story about an Egyptian attack on three Israeli villages, the U.S. representative sat quietly and didn't refute it. And that allowed the situation to continue until the Security Council eventually, some months later, issued Resolution 242, in which it stated that territory cannot be acquired by force, but also said that the Arab states should recognize Israel. Resolution 242 thus could be read to put those two propositions together in a way that allowed Israel to say that until the Arab states recognized Israel, it did not have to withdraw from the Gaza Strip or the West Bank. To this day, the Security Council has not taken action to force Israel to withdraw, thus allowing Israel's occupation to continue.

Israel had no evidence to support Eban's story of an Egyptian attack. After early July 1967, Israeli officials no longer used it, falling back on an argument that Egypt had been about to attack, allowing Israel to attack preemptively. This is the story the Israeli Government still uses to rationalize its action in the 1967 war, but this fallback version of the war has no more truth to it than Eban's original story.

Regarding the 1967 war, there is a significant deficit in the implementation of international law. The Security Council should have been dealing with it at that time; it never did, but it still *should* address the violations. In my view, what should be happening today is not the bilateral talks that have been on-again-off-again for the past decade. Rather, the Security Council should be dealing with the occupation as a threat to the peace, even though it is a few decades late. But you don't leave it to the victim of aggression to negotiate with the aggressor, any more than you leave it to a homeowner whose house has been burglarized to negotiate with the burglar over the return of a television set.

The International Criminal Court (ICC) is one of the more interesting developments in international law given the fact that the settlement policy has gone on for as long as it has, and given the fact that condemnations of settlements as illegal by the UN General Assembly and the UN Security Council have not had any impact. When UN resolutions fail, what is left in terms of international law? There is the ICC, a court set up a few years ago to deal with war crimes. The Statute of the ICC—also called the Rome Statute because it was adopted at a conference in Rome in 1998—contains a long list of acts that qualify as war crimes, and one of the war crimes identified is the transfer of population into territory under belligerent occupation. This is language taken directly out of the Convention Relative to the Protection of Civilian Persons in Time of War of 1949, also known as the Fourth Geneva Convention, which deals with the occupation of foreign territory.

That provision in the Statute of the ICC would seem to be applicable to officials of the Israeli Government. The only way they would perhaps be able to argue around it is that the Statute uses the term "transfer," and they might argue they didn't transfer the people, but the people went on their own and officials just helped them out a bit. But I think that argument wouldn't succeed. At the United Nations, both the General Assembly and Security Council have condemned the settlements as being a population transfer by the Government of Israel. The International Court of Justice has also done so. If it is a transfer by the Government of Israel, then the officials who are implementing the policy would also have engaged in the act of "transfer."

The jurisdiction of the ICC is limited; that is, the ICC doesn't have jurisdiction over any war crime committed anywhere in the world. Its jurisdiction is based on the adherence of particular states to the Statute. Jurisdiction attaches, for example, if a war crime is committed in the territory of a state that is a party to the Statute, or if a war crime is committed anywhere in the world by a person who is a national of a state that is a party.

The Statute foresees the possibility that these provisions could apply for a state that is not a party to the Statute if such a state decides to confer jurisdiction on the Court. Under this provision, jurisdiction attaches over war crimes in such circumstances if a state that is not a party to the Statute files a declaration with the Court saying that it grants jurisdiction. The Government of

Palestine acted under this provision in January 2009, following the Gaza war known on the Israeli side as Operation Cast Lead— the precipitating event was not settlement building but the Gaza war. The Minister of Justice of Palestine filed a brief letter with the ICC saying that Palestine confers jurisdiction on the Court for any acts within Palestine's territory, dating back to the time when the Court began to function, which was July 1, 2002.

The Court's office accepted the declaration, but the prosecutor of the court said that he would not immediately initiate an investigation because he was not certain about the status of Palestine. Under the Statute, only a state can confer jurisdiction, so the prosecutor indicated that he would have to decide whether Palestine is a state. I had just written a short article for publication in which I explained why Palestine was a state, so I sent the article to the Office of the Prosecutor. I was also aware that a contrary opinion had been expressed in print, so I wrote a memorandum a few weeks later to the Office of the Prosecutor refuting that point of view. Within a short time, others began sending the Office of the Prosecutor their views on whether Palestine was a state.

In early 2010, I got a message from the Office of the Prosecutor asking if I minded if my memo be posted on the Court's website. The Office wanted to post communications both for and against jurisdiction, so I agreed for my memo to be published, despite the fact that it was quite informally written. If you access the website of the ICC, click on "Office of the Prosecutor," and look for "Summary of Submissions," you'll find my memo in favor of jurisdiction, along with those of various organizations that were in opposition.

A few months later, the Office of the Prosecutor sent another message to invite me, along with others who had written either for or against jurisdiction based on the Palestine declaration, to come to The Hague to argue the matter for the benefit of the prosecutor and his staff. Eight people were invited: four to argue that the Court had jurisdiction, four to argue that it did not. In October of 2010, we gathered for the session, the four arguing against jurisdiction speaking first. They included Malcolm Shaw, who is a British legal academic, and Dore Gold, who formerly served as Israel's Ambassador to the United Nations.

Speaking next, I said that I saw little merit in what they said. My argument was that Palestine had been made a state under Britain in the arrangements that terminated the First World War. Reading back through the treaty that terminated the war—the Treaty of Lausanne of 1923—reveals that it refers to the territories coming out of the Ottoman Empire, which would be Palestine, Iraq, and Syria, as "states." The international community dealt with these entities as states all during the 1920s and 1930s. But in 1948 Israel is established from part of the territory of Palestine, with Egypt keeping the administration of the Gaza Strip and Jordan provisionally annexing what came to be called the West Bank of the Jordan River. Then in 1988 the Palestinian Liberation Organization (PLO) declared itself to be the governing authority of Palestine and referred back to the Treaty of Lausanne of 1923 as the time of initiation of the statehood of Palestine.

The four who were arguing against jurisdiction did not seriously address my analysis of the historical evolution of Palestine, and the prosecutor did not state a view on the matter until April 2012, a full year and a half later. On April 3, 2012, he issued a statement indicating that he did not believe it was appropriate for him to determine whether Palestine is a state. That determination, he said, should be made either by the General Assembly of the UN, or by the Assembly of States Parties to the Statute of the International Criminal Court. So after undergoing this process for three years, giving the impression that he would decide whether Palestine is a state, the prosecutor relieved himself of that responsibility.

The posture of the prosecutor all but invited Palestine to go to the General Assembly or to the Assembly of States Parties, which Palestine did in Autumn 2012. On November 29, 2012, the General Assembly adopted Resolution 67/19 in which it affirmed, by a large majority, the upgrade of Palestine from "non-member observer *entity*" to "non-member observer *state*." Previously, the General Assembly had not explicitly characterized the Palestine mission, but through Resolution 67/19, the General Assembly expressed its view that Palestine is a state.

This leaves the potential that government leaders in Israel would be prosecuted for the war crime of transferring population into territory under belligerent occupation. Currently, the case is under advisement by the prosecutor's office; that is, even though the General Assembly has said Palestine is a state, the prosecutor's office has not gone ahead with prosecution. In June 2012, Fatou Bensouda took over from Luis Moreno Ocampo as Prosecutor of the Court, and she has not made formal moves to prosecute. One thing she has said is she thinks the court has jurisdiction over war crimes in Palestine starting from November 29, 2012, which is the date of General Assembly Resolution 67/19. But the General Assembly Resolution 67/19 did not purport to create a state; instead, it made a statement that Palestine *was* a state, which clearly meant that in the General Assembly's view Palestine had been a state prior to the resolution. The statement of the previous prosecutor on April 3, 2012, made it appear that should the General Assembly say that Palestine is a state, then Palestine's declaration of jurisdiction (January 2009) would be valid.

The other thing the prosecutor has said is that she is perplexed why the Government of Palestine has not come forward, as if that must happen before she can investigate. The prosecutor has jurisdiction without any additional action by the Government of Palestine; in fact, under the Statute of the Court, the prosecutor is to take action *proprio motu* [Latin: "by one's own motion"] when the prosecutor finds evidence from any source that a crime has been committed within the jurisdiction of the Court. This is the same procedure one finds for criminal prosecution anywhere in the world: prosecutors can proceed to investigate and deal with crime based on information that comes from any source. I would say that the prosecutor is shying away from dealing with this in the way the Statute requires.

The proposition that war crimes have been committed by Israel is based in fact. Israel initially signed the Court's Statute but then issued a statement saying it does not intend to ratify it, and one of the reasons it gave for not ratifying is the provision in the definition of "war crime" that cites the transfer of persons into territory under belligerent occupation. The Israeli Government apparently understands the purport of the provision on transfer of civilians into occupied territory.

That is the current situation, but there is a real possibility of using the ICC if this negative political pressure can be counteracted. The Court is already considering another possible war crime related to the Gaza flotilla incident in 2010, during which Israeli navy personnel went out into international waters to board the vessel *Mavi Marmara* and killed nine people on board. Since the prosecutor has not decided whether Palestine is a state, the Court has jurisdiction based on war crimes committed in the territory of a state that is a party to the Statute. One sub-paragraph in the Statute says that the Court has jurisdiction if a war crime is committed on a vessel that is registered in a state that is party to the Statute.

When this incident occurred in June 2010, the vessels were all coming from Turkey and were being referred to in the press as "Turkish vessels." Turkey is not a party to the Statute, so if the vessels were registered in Turkey the Court would not have jurisdiction. But vessels can be registered anywhere, and in many states of the world it is quite easy to register a vessel by paying a fee. So I checked online about the registration of the *Mavi Marmara* and found information about its ownership and registration. It turned out the *Mavi Marmara* had previously been registered in Turkey, where it was used as a ferry boat around Istanbul. But in May 2010, it was re-registered by new owners—the people who were planning the flotilla action—in Comoros. Upon checking the Court's Statute, I found that Comoros is a party to the treaty, and therefore, the ICC would have jurisdiction over crimes committed on the vessel. In 2013 the Government of Comoros, working through lawyers in Turkey, formally referred the matter to the Court, where it is now before the prosecutor.

If the Court could act to deal with war crimes, would that be a way to resolve the whole conflict? It's unlikely, but the issue also highlights the importance of Palestine's status and of its being considered a state. After the vote in the General Assembly on Resolution 67/19, it seems clear that the State of Palestine is widely accepted, even though the United States maintains that the vote doesn't grant Palestine statehood. When an entity gains such widespread acceptance as a state, however, it is not plausible to argue that it is *not* a state. Some people will refer to the so-called "criteria for statehood"—that before being considered a state, an entity must have a population, a territory, and control. These criteria are sometimes cited as reasons to conclude that Palestine is not a state, but these criteria don't apply when a state's territory is under belligerent occupation, as is the territory of Palestine.

There was a rather interesting statement made on the floor of the Knesset in 1993 by an opposition member who didn't like the fact that Yitzhak Rabin was coming to an agreement with Yasser Arafat to begin talks about status. That Member of Knesset was none other than Benjamin Netanyahu, and he complained that as soon as Israel decided to sit down with the PLO and discuss borders, and once Israel demanded that the PLO recognize Israel, Israel was accepting the fact that Palestine was a state. Because you don't negotiate borders with organizations, you negotiate borders with a *state*. Netanyahu said that if you have an animal that looks like a horse and has black stripes, you call it a zebra; Rabin was doing things that in effect accepted the status of Palestine as a state. Prime Minister Benjamin Netanyahu doesn't say the same any longer, but that was what he said at the time.

Post script from John Quigley regarding International Criminal Court:
On November 25, 2013, the prosecutor of the ICC issued a report in which she indicated that, in the view of the Office of the Prosecutor, the Palestine declaration of January 2009 was not valid when filed, that General Assembly Resolution 67/19 does not validate the declaration, and that she does not plan to conduct any investigation on the basis of the declaration.

PART IV
CONTEMPORARY ISSUES

"Women, Colonialism, and Human Rights"

Maha Abu-Dayyeh

"No existing legal system can protect you. Let's see if we can get help through your family networks and tribal power agents."

After 20 years in the business of providing legal aid and counseling to Palestinian women in the occupied Palestinian territories, more and more often we find ourselves in situations where our clients are falling through the cracks of existing legal and protection systems. To help specific cases, we are forced to resort to tribal and family networks. These, if available and accessible, proclaim that their priority is to establish family and community peace rather than to mete out justice for the individual. This puts our clients, especially women, in a compromising and vulnerable position.

Since the signing of the Oslo Accords[25], the Israeli authorities gradually applied a well-integrated political, military, and economic strategy, supported by religious ideology, to control land and water. In the process, they divided the Palestinians into disconnected communities with jurisdiction multiplicity and no executive power as an accountable authority. This was done

---

25 In September 1993, the Oslo Accords, officially called the Declaration of Principles (DOP) on Interim Self-Government Arrangements, were signed and hailed the creation of the Palestinian Authority (PA), the governing body separate from the PLO, to assume control over and responsibility for internal Palestinian affairs. The DOP set the framework for relationship between the PA and the State of Israel for an interim period of five years, during which a permanent agreement between the PA and Israel would be negotiated (beginning no later than May 1996). Permanent-status issues, such as jurisdiction over Jerusalem, status of refugees, Israeli settlements, security and borders, environment and water resources, were deliberately left to be decided at a later stage.

without any sense of responsibility for the population's well-being; to add insult to injury, Palestinians found themselves subject to state-sanctioned settler terrorization. This status quo places the Palestinian family—whose core is women and children—in the most vulnerable position.[26]

Colonialism has clearly framed the Palestinian legislative and jurisdictional scene in order to maintain social fragmentation. This dates back to the Ottoman period. In terms of family life, the Ottoman *milleh* system is still used in order to regulate family lives according to religious affiliation, whereby *sharia* courts regulate the affairs of the Muslim community, seven ecclesiastical courts regulate lives of the Christian community, and rabbinical courts regulate lives of the Jewish communities. The British and the Jordanians confirmed these systems for Palestinians through legislation.[27] At present, all the Christian courts sit in Jerusalem only, despite the fact that most Christians live in the West Bank and Gaza and therefore have no access to these courts. Jordan remained in charge of the Muslim *sharia* courts after 1967 and the Israeli annexation of Jerusalem, until the Palestinian Authority was established in 1994, creating a Palestinian office for the Chief Justice for Religious Affairs attached to the president's office. However, Jordan is still in charge of the *sharia* courts in East Jerusalem, and East Jerusalemites have to deal with both the Jordanian as well as the Israeli systems to maintain their family status in the city. Consequently, at this point three national jurisdictions are applicable to the Palestinian community in historical Palestine: the Jordanian, the Palestinian, and the Israeli. Given the geopolitical disconnection, this is most crucial in terms of lack of enforcement of court decisions.

The existing world order is organized around states and governments. The international legal system, human rights, and humanitarian laws all deal with state and government responsibility towards their populations and towards each other.

---

26 For more information, see: www.wclac.org.
27 Article 2, 1932, Law for the non-Muslim religious councils, and Jordanian Constitution of 1952, Article 99.

Palestinians, however, are subject to the jurisdiction of three states, but there is no one state that takes or even wants to take responsibility for their well-being.

It is safe to say that the nature of our society and the strength of our common cultural heritage is what keeps us connected. The Palestinian society is a conservative and tightly knit society where kinship relations precede all other types of social organizations. In addition to city, town, and village structures, individuals also belong to tribes or *hamoulehs*. The social networks of all of these communities extend throughout historical Palestine, including Israel. Palestinian families are interconnected through marriage. Family is the main source of support for the individual, especially for women. The family provides all kinds of support, including financial. It also mediates on behalf of the individual in all sorts of conflicts, especially marital ones.

This extensive structure has taken several hits throughout Palestinian history. The 1948 War, the annexation of East Jerusalem in 1967, the creation of areas A, B, and C in the West Bank, the isolation of Gaza after the Oslo Agreement, and now the creation of "area D" as a result of the separation wall which has divided many families, have all battered the social, economic, and cultural networks. The Palestinian family, particularly women and children, are the ones who suffer most due to this artificial division of Palestine's geography. The isolation due to various types of physical barriers (the wall and checkpoints) and non-physical barriers (law and policy) set up by Israel have forced disconnection. Individual families are left isolated from their kinfolk.

The religious court system which touches every individual's life—marriage, divorce, custody, maintenance, inheritance, etc.— is disconnected and does not have complete jurisdiction over the entire population. Marriages between West Bankers or Gazans and Jerusalemites pose a further complication. In addition to the disconnect that one of the family members will experience with respect to the rest of the family based on place of residence, there is court jurisdiction to consider. In case of a conflict, it is difficult to determine which court has the jurisdiction to rule in that particular case; even if there is a court order, there is still the problem of enforcing it.

Challenges in enforcing court decisions also apply to West Bank residents who live in different areas: A, B and C. Israeli and PA authorities coordinate only on military security matters but never on issues that deal with civilian security. Without coordination with Israeli military authorities, the Palestinian police force has no access to the population outside PA-controlled areas.

In Jerusalem, thousands of Palestinian women from the West Bank married to Jerusalemites and Israeli citizens are not protected by any social service system, because the Israelis deny family reunification. In addition to not being part of the health and social service system, they are not actually allowed to be in the city. If they are caught by police, they are arrested and sent back to the West Bank. They are treated as illegal aliens. Jerusalem women married to West Bank men risk their Jerusalem status, which means that they would end up with no legal status that allows them to get drivers' permits, travel documents, etc., so they also end up prisoners in their communities. Children of such marriages are at risk of ending up with neither Jerusalem nor Palestinian residency cards. We are witnessing an increase in the phenomenon of *bidouns*[28] in Palestine. The problem of insecurity and statelessness has been compounded by the Oslo Accords, and further amplified by the phenomenon of persons shirking their responsibilities to their families, not to mention getting away with crimes because of an increase in vacuums in jurisdiction.

For both men and women, but more so for women, justice in Palestine is something that they hope their children and grandchildren will enjoy at some point in the future. The common inter-communal or interpersonal conflicts are exacerbated by the prolonged political conflict due to the Israeli occupation. It is an established fact that the Palestinian community is targeted by

---

28 Those who are without nationality; stateless.

all sorts of obstacles, militarized or otherwise, that are used to hinder its independent vibrant growth and development. In such a context, women's rights advocates and advocates for human rights, justice, and democracy must focus on keeping these principles alive and under public discussion. Violations should remain under scrutiny, paralleled with developing institutions and policies that ensure respect for human rights, women's rights, and the service of justice. To monitor, prevent, and punish criminal behavior, established Palestinian state institutions must work hand-in-hand with civil society and existing social control mechanisms, regardless of whether these social control mechanisms clearly give more value to group rights than to individual rights. The society, the clan, and the family are more important than the individual, and in the context where the prevailing value system is patriarchal, the interests of women are at the bottom of the totem pole. Still, an unjust law is better than no law for women.

The search for justice is a deep-rooted human need, and, in Palestine, surviving with dignity is what has enabled the Palestinian community and civil society organizations to navigate through available local and international mechanisms to make sure that Palestinian human rights, including women's rights and children's rights, are respected and protected. Due diligence measures must be taken to ensure protection, holding accountable all duty-bearers, including international ones, for not assuming their responsibility according to international law, human rights, and humanitarian law, and/or allowing crimes against humanity to be perpetuated without accountability.

"The Holy Books as Guiding Lights"

Mohammed S. Dajani Daoudi

While many books on politics are filled with the call for a "clash of civilizations,"[29] the Holy Books call for a "dialogue of civilizations," and for an "understanding of civilizations." They all share basic Abrahamic moral guidance, and if we search in depth in the sacred scriptures of the rest of the world's religious traditions, we will find much of the same teaching of the Abrahamic faiths in them also. A careful, detailed look at the Hebrew Bible, the New Testament, and the Qur'an makes clear the common religious values and ethics inherent in all three traditions. As the last of the three, the Qur'an urges Muslims to believe in the Holy Scriptures of Jews and Christians that preceded it.[30]

The Qur'an affirms in Aal Imran Surah: "It is He Who sent down to thee, in truth, the Book, confirming what was before it; and He revealed [sent down] the Law [of Moses] and the Gospel [of Jesus] before, as a guide to mankind, and He sent down the criterion [of judgment between right and wrong]" (Qur'an 3:3-4).

Let me begin with the way in which the Holy Books share the belief in the goodness and power of God. The Psalmist states: "God is our refuge and strength, a very present help in trouble"

---

29 Though these negative perceptions have their roots in the past, however, they were intensified by the wave of hate and fear initiated by Samuel Huntington's book *The Clash of Civilizations* (1999) in which he portrays religion as the source of future international conflict between the civilization based on Judeo-Christianity and that based on Islam.

30 The Qur'an was revealed to Prophet Muhammad by the Archangel Gabriel in a series of divine revelations over 23 years. Its 114 surahs comprise 6,346 verses providing the rules of conduct that remain fundamental to all Muslims.

(Psa. 46:1). The Qur'an teaches Muslims to love and worship God and that there is but one God whose message of love and mercy was brought to humanity by a series of prophets, including the Hebrew prophets and Jesus, and ending with Muhammad.

Judaism, Christianity and Islam share the concern for the individual relationship with God and the importance of manifesting that love in relations with others. When Jesus was asked which of God's commandments was most important, Mark records Jesus' response: "The most important one is this: 'Hear, O Israel, the Lord our God, the Lord is one. Love the Lord your God with all your heart and with all your soul and with all your mind and with all your strength" (Mark 12:28-30, citing Deut. 6:4). Jesus continues: "The second is this: 'Love your neighbor as yourself.' There is no commandment greater than these" (Mark 12:31). In loving God and loving others, humanity elevates itself and unites in purpose with God.

The Qur'an promotes positive bonds between people because of their common moral responsibility toward one another. Chief among these are deep ethical commitments to humanity, justice and charity to the poorest and the marginalized.

The Holy Books are filled with hope, love, compassion, reconciliation and peace. The Hebrew Scriptures in the Old Testament provided the people of Israel with the hope that helped them persist to survive and to enrich their lives despite the tragic catastrophes they endured in their long history. No matter how good today is, they continue to have hope that tomorrow will be a better day. It is hope that helped them keep the faith in the midst of the Holocaust death, pain, despair, and tragedy. The American historian Charles Beard once said, "When it is dark enough, you can see the stars."

In Judaism, the essential moral concept of *hesed* means "kindness" and "love." This is love displayed through deeds, doing acts of kindness for others. One classic example of *hesed* is the story in Genesis of Abraham sitting at the entrance of his tent and spotting three strangers approaching. He greets them and brings them inside to give them food and drink. Abraham does not know that the three are angels. But the implication is that Abraham and Sarah, his wife, treated all strangers as if they were angels. The kindness to strangers, the commandment to love "the stranger," was mentioned more than 36 times in the Torah. But the stranger in this context was extended to all Gentiles as expressed in Exodus in which the Israelites were commanded to not afflict the stranger because they were once strangers in the land of Egypt.

In one of his best known observations, Rabbi Akiva said that the greatest principle in Torah is to "Love your neighbor as yourself" (Palestinian Talmud, Nedarim 9:4). Famed scholar Hillel added to this by summarizing all of Judaism in the sentence: "What is hateful to you, do not do to others" (Babylonian Talmud, Shabbat 31a). All world religions teach a similar concept entitled "The Golden Rule."

The Torah affirms Christ's inspiring words: "Love your enemies and pray for those who persecute you, so that you may be children of your creator in heaven" (Mt. 5:44-45). The love of neighbor is one of the main commandments of the Bible (Rom. 13:8-10; Gal. 5:13-15). Paul asserts: "Owe no one anything except to love one another; for the one who loves another has fulfilled the law" (Rom. 13:8). The commandments are focused in this command, "Love your neighbor as yourself." When full of love one can do no wrong to a neighbor. When pressed about who "the neighbor" is, Luke records Jesus as answering in the form of a parable: when a man was robbed, beaten, stripped and left to die, two religious people passed the victim without helping him. Then an "impure outsider," a Samaritan, came to the victim's aid, tending to his wounds and bringing him to safety. Jesus thereby makes the argument that a neighbor is anyone in need.

Love is one of the most central themes of the Holy Books. Early Christians used the term *agape* to mean "Christian love," the kind of self-sacrificing love of God for humanity that Christ exemplified. Christians are called to practice this kind of unconditional, generous, respectful love for God with one another (1 Cor. 10:24; Eph. 4:1-6).

John records Jesus as proclaiming, "This is my commandment, that you love one another as I have loved you. No one has greater love than this, to lay down one's life for one's friends" (John 15:12-13). Jesus' subsequent death on the cross represents for Christians the ultimate act of compassion and love.

Paul urges: "Be imitators of God, as beloved children, and live in love, as Christ loved us and gave himself up for us" (Eph. 5:1-2). This was intended to inform all social relations, from family and marriage to friendships (John 15:13). He speaks of brotherly love and its significance to the community (Rom. 14; 1 Cor. 8:12-14). Christian social values, while centrally based in the cardinal principle of love, also carry over many of the ethical precepts found in Judaism. As Hebrews 13:1-3 explains: "Let mutual love continue. Do not neglect to show hospitality to strangers, for by doing that some have entertained angels without knowing it. Remember those who are in prison, as though you were in prison with them; those who are being tortured, as though you yourselves were being tortured."

Elaborating on Biblical ethics, Jesus proclaims, "In everything, do to others as you would have them do to you; for this is the law and the prophets" (Mt. 7:12). Jesus asks believers to love all others as God loves creation: God sends sunshine and rain on the good as well as the bad (Mt. 5:43-48). As God does not distinguish among his creation, nor should his believers.

The Talmud, as well as the Bible, calls upon the faithful to be peace lovers and peacemakers. Similarly, the Qur'an teaches its followers to be peaceful and to deplore violence and aggression, asserting: "Fight for the sake of God those that fight against you, but do not attack them first. God does not love the aggressors" (Qur'an 2:190); also, "But if the enemy incline towards peace, do thou [also] incline towards peace" (Qur'an 8:61).

The practice of justice and seeking a just society are divine commandments of all religious books. The Torah, the Bible and the Qur'an all make clear that piety must necessarily translate in society through a striving for **charity and justice**. "Learn to do good; seek justice; aid the oppressed; uphold the rights of the orphan; defend the cause of the widow" (Is. 1:17). This teaching compresses the moral guidance of all religions. In Judaism, the Hebrew word *tzedakah* combines two concepts: *charity* and *justice*. In Christianity, the closest phrase to *tzedakah* is *social justice*. In Islam, the word *sadakah* refers to the concept of charity to the poor (Qur'an 17:26-29). The Qur'an says: "You shall give the due alms to the relatives, the needy, the poor, and the travelling alien, but do not be excessive, extravagant" (Qur'an 17:26-29); "They ask you about giving: say, 'The charity you give shall go to the parents, the relatives, the orphans, the poor, and the traveling alien'"(Qur'an 2:215); "O you who believe, you shall give to charity from the good things you earn, and from what we have produced for you from the earth" (Qur'an 2:267). The Qur'an states that the path of the righteous involves conscientious charity: "Ye will not attain unto righteousness until ye spend that which ye love. And whatsoever ye spend, God is aware thereof" (Qur'an 3:92). The Qur'an makes it clear that it is the duty of society's privileged to care for the poor (Qur'an 2:273). The Qur'an simultaneously rewards charitable deeds as among the greatest acts of piety.

In spirit, charity is an act of worship, on par in the Qur'an with *salat* (prayer). Indeed, the two are frequently used together in the Qur'an, representing both personal and social worship of God (Qur'an 2:110, 2:227). The Qur'an frequently extols the virtues of charity (Qur'an 2:261-266), adding that the best use of charity is for caring for parents, kin, orphans, the needy, and wayfarers (Qur'an 2:215; 59:7; 76:8).

Jews, Christians and Muslims are called upon to pursue justice no matter how remote the possibility of achieving it or overcoming injustice. Rabbi Abraham Joshua Heschel wrote, "Indifference to evil is more insidious than evil itself." Rabbi Emanuel Rackman observed that Judaism teaches an *empathic justice*, which "seeks to make people identify with each other—with each other's needs, with each other's hopes and aspirations, with each other's defeats and transformations." He affirms: "Because Jews have known the distress of slaves and the loneliness of strangers, we are to project ourselves into their souls and make their plight our own."

The Psalms speak to the role of the just ruler who would receive divine aid: "That he may judge Thy people with righteousness (*tzedek*) and Thy poor with justice (*mishpat*)." The verse goes on to add: "May he defend the cause of the poor of the people, give deliverance to the needy, and crush the oppressor" (Psa. 72:2, 4).

The Qur'an describes God as just and makes clear that justice itself is a command from God (Qur'an 16:90, 5:8), enjoining believers to that which is just and kind (Qur'an 16:90), as well as forbidding that which is unjust (Qur'an 72:15; 60:8). The primacy of justice among Islamic values is demonstrated by God's command to pursue it above all other considerations: "O you who believe! Stand out firmly for justice, as witnesses to God, even if it be against yourselves, your parents, and your relatives, or whether it is against the rich or the poor, for God can best protect both. Follow not the lusts [of your hearts], lest ye swerve, and if ye distort [justice] or decline to do justice, verily God is well-acquainted with all that ye do" (Qur'an 4:35).

All religions extol moderation, including Islam, Judaism and Christianity. The Qur'an asserts: "We have created you ummattan wasatan (a temperate nation)" (Qur'an 2:143).[31] In other verses it says: "Do not squander [your wealth] wastefully, for the spend thrifts [wasteful] are Satan's brothers" (Qur'an 17:26-27); "And let not your hand be tied [like a miser] to your neck, nor stretch it forth to its utmost reach [like a spendthrift] so that you become blameworthy and in severe poverty"(Qur'an 17:29); "Pray neither with too loud a voice nor in a low voice, but seek between these extremes a middle course" (Qur'an 17:110); "Do not treat men with scorn, nor walk proudly on the earth: Allah does not love the arrogant and the vainglorious. Rather let your gait be modest and your voice low: the harshest of voices is the braying of the ass" (Qur'an 31:19); "Eat and drink, but avoid excesses. He does not love the intemperate [He likes not those who waste by extravagance]" (Qur'an 7:31); "O people of the Book! Do not

---

31 It is interesting to note that this Surah has 286 verses and this verse is number 143, exactly halfway through the Surah. It means that the Muslim nation is just, balanced, moderate, middle-ground, centrist, and temperate.

transgress [overstep] the bounds of your religion, nor say of God anything but the truth" (Qur'an 4:171); "As for those who are scornful and proud, He will sternly punish them" (Qur'an 4:173).

Christianity teaches: "Moderation is the silken string running through the pearl chain of all virtues" (Joseph Hall, Bishop of Norwich [1574-1656] in his introduction to Christian Moderation). "A bishop must be ... sober, just, holy, temperate" (Tit. 1:7-8); "Add to your faith virtue; and to virtue knowledge; and to knowledge temperance" (2 Pet. 1:5,6).

Moderation in Judaism: "The Torah may be likened to two paths, one of fire, the other of snow. Turn in one direction, and you will die of heat; turn to the other and you die of the cold. What should you do? Walk in the middle" (Talmud: Hagigah, 2:1); "Three things are good in small quantities and bad in large: yeast, salt, and hesitation" (Talmud: Berakoth, 34a); "There are eight things of which a little is good and much is bad: travel, mating, wealth, work, wine, sleep, spiced drinks, and medicine" (Talmud: Gittin, 70a).

In Bahaism, Bahá'u'lláh (1817-1892) says: "Whoso cleaveth to justice, can, under no circumstances, transgress the limits of moderation." Also, "It is incumbent upon them who are in authority to exercise moderation in all things. Whatsoever passeth beyond the limits of moderation will cease to exert a beneficial influence." "In all matters moderation is desirable."

In Buddhism, moderation is focused around the middle path with eight tracks in which Buddha's trip in search of wisdom ended.

Forgiveness is a central part of Christian worship and identity, and is prominently and frequently stated in the Lord's Prayer: "Forgive us our trespasses, as we forgive those who trespass against us." Forgiveness brings together the Christian and Muslim values of love, compassion, humility, and mercy. It is a defining virtue and practice of all the believers.

One important moral trait in the Qur'an is forgiveness: "Hold to forgiveness, command what is right, and turn away from the ignorant" (Qur'an 7:199). In another verse, God commands:

"They should rather pardon and overlook. Would you not love God to forgive you? God is Ever-Forgiving, Most Merciful" (Qur'an 24:22). God instructs the faithful in the Qur'an: "The repayment of a bad action is one equivalent to it. But if someone pardons and puts things right, his reward is with God" (Qur'an 42:40). In another verse: "But if you pardon and exonerate and forgive, God is Ever-Forgiving, Most Merciful" (Qur'an 64:14). The Qur'an reveals that forgiveness is a superior moral trait: "But if someone is steadfast and forgives, that is the most resolute course to follow" (Qur'an 42:43). For that reason, believers are forgiving, compassionate and tolerant people who, as revealed in the Qur'an, "control their rage and pardon other people" (Qur'an 3:134).

In Jewish and Christian Scriptures as well as in the Qur'an, greed, arrogance, excess and pride are understood as being idolatrous. As throughout Jewish history, Jesus warned his community of the consequences of corruption, injustice and God's judgment in this life and the next.

Islam teaches that God endowed humanity with a good, purposeful nature and with a deep inner awareness of God. Muslims believe humanity has been given divine guidance through the Qur'an. The Qur'an is understood as a "mercy" to mankind, enjoining Muslims to use their gifts and act on their innate sense of decency in service and obedience to God through the creation of a just and peaceful society (Qur'an 6:157; 21:107, 6:165).

Being a Muslim implies not only a belief in the one God, the Angels, the Prophets, the Holy Scriptures and the Day of Judgment, but also actively upholding a set of personal obligations to community and abiding by clearly defined codes of personal, social and moral conduct that are also embodied in Christianity and Judaism. "Say: We believe in God and what has been revealed to us; and what has been revealed to Abraham, Ishmael, Isaac, Jacob, and the Tribes; We believe in what was revealed to Moses and Jesus and the prophets by God. We make no distinction amongst any of them, and to God we are Muslim in [we surrender]" (Qur'an 3:84).

As God revealed Himself to the Jewish and Christian communities in times of extreme oppression, Islamic tradition holds that God's revelation to Muslims came in a period of oppression by ignorance, corruption and violence tearing apart the fabric of traditional Arabian tribes. This *Asr al-Jahiliyya* (Epoch of Ignorance) ended with God's revelation of Islam and the Qur'an through Prophet Muhammad, whose enlightened and inspirational leadership ultimately united the disparate, warring tribes of Arabia into a unified Muslim community (*ummah*).

The core beliefs in liberty, equality, fraternity, moderation, and social justice—the "Abrahamic ethics"—are foundational religious values which carry significant social and political implications. Some of the social values that emerge from these fundamental principles in Islam include those emphasizing *Ta'aruf* (knowing one another), *Ta'awun* (cooperation, mutual assistance, in transactions), and *Takamul* (complementarity and completion). In Islam, the only differentiation among creation is in piety (*taqwa*) or righteousness (*birr*). In his "Farewell Sermon" delivered on Mount Arafat in the year 632, Prophet Muhammad concluded: "I leave behind two things, the Qur'an and the Sunnah, and if you follow both you will never go astray."[32]

The Qur'anic vision of pluralism is closely related to the belief in fundamental equality of humanity and God's plan for his creation (Qur'an 49:13). The Qur'an states that God sent out different prophets (among them, the Hebrew prophets and Jesus) to different people at different times to reveal the same truth of the oneness of God and of individual moral accountability to God (Qur'an 2:213): "Each apostle We have sent has spoken only in the language of his own people, so that he might make plain to them his message" (Qur'an 14:4); We raised an apostle in every nation,

---

32 The Sunnah is the record of the life, tradition, sayings (Hadith), and speeches of the Prophet. The Hadith was collected and published 150 years after the death of the Prophet. It is important to note that it does not complement the Qur'an since this would imply that the Qur'an is incomplete and the word of the Prophet is of equal status to the word of God.

proclaiming: "Worship God and avoid false deities. Amongst them were some whom Allah guided, and others destined to go astray" (Qur'an 16:36). "We sent forth Noah and Abraham, and bestowed on their offspring prophethood and the scriptures... After them We sent other apostles, and after those Jesus the son of Mary. We gave him the Gospel and put compassion and mercy in the hearts of his followers" (Qur'an 57:27).

Pluralism and diversity are therefore to be approached through the principles of justice and egalitarianism, where the doing of good deeds is the only form of distinction acceptable to God. Diversity exists today as a call to know others, and "view with one another to attain your Sustainer's forgiveness... for God loves those who do good" (Qur'an 3:133-134).

Where religious pluralism is concerned, the Qur'an states: "Had God willed, He would have made you into one community; but [it was His will] to test you in what He gave you. So compete with each other in doing good works. To God you are all returning, and He will inform you about how you differed" (Qur'an 5:48). The Qur'an affirms: "Indeed the more honorable among you, in the sight of God, is one who is more pious among you" (Qur'an 49:13); "Had your Lord pleased, He would have united all mankind" (Qur'an 11:118); "Had it been God's will, He could have made them all of one religion"(Qur'an 42:8); "Had your Lord pleased, He would have made you one nation" (Qur'an 5:48).

The Qur'an confers safety, security and legitimacy to and demonstrates a strong respect for the Jewish and Christian communities living within and alongside the Muslim community. It states: "Those who believe [in the Qur'an], and those who follow the Jewish [scriptures], and the Christians...and [all] who believe in God and the last day and work righteousness, shall have their reward with their Lord; on them shall be no fear, nor shall they grieve" (Qur'an 2:62).

Islam offered "Peoples of the Book" a broad scope of religious freedoms, protections and minority group rights within Muslim communities as a religious moral duty. Muslims are encouraged to invite non-Muslims into a "respectful" and "gentle" dialogue on religion, with "wisdom and beautiful preaching" (Qur'an16:125, 22:67-69), though nothing more. Where disagreement or acrimony enters into dialogue, Muslims are instructed to part ways, saying, "To you your beliefs, and to me mine" (Qur'an 109:6, 1:107-9). On interfaith disputes, the Qur'an reminds Muslims that only God can be the final arbiter on matters of ultimate truth: "God will judge between you on the Day of Judgment concerning the matters in which you differ" (Qur'an 22:76-69). While God endowed humankind with a decent and God-fearing nature, the Qur'an makes it clear that God's purpose for creation is to test humanity in the application and manifestation of our greatest potential and ideals. The Qur'an asks, "Do you think that you will enter the garden while God has not yet known those who strive hard from among you, and [He has not] known the patient?" (Qur'an 3:142).

Numerous verses in the Qur'an promote an ethic of social duty and responsibility toward fellow Muslims and non-Muslims. The Qur'an states that "Verily, the believers are brothers" (Qur'an 49:9).

Islam, Christianity and Judaism seek to provide the moral and spiritual guidance through the Holy Books for individual believers to fulfill their divine purpose in worshipping God and establishing a just and peaceful society. Given the human capacity to know God and choose moral actions accordingly, the Abrahamic ethic speaks to fundamental human dignity. The Abrahamic principles of liberty, equality and fraternity serve as important moral guideposts to evaluate progress in society. The path of Abraham not only provides a means of ennobling the soul, but also bringing believers into harmony with one another and proximity to God. As the Qur'an states: "And who better in faith than the one who willingly surrenders his being to God, and is a doer of good, and follows the way of Abraham the rightly oriented?" The Qur'an emphasizes that Abraham believed in God long before Judaism, Christianity and Islam. "Abraham was neither Jew nor Christian; but he was one of the true religion (*hanif*) who submitted to God" (Qur'an 3:60); "Who can be better in religion than one who submits his whole self to God, does good, and follows the way of Abraham the true in faith for God did take Abraham for a friend" (Qur'an 4:125). Abraham calls upon his sons to be sure that when they die, they do so in state of submission to God. He prays to God to raise up from his posterity a nation *(ummat)* which would submit to God. "Lord, send among them a messenger of their own who may recite your signs to them, teach the Book and wisdom, and purify them" (Qur'an 2:127).

In conclusion, one may ask: If the Holy Books hold similar tenets, then why are we so far apart and how can we close the gap? Interfaith dialogue brings us together, ignorance keeps us apart. We need to support our faith with knowledge. In this climate of increasing religious hostility and prejudice, we need to learn about the religion of the other, to reach out in love and friendship to our sisters and brothers embracing different faiths, so that through this interfaith understanding and solidarity we can establish world peace. In the Proverbs, we read: "If you indeed cry out for insight, and raise your voice for understanding; if you seek it like silver, and search for it as for hidden treasures, then you will understand the fear of the Lord and find the knowledge of God... Then you will understand righteousness and justice and equity, every good path" (Prov. 2:3-5).

"Resistance through Culture"

Rania Elias Khoury

As director of Yabous Cultural Centre, I wish to thank Sabeel for inviting me to participate in this conference which in itself can be considered an example of resistance through culture. Historically, "Yabous" was the name given to Jerusalem after one of the Canaanite tribes that built the first city of Jerusalem 5000 years ago.

Yabous is a Jerusalem-based Palestinian nonprofit organization that was founded in 1995 for the purpose of reviving the cultural life in the city of Jerusalem, which had suffered as a result of its closure after the Oslo Accords. With checkpoints and the separation wall, Palestinians from the West Bank have been denied access to Jerusalem. That is why the mission of Yabous is to develop and promote arts that enhance and assert cultural, national, and human values. After several years of asserting itself in Jerusalem and organizing festivals during the summer that brought life to the city, Yabous was able to rent Cinema Al-Quds on Al Zahra Street, which had been closed since 1987, and transformed it into a multipurpose cultural centre.

Under the prevailing circumstances of the Israeli occupation of Palestine, we continue to struggle to maintain our identity and presence; our cultural heritage is being targeted because it represents the essence of a nation and its enduring ability to resist occupation and to sustain us as a people.

Our identity is reflected in our culture, which is the means through which we challenge and confront crisis. All too often, when we feel helpless in the face of occupation and think nobody is going to write a book or sing a song as bullets are flying around or homes are being demolished, we realize how mistaken we are. Creativity comes out of places and people suffering from hardship and difficult conditions, like Palestine. It is this resilience that gives us the ability to bear the unbearable, not by simply accepting it but by being creative in finding the mechanism that will help us deal with the situation and maintain our steadfastness, or *sumud.*

When there is no justice and the rule of law has been eroded, when social services are missing and there is no freedom of expression, movement, or press, the artist often takes on the role of government critic, people's advocate, community organizer, human rights defender or even movement leader. But more importantly, the artist can create spaces for freedom of expression and encounter, places where people feel safe and can see productivity and tangible result. This is the role of Yabous Cultural Centre and it will continue to play this role until we are all free.

However, the Palestinian identity and culture have been continuously suppressed by the Israeli occupation in different ways and means, and Yabous has documented many times when the Israeli military would prevent a cultural activity, such as a literature festival, children flying balloons, clowns or groups dancing in the streets, using military force. Israel is not only banning these cultural events, but the occupation is trying to quash our imagination and turn us into a helpless population. They have even tried to erode our history as well by changing names of streets. The political situation influences our goals, our programmes and our entire presence as it deprives us of our ability to move, work freely, hence to lead a normal life like all human beings.

But in the face of these measures, our resolve to pursue activities has become a greater challenge. As an assertive society with a rich heritage, we Palestinians have been able to express ourselves through culture and art; it is through cultural activities that we preserve our identity and express our belonging to the land. For us, cultural resistance is carried out in many forms, including establishing a national orchestra, creating an art exhibition, building a school of music, renovating a theater, organizing festivals, conferences, seminars, and lectures, training children to dance traditional *dabkeh*, etc.

From my point of view, resistance through culture is our ability to implement cultural activities and our determination to highlight the occupation's brutality towards even the most peaceful means of resisting occupation. But organizing a concert in Palestine these days is not an easy task, unless you have hope, power, and resources contributing to your efforts. Yabous Cultural Centre as so many other institutions had to cancel two festivals and several concerts for reasons relating to the general political situation and the difficulties of issuing permits to groups and musicians, especially those from the Arab world. Palestinian artists living in West Bank cities such as Ramallah or Jenin, or those living in Gaza which is only a few kilometers from Jerusalem, are not allowed to travel to Jerusalem and vice versa. In 2013, the Palestinian National Orchestra members were not granted permission to come to Jerusalem, forcing a last minute change in program to replace the musicians.

The Israeli occupation also prevents international artists and musicians from participating in cultural events in Palestine. Marwan Abado, the Palestinian 'oud player living in Vienna, was invited to perform in Jerusalem and Ramallah but he was stopped and detained for 48 hours at Ben Gurion Airport and then sent back to Vienna. He has been blacklisted and is no longer allowed to enter Palestine. In 2008, the sixtieth anniversary of the *Nakba*, Yabous planned to organize a festival called "The Jerusalem Festival: Songs of Freedom." We invited the group Inti-Illimani from Chile; one of the artists was from Cuba and was denied entry after being detained for 24 hours at the airport in Tel Aviv.

During the incursion of the Israeli occupation forces into Ramallah on March 9, 2002, several cultural premises were invaded, including the National Conservatory of Music (NCM), the Peace Centre in Bethlehem, the Sakakini Cultural Centre, and the Popular Art Centre in Ramallah. The main door of the NCM was opened using explosives, which caused major damage. The occupation forces broke all the drawers and threw the contents around. Cellos and other instruments were broken, as well as music CDs. Books were thrown on the floor and trampled. Ahmad Al Khatib, a teacher at the NCM, was arrested on April 8, 2002, and was used as human shield by the Israeli occupation forces before being released. During the Israeli assault on Gaza (2008-9), UN schools were bombed, as well as the School of Music. Hundreds of civilians were killed after missiles exploded outside the UN school,[33] where hundreds of people had been taking shelter from the Israeli offensive.

I remember a statement by the Palestinian author Tawfiq Zayad, in which he says, "I never carried a rifle on my shoulder or pulled a trigger. All I have is unshakeable faith and an infinite love for my people in pain." And this is what we always carry in our hearts.

I believe culture and innovation became essential means of the new way of Palestinian resistance, a *nonviolent* resistance. And I also believe that we need a national cultural strategy as a main component of Palestinian resistance against Israeli occupation; we must protect our cultural heritage, education, and identity. It is much needed for the future. It is important that we sustain and protect our children, youth, and ourselves, in order to *stay human* and not lose our dignity. The real challenge for us is to transform culture and the arts into an ongoing reality that will support us to sustain our existence and our humanity.

---

33 For more information, read: McGreal, C. (6 Jan. 2009). "Besieged families flee homes for shelter under UN flag." *The Guardian*. Accessed 19 June 2014. < http://www.theguardian.com/world/2009/jan/06/gaza-palestine-israel>.

Our role at this moment is "to look after or to take care of human beings and not just the stones. Even if the Israelis demolish 1000 houses a day, a time will come and we will build them again. But if they kill the spirit and dignity of one person, it is impossible to have him/her back."

My friends, in South Africa they sang and danced against apartheid.

In Chile they sang against dictatorship.

And in Palestine we shall sing for our freedom, to our own tunes and to the tunes of the friends of freedom.

Thank you.

"Jewish and Democratic?"

Jeff Halper

Can Israel Be Jewish and Democratic?

Israel presents itself as a democracy, and if you look around, it might look like a democracy in some ways. It's a European-type society; the standard of living is European, not too different from the United States. Everybody has cars, the infra-structure is pretty good, and you have a thousand TV channels. It's high-tech. And, in fact, Israel does have elections and certainly is seen by the U.S. and Europe as a country of the Global North.

But Israel is what we call an "ethnocracy" rather than a democracy. That's the academic jargon. In principle, a democracy is a country that belongs to all its people; this kind of nationalism began to develop in the nineteenth century, after the French Revolution and the American Revolution. So countries like the United States and Canada share this: that the country belongs to all its citizens.

We know that there's discrimination and racism; we're not that naïve. During the U.S. Civil Rights Movement in the 1960s, there was a lot of violent resistance, but the wind was at their backs because the U.S. Constitution and "democracy," a government that belongs to all, supported the movement. You could not justify the Jim Crow system because that was in contradiction to the whole concept of democracy. In a sense, the Civil Rights Movement had that advantage.

Another kind of nationalism began in Eastern and Central Europe at the same time, but that was ethnocracy (e.g. Zionism), not democracy. For example, Poland is very "Polish" and there's no place for non-Poles. Actually, a couple of years ago I was invited to Poland by the Palestinian community of Poland. There are 500 Palestinians living in Poland from the days when Palestinians were given scholarships by the communist party to study in the Soviet Union, and some of them stayed. And there's still a small Jewish community in Poland. So when I was in Krakow, I went with a Polish Palestinian friend to visit someone who runs one of the Jewish museums. We went together, and it turns out that they have a program with the Jews and the small Muslim community. The Jews and Muslims are both trying to tell the Poles that they're Polish; the Jewish message and the Muslim message to the kids in the schools is that "we're all Poles." But it's a very hard message because Poland doesn't have a concept of multiculturalism.

And this is true in any part of Eastern Europe. You talk about Romania, or Hungary which are still very xenophobic. And certainly Germany, which before the end of World War II was *Deutschland Über Alles*. Germany belonged to Germans. It wasn't just "Germany, a state;" that was just one part of it. It was the German-speaking people. Ethnocracy is based on tribal, organic people, not a state with citizenship. In a way, the whole concept of citizenship in Central and Eastern Europe was a foreign concept because those countries existed before the states did and were very tribal.

That's the context from which Zionism emerges. Essentially, Zionism is a Central or Eastern European form of nationalism. Theodor Herzl came from Vienna and Ben Gurion came from Poland. Basically then, Israel is a nineteenth century Eastern European country imposed on the Middle East. Just like Russia belongs to the Russians, Poland belongs to the Poles, Germany belongs to the Germans, and the Slavic lands belong to the Slavs. Zionism says that the land of Israel belongs to the Jews. It wasn't a strange concept in terms of the historical context, but as Zionism developed, Ben Gurion and Herzl didn't jump to a Jeffersonian kind of democracy. They had never heard of Jefferson. They took from what they knew and transposed it.

And it has its own logic. The policy of the Israeli government until today is that 72 percent of the people in Jerusalem should be

Jewish. We're judaizing Jerusalem. Judaizing to make Jerusalem Jewish, to make the Galilee Jewish, to turn the West Bank into Judea and Samaria, though, in Western democracies, this is racist. Anytime you privilege one racial group over another, that's racist. The idea that we're going to "WASP-ify" New York City, or something like that, is simply not acceptable. But here, in an ethnocracy, it's not only acceptable, but completely expected.

When you pose this statement to Israeli Jews, that judaizing Jerusalem is racist because Jerusalem should be a multicultural city and should belong to all its inhabitants just like the country should belong to all its inhabitants, their answer is, "Why is that racist? Jerusalem was the ancient capital of the Jewish people. It's in the Bible. And we're reclaiming our ancient capital. What's the problem with that?" Obviously there *is* a problem, but the point is that, in some ways, Israelis don't get it. There's an internal logic to this kind of nationalism, so then the question really becomes: How do you turn an ethnocracy into a democracy?

People here just don't get it. It isn't that they're racist; it's just that, yes, this is a Jewish country that belongs to the Jews. And then, of course, I think that the big problem is that the world lets Israel do this. In other words, I think that ethnocracy is simply unacceptable. It could be acceptable, maybe, if your country was purely whatever you are. Maybe it works better in Poland which is around 96 percent Polish Poles. Or Saudi Arabia. Saudi Arabia would be considered an ethnocratic country. And some people say that China is an ethnocracy as well. The Han Chinese is the dominant ethnic group in China, and the government treats the Muslims, the Tibetans, and others as outside of that framework.

There is a difficult balance to be struck in order to not allow Israel to continue its occupation. Israel is in a worse shape than these other countries because when Zionism began, Zionists were a minority. The Zionists in Palestine were 10 percent of the population until World War I. In 1947, when the Partition Plan was made and the Jews were given 56 percent of the land, they were only a third of the population and most of them were new immigrants. So there you could say, "Look, you can't impose an ethnocracy here because you're not the majority."

What do you do about China? Saudi Arabia? That is a different question, because you have the concept of human rights which says to the Chinese, the Saudis, or the Israelis: You can have your culture. You can think this land belongs to you. God gave it to you. You can do all that, but the other people living in your country have certain human rights that are universal. So you can believe anything you want, but you can't impose it on others.

It is finding that balance between cultures, because on the one hand, you do not want to eliminate cultures. We may not like every culture, but we also cannot impose our culture on everybody else and say that this is how you should be. There is a danger in that. So there is this constant struggle of dialoguing between what is legitimate and what is not legitimate, and so on. In the Israeli case, Israel partly presents itself as a democracy, yet it hoists itself on its own petard. Israel says: "We are the only democracy in the Middle East. We're a democracy; we share common values with the United States. Obama comes here and talks with us." The Chinese and Saudis don't pretend to be a democracy.

Now we have to deal with this in a certain way because Israel's trying to convince you that it's a democracy while, in fact, it is an ethnocracy. And therefore, what Israel is doing *is* racist in a sense. If it really is a democracy, what it is doing cannot be sustained.

Sometimes we talk about a triangle to describe how Israel works as an ethnocracy. The first point: Israel wants to be a Jewish state. So immediately there is a human rights issue: Can you be a country that only belongs to one people? What about the rights of the other people? At any rate, Israel claims to be a Jewish state and Israel uses the term "Jewish democracy." We say to the world that we're the only democracy in the Middle East, but inside, in Hebrew, we talk about a "Jewish democracy." These are very different things. Israel wants to be a Jewish state, but also it claims to be, or wants to be, a democracy (the second point). But it also wants the entire land of Israel (the third point). That is the direction the state is obviously going. The settlements and permanency of the whole occupation are obviously a claim to the entire land of Israel.

And this is the essence of an ethnocracy: it looks at the land, not at the state. It doesn't define itself as a state; instead it's a people with a turf (like Germany). A big problem today in the negotiations with U.S. Sec. John Kerry is that the negotiators are trying to nail down each party's basic position, but Israel will not define its borders with Palestine because the whole idea is that this is *all* the land of Israel. "It all belongs to us, so how can you put borders on us?" It's a very real part of the political dilemma.

This brings us back to the triangle. Israel wants these three things: Jewish state, democracy, and the entire land. The issue is that you can only have two out of the three. You can be, in a way, a Jewish democracy. That's also problematic, of course, because of the demand by Israel that the Palestinians recognize Israel as a Jewish state. Twenty-five years ago, in 1988, the Palestinian Liberation Organization (PLO) recognized the State of Israel. But now Israel says, "That's not enough. You have to recognize Israel as a *Jewish* state." Almost a third of the population of Israel isn't Jewish. They're Palestinian Arabs, Bedouins, Druze, Russians, or foreign workers who stayed and married. Almost 30 percent aren't Jewish, which compromises their civil status living in a Jewish state, and this is a problem unique to ethnocracies.

But let's leave that aside. Jews are roughly 72 percent of the population of Israel. Let's just say for the sake of our discussion that to have a Jewish democracy (in the sense that the Jews are the majority, but ignoring all the other civil rights issues), you cannot have the whole land of Israel. You cannot incorporate another four and a half million Palestinians and still have a *Jewish democracy*. So, you can have a Jewish democracy, sort of, but it has to be a two-state solution. This is what Israeli President Shimon Peres and some of the other people argue: Israel needs a two-state solution in order for there to be a Jewish state, to save Zionism.

Or you can be a Jewish state and you can have the whole land of Israel. But then, you can't be a democracy. Obviously, Palestinians aren't going to vote for Israel as a Jewish state, so though Israel has the power to claim the land (and this is where Israel is going), it *is* giving up democracy. As a matter of fact, there is a law being shepherded through the Knesset that says, in all legislation, "Jewish" trumps "democratic." Jewish interests become the basis of our legislation instead of democratic concepts.

The third possibility is that you can have the whole land of Israel and it can be democratic, but it cannot be Jewish. This is what people like me want to see. But this is a dilemma: you can't have all three. You're in an impossible situation.

What's the answer according to the Israeli government? The answer is that it stays very carefully within the parameters. It doesn't push too hard in any direction. Right now, it has its cake and can eat it too. Right now it has all three. Israel is seen as democratic by the United States and by Europe. It does not push the boundaries in any direction.

The name of the Israeli policy towards the Palestinians is the *status quo*. It maintains the status quo. Now it's not *really* maintaining the situation; it is building settlements all the time, changing. It's a *dynamic* status quo, but a status quo from the point of view that it doesn't negotiate its goals. Israel might enter into talks with U.S. Sec. John Kerry, but it's not real. Israel is just delaying things. Any direction it goes is unacceptable, because it risks losing one of the three goals. So it simply keeps going, delaying negotiations, prolonging negotiations. Some years, there are no negotiations, but this has been going on now for 46 years, and has to keep going. And this is the whole idea.

"The Future of Jerusalem"

Raffoul Rofa

I think it's important to know the local legal challenge that Palestinians in Jerusalem face, and the legal complexities they have to go through in their daily lives.

Let me give you a brief introduction about my organization. Saint Yves is a Catholic human rights organization, established by canonical decree by the former Latin Patriarch of Jerusalem, Michel Sabbah, to provide legal aid and assistance to the poor and oppressed of the Holy Land without regard to religion, gender, or race. We work in Jerusalem and in the southern West Bank, in matters related to residency rights, house demolitions, social rights, land confiscations in the southern West Bank, matters of freedom of movement, and, most recently, the building of the separation wall.

I'd like to talk about Jerusalem, particularly the issues of residency of Palestinians in Jerusalem, house demolitions, and social rights. I choose to talk about these issues, and particularly the issue of residency, because not many people know about this issue, yet it is a challenge that Palestinians in Jerusalem face on a daily basis.

Residency

In 1967, when Israel occupied East Jerusalem, the Palestinians living in East Jerusalem were given a status that is different from Palestinians living in the remainder of the West Bank. Palestinians in Jerusalem were given the status of *permanent residents* of the State of Israel, and not citizens of the State of Israel. The Palestinian population of the West Bank remained protected persons under international law, and the institution responsible for protected persons is the occupying army, in this case headed by the commander of the Israeli army. Nowadays, this institution is called the Civil Administration.

In Jerusalem, because of this status and under Israeli law, it is possible for the Minister of the Interior of the State of Israel to cancel or revoke the residency of permanent residents if they leave the country for seven continuous years, or if they acquire permanent residency or citizenship anywhere else in the world. As a result of this policy, it is estimated that more than 14,000 Palestinians from Jerusalem have lost their right to live in the city since 1967. Now if you consider these 14,000 and think that they got married and had children, we're talking about much larger numbers of Palestinians losing their right to live in Jerusalem.

When I mention these facts, many people respond, "It is the prerogative of any country to allow whomever it sees fit into its borders, and to deny access to those it deems not fit. Therefore it is the prerogative of Israel to revoke the residency of any non-citizen who may choose to leave the country." I answer that Palestinians in East Jerusalem are the natives. Palestinians from East Jerusalem did not immigrate to Israel. Palestinians from East Jerusalem lived for thousands of years in East Jerusalem and all over Palestine. It was Israel that occupied *them* in 1967; it was Israel that chose to give them this legal status, and it was Israel that chose to revoke their residencies despite the fact that the Palestinians are the native people. This is very important. Palestinians are not immigrants; they are the natives.

Family Reunification

A matter that is very closely related to the issue of residency is the issue of family reunification. Because of the different legal statuses that the Palestinians have in Jerusalem and in the remainder of the West Bank or Gaza, when someone from Jerusalem marries someone from Bethlehem, for example, the couple has no choice because of the different statuses and IDs. They have to live in Jerusalem. If they go to live in Bethlehem, the spouse from

Jerusalem loses his or her residency in Jerusalem. They have to live in Jerusalem, but in order to live in Jerusalem, the spouse holding the Jerusalem residency card has to apply for family reunification for his or her spouse.

Family reunification was a simple process until the first Netanyahu administration in the middle of the 1990s. Up until then, it took a maximum of a year and then the person from the West Bank would get a Jerusalem identity card or become a permanent resident, like his or her spouse from Jerusalem. The first Netanyahu administration changed the laws and introduced something called *the gradual process* whereby, in theory, it took five and a quarter years for the spouse from the West Bank or for whomever—citizen of the United States, European citizen, Australian—to attain the legal status of their Israeli spouse (Israeli according to law). "Israeli" can either be Israeli citizen or permanent resident.

In practice in East Jerusalem, this was not true. The offices of the Ministry of the Interior were not fit to absorb the numbers of Palestinians living in East Jerusalem. The offices and the building itself were not suitable; it was under-staffed and it was on many occasions physically impossible to gain access to this office. And even if you could gain access and were able to apply for family reunification, most probably your papers would be lost and you'd be asked to bring your papers over and over again. Or, surprisingly enough, this office has suffered from many fires, and a lot of family reunification applications have been lost in these fires, so people have had to apply again and again. The result is that many couples who have been married for 20 or 25 years are still going through the family reunification application, though the spouse from the West Bank should have attained the legal status of their spouse after only five and a quarter years.

The situation got even worse in 2002 when the process of family reunification was suspended due to Israel's claim that those who acquired legal status through family reunification used this status to carry out terrorist attacks. This despite the fact that statistics show those who were involved in any attack against Israel could be counted on the fingers of one hand. And if you go back to the discussions in the Knesset that relate to the law, it is clear that the main reason for this law is demography: Israel does not want Palestinians in Jerusalem and it sees the whole process of family reunification as Palestinians practicing the right of return.

In 2003, the Citizenship and Entry into Israel Law was enacted. It was meant to be a temporary law, only lasting one year, but that "one year" has continued until now. The law is still in effect. This law has been challenged in the High Court of Justice three times, but in all three occasions the High Court of Justice upheld that this law is legal and should remain in place, despite the fact that it is, to say the least, discriminatory, if not an apartheid law. This law, first of all, prohibits altogether the family reunification of Palestinians who have different legal statuses. Palestinians can either be citizens of the State of Israel, permanent residents of the State of Israel, or residents of the Palestinian Authority areas. But this law prohibits family reunification not only between Palestinians, but also between Israelis (according to law) and citizens of Lebanon, Syria, Iraq or Iran.

For the residents of the Palestinian Authority, the Israeli law makes two exceptions: Firstly, persons requesting to live in Israel who can prove they have been working for the "benefit of the State of Israel," i.e., as collaborators and others. Secondly, spouses of Israelis who fit within age categories. If we are talking about the husband, he must be 35 years or older; if we are talking about the wife, she must be 25 years or older. If the person doesn't satisfy the age requirement, the family reunification application will be rejected at this point.

If they satisfy the age category, they have to then satisfy the residency category, which means they have to prove they are living in Jerusalem or in Nazareth or in Tel Aviv or wherever. They prove this by producing documents like a lease contract, electricity bills, water bills, or certificates of school for the children. If they have babies, the documents must prove that the baby is being inoculated and that the family is using the mother-care units in Israel, not in the West Bank. If the applicants don't satisfy the residency category, the family reunification application will be rejected and they will have to wait two years before they can reapply.

Most importantly, the applicants must also satisfy the security and criminal requirements. Up until 2007, it was just the couple applying who had to satisfy this requirement. In 2007, the Knesset introduced an amendment to the law requiring that the parents, their brothers and sisters, their spouses, and their children (either their own adult children or children that they might have had from other marriages) satisfy the security requirement. If any of these people have a security or criminal record, the family reunification application will be rejected, even without consideration that the couple applying is free of such a record.

And if a family reunification application is approved, the spouse from the West Bank gets a permit for only one year. It's temporary. They have to renew it on a yearly basis, and if any of these hindrances or requirements of the law come up, the family reunification application will be rejected. And this permit doesn't give the spouse from the West Bank any rights whatsoever: they can't drive a car, they are not entitled to any of the social benefits, and only recently—a few months ago—were they able to work legally. Before this, they were not allowed to work.

Of course, we and others challenge this law. On one occasion we were in court challenging the refusal of a family reunification application, which was initially approved with the husband getting a permit. Now, in this case, we challenged the denial of the family reunification application in front of the administrative court. The lawyer representing the Ministry of the Interior said that he wanted to present evidence to the court, given by three witnesses who were secret agents, and that because this evidence was secret, my beneficiary and I should leave the courtroom. This is a criminal procedure and not an administrative procedure, so the lawyer imported it from criminal law into the administrative law. When I objected, the judge answered, "You either trust me and my judgment, or I dismiss the case on this point." After consulting with my beneficiary, we left the court. An hour later, we were called in and the judge dismissed our case, saying there was a security threat and the evidence presented by three secret agents was locked in the court safe, not part of the public record of the hearing.

An amendment was introduced to this security requirement. I don't know if it's for the best; I'll leave it for you to judge. Now it's possible for those people whose family members have a security record to sign a document stating that they will cut all ties with those family members, not visit them or talk to them again. If they sign this document, the applicants will be given family reunification.

Another issue tied to both previous issues is child registration. When these mixed-couples (Israeli or Jerusalemite with West Bank Palestinian) have children, their children are not automatically registered in the population registry. At best, if the couple does not have any problems and can prove residency in Jerusalem, etc., it takes up to six months to register the child. During this time the child is without any rights. Officially he or she does not exist, is not entitled to status benefits, is not entitled to anything. With couples who have problems, it can take years to register the child. If the child gets to school age and is still unregistered, he or she will not be able to attend school because officially he or she does not exist. And if the child reaches the age of 14 and still is not registered, he or she can only get a temporary permit—like the parent from the West Bank. If the child reaches 18 without being registered, he or she must leave Jerusalem and go to the West Bank. Residency and family reunification are major problems and affect not only adults (i.e., the couple, the parents), but also young children, because it leaves them vulnerable, without proper healthcare or education.

Social Rights

Palestinians in Jerusalem must prove residency under two separate laws: the National Insurance Law, and the Entry into Israel Law. In order to claim their rights from the National Insurance Institute, Palestinians have to be residents of Jerusalem. If they're not residents, they are not entitled to health insurance; they are not entitled to any of the benefits given by the National Insurance Institute. If Palestinians fail to prove that they are residents under the National Insurance Law, then the seven year period which is needed under the Entry into Israel Law will start running. If the person concerned does not remedy his or her legal position within the seven year period, then his or her residency under the Entry into Israel Law will be revoked. This is not necessarily automatic. Many people lose their residency far beyond the seven years, when they cannot furnish evidence that the National Insurance Institute recognizes them as residents. The Ministry of the Interior revokes the residencies retroactively in these cases. So it's all connected.

House Demolitions

After 1967, when Israel annexed East Jerusalem, the state stopped the process of land registry that was initiated by the Jordanian government, halting the process not only in East Jerusalem but in the West Bank as a whole. Because Israel stopped the land settlement process, it became very difficult for Palestinians to get building permits. Before anyone is able to get a permit to build a house or any other building, he or she must be a landowner. Palestinians found a solution. Now heads of communities sign that "X" or "Y" is the owner of the land; the neighbors sign, and it is possible to apply for a building permit.

However, most of the land in East Jerusalem that is left for Palestinians is designated as "green land" or open-space land, and it takes on average 10 years to change the status of this land from "open-space" to "building." And the process is so expensive that people cannot afford to pay the huge amounts of money required. If they succeed in changing the status of the land from green land to building land, then they must apply for a building permit. On average, for a Palestinian to get a permit takes three to five years, and, again, is very expensive. To get a permit, people pay the equivalent of hundreds of thousands of American dollars.

Statistics say that on the eve of the occupation in 1967, the

Palestinian population in East Jerusalem was around 66,000, and now they are more than 300,000. With the growth of the population, people need places to live. So people started building without permits, mostly on their own privately owned land, and the result is that now there are over 20,000 housing units that are under threat of being demolished because they were built illegally under Israeli neighborhood planning laws.

And another thing: those who build illegally and are caught get a criminal record, because criminal procedure applies to these issues. So people are indicted, they receive heavy fines, and they get suspended prison sentences. If they get indicted for a second time, they are fined again. Normally the second indictment is for non-compliance with the judicial order stating that they have to demolish their own home. And if they are indicted for a third time, they go to prison and the fines shift from a single amount to daily fines, so they pay huge amounts in fines. And many people end up going to prison. But sometimes you are talking about people who are elderly or very sick. In one case, the judge sent a severely disabled man to prison because the law requires prison time for the third indictment. And the judge's comment was, "Well, at least he'll get proper medical treatment in prison."

The planning policy of the Jerusalem municipality and the Israeli Ministry of the Interior results in the Palestinians being gathered in neighborhoods, separated from each other. So if you look at East Jerusalem, you find Beit Hanina and Shu'afat in the north and they are separated from Issawiyye, the Old City, and Sheikh Jarrah, which are separated from the neighborhoods in the east (at-Tur and Jabal al-Mukkabir). And these are separated from Beit Sahour. And everything in-between is filled with settlements.

These are some of the issues that Palestinians living in Jerusalem face on a daily basis. There is a great need to educate people about their rights, and we at St. Yves run awareness-raising sessions to help people protect themselves from falling into the trap of losing their Jerusalem residency.

"The Militarization of Israeli Society"

Moriel Rothman

Let me begin my presentation with four declarations:
1) I am a violent person
2) I am a privileged person
3) I am not an expert
4) I am a conscientious objector

Beginning with the first declaration: I am a violent person. Recently a friend sent me the work of Walter Wink, a Christian theologian and activist. In this work, Wink talks about what a relief it would be if we could live in faith communities where we could recognize ourselves as containers of all opposites, recognize that we, as non-violent activists, often possess the exact same instincts and impulses toward violence as the systems and individuals whose actions we are protesting. When I'm afraid, my hands clench into a fist, and when something makes me angry, I want to hurt that thing. A person can't hurt a thing, so often that anger morphs into a desire to hurt another person. That's the context with which I want to begin this discussion.

My second declaration is privilege. I am privileged. Compared to most of the world, I am extremely well-off economically. I am also light skinned. Growing up in America I was privileged as a White person, and living in Israel I am privileged as a White Jewish person. I am privileged to have American citizenship and also Israeli citizenship, complicated privileges that became significant in my story.

My third declaration: I'm not an expert. I don't say this as a point of false modesty. I know what I've learned from reading and experience, from study on the ground, study with my feet, but I don't hold a doctorate and I haven't researched these subjects. I was speaking with someone in the hallway and they said, "Oh, you're speaking on Israeli militarization. I'm writing a book on that." He should do my presentation! But I'm honored to be here with you to tell my story and how that story reflects broader trends of Israeli society.

And so the fourth declaration is that I'm a conscientious objector. I'm going to tell you the story of how I came to this decision, to this identity, and the ways in which this intersects with society and with militarization.

I was born in Jerusalem but lived a lot of my childhood in America, in a small town in southwest Ohio, thus the American English and the American passport. Growing up, I had this ideal of using violence to stop what I saw as bad. I wanted to use "good" violence and thereby become good myself, in my own eyes, in the eyes of the world, in the eyes of God. To justly wield violence to stop evil. This was the concept I had, and at the same time, I had very strong concepts of what was "bad." I was against oppression, against discrimination, against racism. I was against "bad" violence and I wanted to wield "good" violence. As a young teenager this manifested as a desire to join the Israeli army, to become a soldier, and to wield good violence against those who were doing bad things.

I don't wish to draw a caricature of myself, though. It's easy to tell this narrative of radical transformation, that as a teenager I hated Palestinians and as an adult I grew up and learned that Palestinians are people just like me. But that's too simple. I never hated Palestinians, which I think in some way is more troubling. I never felt hate towards the Palestinians at large, and yet I desperately wanted to become a soldier in the Israeli army.

Fast forward a few years. I am living in Jerusalem, going to an Israeli high school, and all my friends are preparing for army service. We talk about it every hour, if not every minute. We talk about what everyone is going to do, what unit they'll join and what it'll be like. I don't think we ever stopped and thought, "What about the Palestinians?" It wasn't that we were all thinking,

"Let's all join and kill our enemies." It wasn't that we were saying, "Let's get together and join the army so we can crush the Arabs."

The Palestinians and the Arabs were basically an issue that had nothing to do with our discussion. We knew of the conflict and occupation and such things "over there," and even then, as a 17-year-old, I was (relatively) on the political left. The conflict was sad, the occupation was bad, the Palestinians should have a state and we shouldn't hate each other, but that was separate from us. That was *over there* and the Israeli military was *right here*.

I remember when I was 16 years old, I thought of my book title. I thought I would write a book called *Memoirs of a Soldier, Memoirs for Peace*, because I wanted to show that I'd been a soldier, I'd been through war and knew that war is bad and that I believe in peace. And looking back on that now, it's wild that even though I knew war was bad in a vague sense as a 16-year-old, I still wanted to go through war so I could justify saying "no more war."

And here's where privilege ties in. Had I not been an American citizen, I would have joined a combat unit, served my three years in the Israeli military, and then, perhaps, would have realized that troubling things happened. Maybe I would have joined "Breaking the Silence," which is an excellent organization of Israeli veterans who have chosen to speak out against the occupation, what they witnessed and, in some cases, carried out as soldiers in the army. But, as an American citizen, I decided to take a year and go back to the U.S. to study, see what I wanted to do: whether I wanted to join the military at age 22 or at age 18. So, I went back to the U.S., went to college, studied Arabic, and during this time, some of my conclusions began to shift, particularly during the 2008-2009 Israeli bombing campaign on Gaza, known as Operation Cast Lead.

Witnessing this campaign, even from afar on a computer screen, really shook some of my deeply held conclusions. I very much supported peace; I very much supported fairness. And in my Israeli high school it was okay to criticize the government, it was okay to criticize the prime minister, it was okay to criticize the school systems, and it was okay to criticize virtually everything, except the army. In Israel whether you're for peace or you're for war, you join the army. Whether you're a leftist or you're a rightist, you join the army. Whether you believe the occupation is good or the occupation is bad, you join the army. Afterwards, you talk about whether things should remain as they are or change.

So again we fast forward a few years. I returned to Israel after graduating college and quickly got involved in various forms of activism against the occupation, against the expansion of settlements in the Sheikh Jarrah neighborhood, and some work in villages in the South Hebron Hills of the West Bank.

And I want to tell you about one moment. One moment. I was standing in Susiya, a small Palestinian village in the South Hebron Hills. I was standing there and I remember the smell, a strange mixture of sweat and dust and tear gas I'd gotten used to at this point. And some people were yelling and some people were silent, and they were holding signs. Across from us, a line of soldiers stood, watching our massive demonstration against a recent declaration by the Israeli government that it planned to demolish Susiya. In many cases you hear of a house being demolished in this village or a structure being demolished in that village, but in this case, the entire village of Susiya had been given demolition orders because it was built "illegally." With the explanation being that if you're a Palestinian living in the occupied West Bank, it's virtually impossible to get a building permit, so of course the village was built "illegally." I drew the conclusion that Susiya was threatened with demolition because it was a *Palestinian* village, nothing more.

And so, I stood there, angry, the people around me also angry. Angry and yelling, and across from us this line of soldiers, just young kids wearing sunglasses, so we couldn't see their eyes. And then I noticed a soldier not wearing sunglasses, and as I looked at him, I recalled a piece I'd studied in college by a French Jewish philosopher, Emmanuel Levinas. He writes, in essence, that when we look into someone's eyes, when we truly see someone's eyes, the only part of the inner body that's exposed to the world, we see our capacity to murder them. And in this same capacity to murder them, we see their infinity, their fragility, and from that point we can truly love them. At this moment I think I felt something similar to what Levinas describes. I saw this soldier and I understood my capacity to murder him, to kill him. Though the demonstration was non-violent—no one was shooting weapons—there was still an anger boiling under the surface of my being.

At that moment, I deeply understood that the violent instincts I have and this anger I directed at this person, this soldier, this kid, were not true manifestations of myself or my ideals. And that moment was made all the more poignant and powerful because two days before I had received my draft notice for the Israeli army. With the draft notice sitting on my desk at home and the protest raging around me, I came to this ideal that would recognize the humanity of the soldier standing in front of me without ignoring the fact that the Palestinians standing next to me were equally fragile, equally human, equally deserving of love and fairness, and that their entire village was waiting to be demolished by the system in which this soldier participated.

A few months later, I decided to apply for conscientious objector status, which does exist in the Israeli military, although I can't tell you the process because my application was rejected three times, without explanation. The final time, I got a phone call from an unknown number, ten days before my draft date, saying, "Moriel Rothman, your application has been rejected. We can't explain why. See you at the draft station." At that point, I was riding on the heels of a movement much bigger than myself, and without which I would not have been able to take the stand I did. The movement started in the 1980s during the First Lebanon War and then, of more relevance to my context, continued during the beginning of the Second Intifada. At that time, Israelis, by the hundreds and sometimes thousands, refused to serve in the military, sometimes just in the occupied Territories, but sometimes in the military generally. These public refusals supported me and made me feel I had a community within Israeli Jewish society, as well as in Palestinian-Israeli society and Palestinian society in the

West Bank and East Jerusalem. I had supporters and friends, and so I decided to refuse publicly.

The day before reporting to the draft station, I published a letter stating my refusal to enlist. The next day, I arrived at the draft station and I stood in line, waiting for the commander to call each of us, one-by-one, into the next room for our uniform and gun. He came to me and said, "Your turn."

"I refuse to enlist."

"What are you talking about?"

"I refuse to enlist in the Israeli army because I'm opposed to violence and opposed to the violence of the occupation."

He looked at me. "That's nice. Go and put on your uniform. We'll talk about it afterwards."

"I won't put on the uniform."

He shook his head, called a higher up official, and took me to a room where I waited for three or four hours with other people who weren't fitting into the system. Finally I was brought before a commander, a high ranking officer, who asked me what I was doing.

"I refuse to serve in the army."

"Do you realize you could go to jail for this?"

"I realize."

The next thing I knew, I was in military prison outside the town of Atlit in the North. I spent a week and a half there during this first sentence, and then was released for the weekend and told to report back to the draft station on Sunday morning.

"Okay," I said. I wrote another letter, found a lawyer to notarize it, and applied again for conscientious objector status. This time I brought the letter with me and before the commander even called me, I said that I was refusing the draft. Again their answer was, "That's nice," and they brought me to the same waiting room as before. I waited another three hours and then was brought to the same commander.

"Are you refusing again?" he asked.

"I'm refusing again." And I was sent back to jail.

At that point I realized the process could go on as long as

they wanted or as long as I wanted, which is another element of privilege. Essentially I was faced with the choice of continuing indefinitely or going to a psychologist, which is what most Israeli political refusers do either before service or after they've been jailed for some time.

I chose to go to a psychologist. I don't know what was written on his computer screen; it could have been, "As soon as Moriel Rothman comes to you, let him go," because this way the army maintains perfect statistics. Everyone who is physically and mentally sound—not spouting "unacceptable" positions like opposition to violence and the occupation—serves. "Of course, there are examples of people who aren't mentally sound, aren't physically sound, and they don't serve. But aside from that, every member of Israeli society does their mandatory service," says the army. So, I was quickly released on psychological grounds after spending less than a month in jail.

In all that I've shared, note that what I know best is what I know best: my story and my experience.

"Palestinian Christians in the Holy Land"

Sami El-Yousef

Given the history and given the politics, it's a challenge for Christians living in the Middle East; I would like to briefly discuss the broader situation of Christians in the region, and then particularly address the local situation (Palestine and Israel) because it is descriptive of the challenges in the whole Middle East.

Christians in the Middle East are concentrated in the Levant, composed of our immediate neighborhood (the West Bank, the Gaza Strip, and Israel) and Egypt, Jordan, Syria, and Lebanon. The further out from the Levant you go, the fewer Christians you find. In the Emirates and some of the Gulf countries, you may have a 13, 14, or 15 percent Christian population, but these are not indigenous Christians; these are mostly expatriate workers who are there temporarily before they go back to their home countries.

We do not have exact numbers of Christians scattered in these countries; all of these percentages are questioned and debatable.

Lebanon: 36 percent, the highest percentage of Christian presence

Egypt: 10 percent

Jordan: about 6 percent

Syria: 5 percent (pre-Syrian war numbers)

Israel: about 2 percent

Palestine: well under 2 percent

In Palestine, we used to say 2 percent confidently, but we cannot make that claim anymore. At the time of the conflict that led to the creation of the state of Israel in 1948, the Palestinian population was 1.2 million, of which 8 percent were Christian. That means roughly 100,000 Christians lived in the Holy Land at that time. If we maintained our Christian presence of 1948 and do not account for natural growth, today there would be one million Christians between the combined states of Israel and Palestine. But this is not where we are today.

The worldwide Palestinian population is around 11.5 million, with 38 percent in Palestine (the West Bank and Gaza Strip), 12 percent in Israel, 44 percent refugees, and 6 percent elsewhere around the world.

Compared to the challenges faced by Christians in many countries of the Middle East, particularly in Syria and Egypt, our situation in the Holy Land does not seem so bad at first glance. After all, there is no war or intifada or major crisis, and thus for all practical purposes, we seem to be doing well for now. However, the history books are rich with the upheaval that has become a way of life in the Holy Land. In many ways, we live a perpetual and chronic emergency situation. Between wars and intifadas and crises, we get a little bit of rest, some short-term peace and tranquility, even some limited economic development; and then the cycle kicks in again, and we find ourselves in a new low that seems worse than anything we have witnessed before.

On the one hand, we as indigenous Christians have a lot of which to be proud given our many contributions to Palestinian society over our long history. Thus, I will focus on some of the challenges that we face living in the Holy Land, which for many of us is also very rewarding. I will summarize such challenges in a few points breaking them down into four geographic areas, three in Palestine and the final one in Israel:

West Bank

In terms of demographics, 2.65 million Palestinians reside in the West Bank, and the Christian population is a mere 50 thousand. The consecutive governments of the West Bank have been and still are very supportive of Christians and the Christian presence in the Holy Land. In particular, there are assurances of participation at the various levels of the government to ensure that Christian voices are heard and that they are an integral part of Palestinian society. A quota system ensures that six out of sixty-six seats of the Legislative Council are reserved for Christians. A presidential decree guarantees the local council and local government in ten locations—ten villages and local councils—to Christians, even if there is no Christian majority in those towns. In some areas, only 30 percent of the population is Christian, yet the mayor and the majority of council seats are reserved, by law, for Christians. Thus, Christians have assured participation in the local government with 10 local mayoral posts and majority rule in village councils reserved for Christians, as well as assured participation in the legislative council and no fewer than two seats in most governments formed since 1994. In addition, there are always calls by various political and religious leaders to preserve the Christian presence in the Holy Land.

However, the problem is that on the street level, one sees more and more polarization between Christians and Muslims and a receding level of interaction compared to just a few years ago. Political Islam is certainly taking its toll with less and less tolerance of the Christian presence, and a greater sense that Christians are part of the West rather than equal citizens with equal rights and responsibilities. One finds more and more segregation rather than integration between Muslims and Christians. Having said that, life for a Christian in the West Bank is probably the best ranked compared to the surrounding countries, despite the continuing brutal occupation and the endless associated restrictions that come with it. Palestinians continue to live under an occupation in which the methods of control shift on a daily basis and continually disrupt daily life. Christians face limited access to holy places and sites, which are restricted during Christian holidays. This past Easter, for example, saw the Palestinian community struggling to receive permits from the Israeli government, both to come from the West Bank to Jerusalem and also to enter the Church of the Holy Sepulchre on Holy Saturday. The Israeli police set up checkpoints around the Old City to restrict access to the church.

The issue of family reunification disproportionately affects Palestinian Christian families. Because Christians make up such a small percentage of the population of Israel and Palestine, and Christians tend to marry other Christians, the pool of eligible people is rather small. Palestinian Christians from the West Bank must marry across borders, to Jerusalemites or Palestinian citizens of Israel, but the families are then faced with the impossibility of living together inside Jerusalem or Israel because of Israel's ban on family reunification. Rather than suffer through the indignities of this discriminatory system—applying annually for permits to live together, often having these applications denied—many families emigrate, further lessening the number of Christians remaining in Palestine and Israel.

Gaza Strip

Since Hamas took over the Gaza Strip in 2007, life for Christians and Christian institutions in Gaza has become very uncomfortable; emigration of Christians continues, and their number is now less than 2,000 among a total population of close to 1.8 million. New legislation is introduced every day to ensure that Islamic law is imposed on all, which not only makes it difficult for Christians but also for moderate and liberal-minded Muslims. One example is the new education law[34] passed in 2014 that calls on all schools to be segregated by gender; this would have a tremendous impact on Christian schools since all of them are coeducational and offer a superior liberal arts education. If Hamas continues in this way, all of Palestinian society loses since the majority of the students at Christian schools in Gaza are Muslim. Thus life for the average Christian living in Gaza is very challenging, especially since these internal difficulties are exacerbated by the continuing Israeli (and now Egyptian) blockade that has turned Gaza into the biggest open air prison in the world.

---

34 For more information, read: Balousha, H. (4 April 2014). "New Gaza education law imposes gender segregation." *Al-Monitor*. Accessed 17 June 2014. <http://www.al-monitor.com/pulse/originals/2013/04/gaza-education-law-gender-segregation.html>.

East Jerusalem

The third geographic area is very unique in many ways. Jerusalem has become a large city with a population of close to 800,000 people. The Jewish population is about 64 percent (almost 500,000), and the Arab population is roughly 36 percent (close to 280,000). There are approximately 9,000 Christians, which is 3 percent of the Arab population that resides inside Jerusalem and 60 percent of those who live inside the Old City. So a significant percentage of the Christians of Jerusalem reside inside the Old City.

Palestinians consider East Jerusalem part of the land occupied in 1967 and the capital of the future State of Palestine. Israel annexed East Jerusalem after its occupation in 1967 and considers it part of its undivided capital. Since 1967, Israel has been moving consistently to both assimilate East Jerusalem's Palestinian population with the Israeli system—granting residency, freedom of movement and including them in Israel's social and health care system—but also to minimize the non-Jewish presence in the city. Israel also provides generous government subsidies to various institutions working in education, health care and social services, making them very dependent on these subsidies. Now we are entering into a new phase whereby Israel is imposing new policies, such as requiring Palestinian schools to change from the Palestinian curriculum to an Israeli-approved curriculum or risk losing the government subsidy. This certainly will have a negative impact not only on schools but also on many Christian institutions now that they have been co-opted into the Israeli system. This was made possible by the inability of the Palestinian Authority to keep Jerusalem as a priority in negotiations.

One of the most critical problems facing the youth in particular is the proximity of the East side to the West, and the availability in West Jerusalem of many minimum wage jobs. This has led many youth to drop their last few years of education to join the workforce, only to find themselves out of a job within 12 months and without long-term benefits. They lose the opportunity for an education as well as decent work opportunities. Thus there is a whole generation of youth who are lost and unsure of their affiliations. Many of these youth are Christian, since over 50 percent of the Christians of Jerusalem live in the Old City, in close proximity to West Jerusalem.

Christians and Muslims face other policies under occupation: denial of residency, house demolitions, confiscation of land including restricting the expansion of Palestinian neighborhoods in East Jerusalem, and poor and neglected government-run social, educational, and healthcare services in East Jerusalem. Palestinian East Jerusalemites suffer from unemployment and poverty rates that are among the highest in Israel.

Israel

The total population of Israel is about 8 million people. The Jewish population makes up 75 percent (6 million Jews in the State of Israel). The population is made up of approximately 20.7 percent Arab citizens of the State of Israel; this is 1.66 million Arabs, including 158,000 Christians (about 2 percent of the total population of Israel). Additionally, there are another 300,000 non-Arab Christians (another 4 percent of the total population) who are not indigenous Christians, but come mostly from the Soviet Union.

In Israel proper, the Arabs remaining after 1948 were granted full citizenship with benefits, and thus the socioeconomic status of these individuals is much higher than that of an average Palestinian in the West Bank and Gaza. Additionally, Christian institutions in Israel working in education, healthcare, and social services receive generous subsidies from the government which cover most of their operating costs, in lieu of providing quality services. The challenge for these institutions comes with capital development projects, equipment needs, and the like. In many instances, these institutions are subjected to various inspections by the relevant government ministries and huge investments are needed to ensure that they meet standards and remain licensed; otherwise they risk being shut down. The government does not provide any support beyond operating cost support.

Christian Palestinians in Israel are a minority within a minority, with all the pressures that come with that designation. In the eyes of the Israeli government, Christians are Arabs and thus cannot be trusted; in many instances, the government imposes policies that deliberately discriminate against them (e.g. education and job opportunities connected to military service; low subsidies to local councils). In legislation passed in February 2014, the Israeli government declared Christian Palestinians to be different from Muslim Palestinians, recognizing Christians and Muslims as separate ethnic identities in order to establish a discriminatory employment system. This system of multiple identities imposed by Israel becomes even more complicated when one looks at the Muslim-Christian-Druze relations in Israel, where tensions are high and Christians are viewed with a different set of eyes. A number of religiously based violent interactions have occurred recently in many villages.

A systematic push by the government of Israel (including the prime minister himself) in encouraging the Christian youth to join the army has complicated matters further. These moves are certainly a continuation of the "divide and rule" mentality common in colonial enterprises, and represent an attempt to capitalize on the serious identity crisis faced by many Christian youth. These youth try to make sense of the complex Israeli-Palestinian-Arab-Christian make up of their identity, where each component pulls in a different and conflicting direction.

Finally, it should be noted that Jewish right-wing extremists have vandalized various Christian institutions in the past year. In most instances the perpetrators are never caught or brought to justice. The increasing number of attacks even prompted the Latin Patriarch in Jerusalem to comment[35] on the questionable safety of the country right before Pope Francis was scheduled to visit in May.

---

35 For more information, read: Gavlak, D. (13 May 2014). "'Price tag' Israeli extremists target Christians." *Christianity Today*. < http://www.christianitytoday. com/ct/2014/may-web-only/price-tag-israeli-extremists-target-christians. html?paging=off>.

Institutional Presence and Witness

With this brief background about each of the four distinct regions that make up the Holy Land, allow me to highlight some of the Christian contributions. According to a study conducted by Diyar Consortium in Bethlehem, a full 45 percent of the NGO sector in Palestine working in education, health, and social services belongs to various churches. In many ways, the churches end up doing the work of governments. These contributions cannot be underestimated; neither should we underestimate what it takes to keep these institutions open and providing services to all segments of the population, nor the value of these institutions in practicing interfaith dialogue.

If we consider the contribution of our various institutions in education, there are students from all faiths getting a quality education imbued with Christian values. Graduates of all faiths from Christian schools have ended up in leadership positions where they practice these core values, including the importance of respect, tolerance, peaceful coexistence, and dignity. They are better citizens for it. When it comes to health and social services, our Christian institutions are open to anyone seeking their services, especially the poor, marginalized, and weak. Again, it is in these institutions that dialogue is practiced rather than preached and everyone receives the service with dignity and respect. Finally, these various institutions of the Church provide important employment opportunities for the young, helping stop emigration.

Christians of the Holy Land have a great responsibility to live and uphold Christian values; their contribution to the building of their society and country is needed more today than at any other time in history. Emigration is certainly worrying, and as our numbers continue to decrease, additional problems arise. However, we must continue to learn how to adapt to the new realities and maintain our belief that what we do makes a difference, even if it is in the life of only one person at a time.

I firmly believe that if we are to maintain a healthy Christian presence in the Holy Land, we must support the various institutions of the church working in education, healthcare, and social services, and ensure not only that they survive but that they thrive. It is through these institutions that we find our identity and confirm who we are and why we are here. I cannot envision the Holy Land without its Christian institutions. Churches and holy sites are wonderful and we need them for the spiritual dimension, but our institutions represent today's Christian community and how Christians of the Holy Land translate the teachings of Christ into reality. The Holy Land would not be the same without its indigenous Christians and without its Christian institutions providing quality services to the poor, weak, and marginalized.

PART V
REMEMBERING AND LOOKING FORWARD

FINAL SERMON

Don Wagner

Let me begin with a sincere thank you to all the Sabeel staff for the remarkable week you have given us. We leave this place changed. Allow me to add a word of gratitude to all who came from near and far to experience this week. And especially to the local community in Palestine: we salute you, and we leave, *insha'allah,* to work on your behalf.

In many ways this week has been like building a family. I think we leave with a sense of connectedness to one another and particularly to you who are local at Sabeel. We are on a journey together and we have been charged with an enormous ministry which I would like to address this morning.

On our very first evening, Dr. Mustafa Barghouti quoted Nelson Mandela, saying, "The Palestine question is the greatest moral issue of our time." I think we agree that this is the case and that's why we are here. But at the same time, we see and feel what Dr. Mary Grey said: "We are being squeezed with you in an occupation that is systemic evil."

This morning as we think about the occupation and our invitation to ministry, I'd like to reflect on how baptism and Eucharist call us to three movements.

First, a movement of dying: dying to Christ as Christ died for the world. Second, a movement of resistance: standing firm against all that is evil, and doing it corporately. And third, a movement of rising, renewal, and resurrection, which is an ongoing, daily process.

Baptism has both a personal and a corporate dimension. I'd like to speak to both aspects as we move through these three movements, because we so often forget the corporate dimension

273

of sin. Coming from an Evangelical background where the individual dimension was overstated, I believe that the mark of Christ is on me and upon all of us in baptism. In Christ we have been liberated from sin and freed for the ministry of liberation, love, and reconciliation. However, the bad news is that the majority of the world and its governments do not know this. So we have an enormous task in front of us.

As we move into this daunting, difficult task, justice fatigue can become a challenge. How do we stay the course? How do you from Palestine remain steadfast within this evil system of occupation? How do we internationals stand with you and not give up hope? How do we maintain our commitment to be actively engaged for the long struggle ahead? We have much to learn from the Palestinians, because you have to deal with it on a daily basis and we will fly home tomorrow.

We see systemic evil at work here. There is often an overwhelming nature to the corporate dimension of sin, as the Kairos document so succinctly states: "The occupation is sinful." It is not benign nor is it accidental. It is raw, intentional evil at work every minute. Corporate evil manifests itself in sinister ways. Last week, a small Friends of Sabeel witness group and I traveled to villages, speaking to villagers and grassroots leaders in the West Bank about popular resistance. We saw settlements encroaching on villages, dumping raw sewage, yet no one stops these insidious actions. Rather, my government is sustaining it, paying for it, covering it up. So we go back to the States, to live in the corporate beast of empire, with full recognition of the sinful nature of our government and our complicity in the crimes being committed here.

So though this task is difficult, we cannot avoid our responsibility. I was so struck when we went to Ofer Prison and heard that an average of two children a night, 18 years and younger, are literally kidnapped, brought to that prison, put on trial, and often tortured. This sickness is corrupting Israeli society, and somehow we need to hold onto the power of justice and a love that liberates, lest we fall into despair and raw hatred.

I want to share Cedar Duaybis' prayer as we prayed at Ofer Prison:

Lord Jesus, our hearts cry out in pain as we stand
before the walls of this prison. Lord, you have known
the inside of a prison cell. You have suffered torture
and humiliation for speaking truth to power. Give all
the prisoners of conscience, especially the children,
your strength to sustain them through this ordeal.
Break the chains that bind the occupier to a sick
ideology, so that the chains of these children will fall
one day and they will be free.

This captures the corporate sin that is breaking the soul, not just of Palestinians and children here, but also of Israeli society. This is what Christ came to die for, and we are baptized into that death that liberates.

But the task is daunting and long. When I was a professor, I brought several groups of students here, and we would often sit with Sabeel and debrief on our final day. One group spent three weeks covering the West Bank, Galilee, and Gaza (let us not forget Gaza). The students lived in Palestinian homes, and they worked with NGOs and Palestinian organizations for a week. And by the last night, their reactions were all over the map; some were depressed, some were crying, while for others anger spewed out. And they said, "I don't know what to do when I go back. My parents won't even listen to me. How do we move from here and take this message back?" And it was Cedar who said: "Look up on the arch above you! What does it say?" We looked up where it was written: "You shall know the truth and the truth shall set you free" (John 8:32). Cedar said, "Now you are stuck with the truth. Go and figure it out. How are you going to take back and use your best gifts to change your own country and your families?" So we leave like these students, stuck with the truth.

But we're also stuck with a baptismal power that we often forget. In our baptism we take on the Christ who died and calls us to identify with the forces of death, and work with His power and the Holy Spirit to defeat the death-dealing systems that destroy life today.

Resistance to evil is part of the call to baptism and to Eucharist. In a few moments, we will participate in the baptismal covenant renewal, and be asked a series of questions to reaffirm our faith.[36] Many of us were baptized as children and our parents took those vows on our behalf; we grew into them and we renewed them at our confirmation.

We can all use the reminder that we are called to resist and stand against evil. That's one of the vows that we were given. In the early Orthodox liturgies, there's even a sense of exorcism that comes through. In baptism, we have been liberated through Christ to bring good news to the world. The dominating power of corporate and personal sin has been broken. Clearly, sin is still present in us and in the world, but we are called by Christ to be renewed and give our lives to be stewards for a world that God loves. The power of evil is often overwhelming, so we must constantly seek renewal so that we can go back into our broken societies; and not just to speak and educate, but to live at the margins of society to bring about change.

During our Friends of Sabeel witness trip last week, we read Walter Wink, that late, great theologian, who reminds us that we live in a day of the myth of redemptive violence, the mythology that might makes right, and assumes it will always "win." And don't Zionism, the power of the empire, and so many forms of Christian Zionism embrace that myth of redemptive violence? However, we are called to liberate our theologies, our narratives, and take up a new narrative that calls us to stand against these systems, ideologies, and theologies that oppress, and begin to resist. When you take that vow today, you are stuck with the truth, and you are called to stand firm and continue to stand firm in a long process of resistance to evil. The Greek word which is used throughout the text, and Jesus used in Aramaic, is *anthistemi*, "to stand firm and to resist." And it's just one response to the occupation, but it has tremendous power, and is something everyone can do in small or large ways.

---

36 Refer to *Appendix III: "Baptismal Covenant Renewal"*

In a speech to the French Foreign Minister, Netanyahu mentioned two issues that are threatening Israel. Of course Iran, that great diversion away from Palestine. What was the other? Boycott, Divestment and Sanctions (BDS). BDS is beginning to bite. It's beginning to cause many in Israel to reflect on the need to change course. Still the majority are so trapped in the myth of redemptive violence that they're going to fight us tooth and nail every step of the way. But this is one way for the Palestinians and for us to work together across continents to bring liberation to Palestine and eventually Israel, too.

Finally, let me turn to the rising, renewing, resurrecting aspect of the message. We are called daily to be reminded that we have been liberated by the power of Jesus Christ not only within our own personal struggle, but also for our world. And it takes a daily commitment, a daily reminder of what we're called to, through prayer, worship, our own emotional life, yoga, meditation, whatever works for you. We need to step back and reflect so that we will be standing firm for the long haul.

Dr. Craig Barnes, president of Princeton Seminary, is someone who gets what's going on in Palestine. He wrote a wonderful article in the recent *Christian Century* magazine, where he reflected on Benedict's Rule (Benedict of the Benedictines). In Benedict's Rule something amazing happens. The novice is called into the Oratory to take the vow of "stability, fidelity and obedience," or the familiar "poverty, chastity, obedience." Then he must answer with this phrase: "Uphold me, O Lord, according to your promise that I may live, and let me not be put to shame in my hope." The novice is called to live, to bring good news and a word of hope to a broken world. But then Barnes notes that the novice goes to his room, takes off his street clothes and hangs them in the closet, and puts on the robe signifying his new monastic vocation. Barnes adds, "I was really puzzled by that. I thought the street clothes were burned or handed over to the family." But the street clothes are there for a purpose. Every morning when the novice puts on the habit, he has a choice in freedom to put on the street clothes and walk away from his commitment. And then he goes to prayer, to be reminded of his calling to be renewed, to be blessed. It's a daily journey and a daily decision.

The road ahead for justice in Palestine is going to be rugged and it's likely to get worse. The Israelis are now putting staff in embassies and consulates, armed with millions of dollars, to fight the churches, universities, and even our theologies, to stop the march for justice, to defeat BDS and other forms of legitimate nonviolent resistance. It's going to get nasty. Last night we were sitting with a Palestinian human rights and community organizer who told us what could result from these false peace negotiations. Unbelievable things are coming. Raw and blatant evil will continue. But we must affirm daily that God is in charge, and we have the responsibility to bring the word of liberation, of hope, to a broken world.

Let me close with these words from Kairos Palestine, and I'm reminded that Naim Ateek and Mitri Raheb and others continue to emphasize the difference between optimism and hope. Optimism is how we might feel. And when the situation is daunting, children are being marched off to prison, and we're losing land, we feel destroyed. But hope is different. Hope is not only anchored in the loving, liberating God; it is also what we do about the evil around us and what we're called to do as a community. Hope is a very deep and profound power that goes beyond our feelings of being optimistic or pessimistic on a given day. It empowers us to be reengaged and reenergized for the difficult journey ahead.

Here's how Kairos Palestine closes:

> In the absence of hope, here, we cry out our cry of hope. We believe in God, good and just. We believe that God's goodness will triumph over the evil and over death that still persists in this land. One day we will see here a new land, a new human being, all equal, capable of rising up in the Spirit to love one another as brothers and sisters.

Romantic? Not really. But that's the kingdom of God that we are to hold onto and help grow, to bring its liberating power into our lives and our communities. So let us stand firm, resist, and be renewed: to the glory of God. Amen.

TWENTY-FIVE YEARS OF PALESTINIAN LIBERATION THEOLOGY

Naim Ateek

Brothers and sisters, we have come to the time of celebration. We at Sabeel are celebrating 25 years since the beginning of the Palestinian Liberation Theology (PLT) movement. Thank you for being with us, and it is only by the grace of God that we are here today.

The beginnings of PLT preceded the establishment of Sabeel, developed back during the height of the First Intifada. On December 9, 1987, the intifada started, and by 1988 it was in full force. I was the parish priest at St. George's Cathedral in Jerusalem. The intifada engulfed the Palestinian community throughout the Gaza Strip and the West Bank including East Jerusalem, and touched our small Palestinian Christian community at St. George's.

In the midst of this turmoil, we decided to try something new. While simultaneously the Islamic resistance movement Hamas was emerging and choosing the way of armed struggle, we chose the way of nonviolence as the path to liberation. Every Sunday morning after the worship service, a group would gather in the small parish hall for an hour to discuss the sermon and focus on aspects of our faith in light of the intifada and the occupation. *What is Christ saying to us and asking us to do as people living under occupation? How did Christ respond to the occupation by the Romans? How should we respond today?* The parish hall was packed every Sunday, even including people from other churches. This marked the beginning of PLT.

In 1989, I published my first book, *Justice and Only Justice*. It was launched at St. George's McInness Hall. In March 1990, we organized the first Palestinian Liberation Theology conference, held at Tantur. We didn't adopt the name Sabeel until 1992 when we felt that God was calling us to continue developing this movement and this theology.

It was not an easy process; many Palestinian Christians had been hurt by Zionist interpretations of scripture and the difficult command to "love your enemies." One member of my congregation, who had suffered very much in her life, was upset with me when I preached about the need to "love one's enemies." I challenged her to write her own version of the gospel, saying, "You want to pull down the gospel to your way of thinking, but the gospel wants to pull you up to Christ's way of thinking." Months later, she indicated to me that she was beginning to understand what Jesus said and to slowly rise to the demands of the gospel.

PLT movement

PLT was never a movement with purely political motivation. It was and is a movement that reclaims the Jesus movement. From the beginning, it was a movement of people who wanted to live their faith in community, in action, and in context. PLT is following Jesus Christ; it is discipleship without many of the unnecessary trappings of tradition. In essence, it is servant leadership, in the style of Jesus, serving others through working for justice and peace. And from the very beginning we had people from other faiths or of no faith. Our commitment was and always will be for justice and peace through nonviolent resistance.

PLT is inspired by Jesus' life. Christ is its hermeneutic: Jesus Christ living under occupation. We did not need to import a theology of liberation from abroad. We had the Bible, we had the gospels, and we had the occupation. We had only to reclaim and rediscover the original revolution of Jesus Christ in our land. He is our liberator par excellence. Once people saw Jesus Christ in this way, they were able to recognize the evil of the occupation, contrast it with God's kingdom, and critique it. Once we opened the eyes of our people, they were theologically aware; once they placed themselves in the sandals of Jesus, they were thinking and talking theologically.

Throughout this process of reclamation, we rediscovered Jesus' humanity. The humanity of Jesus was buried under many layers of his divinity, due in part to early Christian controversies of the church. But we discovered Jesus, in his flesh and blood, as a human being who suffered the oppression of an occupation. We had to rediscover the spirituality of justice and love which he embodied and exercised.

Jesus emphasized several points which became immensely important for the development of our theology of liberation:

1. **God's reign:** When we see humankind's reign, in its oppression, ugliness, and de-humanizing reality, our faith inspires us to contrast it with God's reign, God's kingdom of justice and righteousness, of peace and love.

2. **The meek will inherit the earth:** When we see the violence and wars, the conflicts, the corruption, the injustice, people's domination of others and of the land, we remember the words of Christ: *Blessed are the meek.* From God's perspective, the land belongs to the meek of the earth. So we work for God's will to be done on earth. The meek are those who are resilient and strong, who love and trust God and serve others with humility.

3. **Nonviolence:** When we see the violence of the powerful, we remember that God's will for us is to live the nonviolence of Jesus Christ.

4. **Live out the prophetic:** This means championing justice and liberation, resisting evil wherever and whenever it shows its ugly head, and speaking courageously against oppression.

This is PLT; this is what it is all about. It is living a simple life that emphasizes service to others rather than domination. The unique contribution of Sabeel has been and continues to be its biblical and theological foundation. It is from the basis of our faith that we are involved in politics. We believe that we live in God's world and whenever the political, economic, and religious powers act contrary to the health of the community, we as people of faith must take a stand. We take a stand on behalf of the God of justice, mercy, and love.

Vision for the future ministry of Sabeel

From the very beginning of Sabeel's ministry, the vision has been clear:

- So long as there is injustice, we must continue to lift up the cry for justice. Our motto echoes the cry of the woman in Jesus' parable of the Unjust Judge: "Grant me justice!" (Luke 18:1-8)

- When justice as demanded by international law and UN resolutions is achieved, peace will be achieved. The conflict must be resolved on the basis of international law. It must be a just solution so that it can lead to a viable peace. Ancient history does not give Israel any right to take the land; there is no *a priori* right. Israel has taken the land through brutal military force, so international law must be involved in redressing the injustice and implementing a just solution.

- The verse that inspires us most is found in 2 Cor. 5:18: "All this is from God, who reconciled us to himself through Christ, and has given us the ministry of reconciliation." The achievement of peace will open the way for reconciliation, and we have been entrusted with this ministry, though it takes many forms. The most important form is between Palestinians and Israelis for the health of our people and the well-being of our country, but it must also include reconciliation among the religions represented, and ecumenically within the Christian community. As Christians, we must learn how to fully become the body of Christ in the land.

Gratitude

I would simply like to thank all our friends, whether local Palestinians or internationals, for accompanying us along the *sabeel* of justice, peace, and liberation. For me personally, I would now like to go to the back of the line and join my friends who are walking more slowly. But we will continue walking the way together.

My prayer is that everything we have done so far and will do in the future is for the glory of God.

We praise and thank God for the past as we celebrate it.

We praise and thank God for our ministry today.

We pray for God's guidance to Sabeel as it moves into the future.

The charge for the new generation

I believe it is time to pass the mantle to a younger generation:

"Discipleship requires us to put aside personal ambitions and whatever lofty ideas we may have about what it means to be a follower of Christ. Authentic discipleship always requires sacrifice and a great many challenges. Seeking justice, promoting peace, and going against the flow are just a few of the things disciples are called to do. Are you ready for the challenge?"[37] I know that many of you took up the challenge when we started to walk this *sabeel* together, and we thank God for that.

Glory to God whose power, working in us, can do infinitely more than we can ask or imagine: Glory to God from generation to generation in the Church, outside the Church, in Sabeel, and outside Sabeel, and in Christ Jesus for ever and ever.

Amen.

---

37 Cutié, A.R. (2013). "Tuesday, October 15." *Forward day by day.* (pp. 78) Cincinnati, OH: Forward Movement.

TWENTY-FIVE YEARS OF PALESTINIAN LIBERATION THEOLOGY

Rosemary Radford Reuther

The journey of Rev. Naim Ateek in the creation and development of a Palestinian liberation theology has been very important in shaping my meaning of redemption, and many others who have been drawn to the Palestinian story of oppression. I have followed the development of Rev. Ateek's thought since I first encountered his work in Palestine in 1987. I have attended most of the Sabeel conferences since its founding in 1990. I have also taught courses on the conflict in theological seminaries for over 21 years and have taken students and faculty on trips to Israel-Palestine. Rev. Ateek's Palestinian liberation theology has been a key guide in those courses.

In the 1960s, I was involved in critique of Christian anti-Semitism, and in 1974 published a book about it, titled *Faith and Fratricide: The Theological Roots of Anti-Semitism*. But in the late 1970s, I became aware of how the critique of anti-Semitism was being used to justify Israeli domination. In 1980, I participated in a trip to Israel-Palestine sponsored by a Jewish women's group interested in dialogue among Christians, Jews, and Muslims. I spent some time in Jerusalem and Ramallah encountering the Palestinian perspective. This experience deepened my concern to see this issue from the Palestinian context.

In 1987, my husband, Herman J. Ruether, a scholar of Islam, and I decided to pursue this question by spending some months at the Tantur Ecumenical Institute in Jerusalem. One day, I overheard several staff at Tantur discussing Rev. Ateek's thesis on the Episcopal Church in Palestine. This church was founded by British imperialists in the mid-nineteenth century, inspired by a vision of Christian Zionism. Hoping that Jews would convert to Christianity—specifically the Anglican Church—and thereby usher in world redemption through the British Empire, imperialists appointed a converted Jew, the Rev. Michael Solomon Alexander, as the first Anglican bishop of Jerusalem. Rev. Ateek's thesis, written for his doctoral degree at Berkeley, California, discussed the irony of these roots of the Episcopal Church in Israel for Palestinian Anglicans such as himself.

Fascinated by this story, I checked out Rev. Ateek's thesis at the Tantur library, and decided to go over to St. George's Cathedral in Jerusalem to meet him. I encountered him in his office, and we quickly engaged in a conversation. He shared his desire to develop a Palestinian liberation theology. This vision inspired me, and I have been in contact with Rev. Ateek and his developing thought ever since.

In the spring of 1987, I taught a course at Tantur on Christian Zionism and the Israeli-Palestinian conflict while my husband taught a course on Islam. Through these lectures we developed a plan to write a book together on how Western Christian relations to Jews and Judaism were being reshaped by the Israeli-Palestinian conflict; we published the book, titled *The Wrath of Jonah: The Crisis of Religious Nationalism in the Israeli-Palestinian Conflict*, in 1989.

Meanwhile, Rev. Ateek continued to develop his thoughts on Palestinian liberation theology and published his first book on this theme this same year, titled *Justice and Only Justice: A Palestinian Theology of Liberation*. Rev. Ateek very kindly asked me to write the foreword for this book which has been foundational for the movement for a Palestinian theology of liberation, and the development of Sabeel chapters worldwide.

In the foreword, I discussed the challenge raised by Palestinian liberation theology to the use of Exodus and "Promised Land" motifs in other liberation theologies.

> A Palestinian liberation theology reveals the dangerous shadow side of these images of liberation from former oppression. Palestinians are victims

of a Zionist liberation theology and ideology. The Jewish exodus from oppression in Europe is the rationale for their conquest. The Jewish claim to the promised land is [the Palestinians'] dispossession from their land of Palestine. Jewish peoplehood excludes the existence of Palestinians as a people. Jewish redemption is Palestinian oppression. . . . The critical issue for every liberation theology, every liberation movement, is not simply to throw off oppression and empower the formerly victimized, but how to do so in a way that does not make former slaves into new slave masters.[38]

The critical contribution of a Palestinian liberation theology is the struggle to answer this question. Only such a theology "can save us from repeating the cycle of violence, from empowering one oppressed people only by making them oppressors of another people." Only when we understand, "as Father Ateek affirms, that the earth belongs finally to God and not to us as private property," can we learn to live together in peace, by sharing it with one another, "as sisters and brothers, children of one God who created us and chooses us all."

---

38 Ruether, Rosemary Radford. (1989). "Foreword." In Ateek, Naim Stifan, *Justice and Only Justice: A Palestinian Theology of Liberation*, (pp. xi-xiv). Maryknoll, NY: Orbis Books.

TWENTY-FIVE YEARS OF PALESTINIAN LIBERATION THEOLOGY

Mary Grey

It is a great privilege to be asked to reflect on the achievements of Palestinian Liberation Theology (PLT) 25 years on. Like Rosemary Radford Ruether, who has spoken about her involvement since the earliest days, I have also been deeply influenced by Canon Naim Ateek's theology and the work of all his colleagues in Sabeel, and have personally found all of Sabeel's conferences completely transformative.

But I'm aware, sadly, that we celebrate these 25 years tonight still in the midst of the continuing illegal occupation. There's a shadow over us because of what the occupation means for the Palestinian people's struggle for survival and the increased suffering of Christians across the Middle East since the Arab Spring. This tragic situation points to how distinctive PLT is from other contexts. I want to highlight this first, and then suggest some later developments.

From the very beginning of PLT until now, the cry has been: "How can we live under occupation and maintain faith? How can we not lose hope? What is God saying to us today in this context?"

Like many British Christians, I first heard this cry when Christian theology was coming to terms both with its own endemic anti-Judaism and the Church's actions, or inactions, during the Holocaust. The work of Sabeel and Marc Ellis, and Rosemary herself, awakened us to another narrative, the Palestinian narrative. I came also from another experience, not of Latin American liberation theology, but from involvement in Indian liberation theology, or more specifically from Dalit liberation struggles. Dalits are the former Untouchables, who are still outside the caste system in India. Though Untouchability is illegal, outlawed first by the British in India, discrimination and violence continue on a daily basis. So it contains both similarities and differences with the Palestinian situation.

What I have valued in Sabeel's development of liberation theology is that although the priority is justice, there is a built-in dimension of reconciliation. Sabeel has continually reached out and offered forgiveness to Israelis who want to live in peace. In every conference we have been introduced to such groups as Rabbis for Human Rights, etc. In 2008, Sabeel highlighted the story of the late Joseph Ben-Eliezer[39], who was part of the 1948 massacre at Al Tantura. He later came to understand the wrong he committed in the *Nakba*, and repented, converting to Christianity. He and his family were present at the Sabeel conference in 2008 when he told his poignant story. But this is only one story. Other Palestinian Christian groups like the Holy Land Trust and Wi'am in Bethlehem also work, together with Sabeel's initiatives, on different aspects of reconciliation.

As part of this same theme of reconciliation, Sabeel has developed a non-violent theological and practical response to the situation of oppression. This has been a vital part of counteracting the cruel and false stereotype of Palestinians as terrorists. During the First Intifada, in the early days of PLT, this was a striking dimension, often forgotten by the world. I would say that this nonviolent response, resistance, and commitment stressed by Naim Ateek in *A Palestinian Christian Cry for Reconciliation*[40] is something that PLT has offered to the world. Rediscovering the Bible as a source of inspiration and liberation is at the heart of Sabeel's theology. It focuses on the Sermon on the Mount, and the Beatitudes are the beating heart of Sabeel's theology, of Naim's theology, of Archbishop Elias Chacour's theology, and so on. And the words of Mitri Raheb at Sabeel's 2011 Conference on *Challenging Empire* in Bethlehem still ring in my ears: "The meek will inherit the earth because there will be no one left! The

---

39 Died 2013
40 Naim Ateek, *A Palestinian Cry for Reconciliation*, (Maryknoll: Orbis 2008), p.139

Ottomans have gone, the British have gone, the Jordanians have gone. The Israeli Empire will go too. *Only the meek will be left!"*

The concept of nonviolent resistance, as a distinctive part of PLT, has many dimensions. Sabeel's unique contribution has been to reread the Scriptures with new eyes in order to highlight nonviolence on many levels: with young people, with women's groups. And I salute Sabeel for its gender focus and this conscientious sensitivity to the role that women play at every level of the organization. And Sabeel is developing this focus amidst the daily humiliations experienced by so many people. Reading Scripture through the eyes of nonviolence inspires not only nonviolent *public* resistance, but resistance *lived out on many levels,* as Professor Mazin Qumsiyeh of Bethlehem University, a good friend of Sabeel, wrote so passionately:

> We could write volumes about resistance by simply living, eating, breathing in a land that is coveted. We resist by going to school, by cultivating what remains of our lands, by working under harsh conditions, by falling in love, getting married and having children. Resistance includes hanging on to what remains of Palestine when it has been made crystal-clear in words and deeds that we are not welcome in our own lands.[41]

But underpinning the movement of nonviolent resistance is a spirituality that PLT has also offered to the world; the spirituality of *sumud:* steadfastness, resilience, endurance. Jean Zaru, a founding member of Sabeel from Ramallah, writes of the importance of *sumud* in the context of occupation: "To practice *sumud*...is to remain steadfast on one's own land...to remain steadfast in service to one's homeland to the struggle for freedom."[42]

Sumud, as Palestinians teach us, is *the gift of living peacefully when there is no peace.* For me, there is something mystical about

---

41 Mazin Qumsiyeh, *Popular Resistance in Palestine: A History of Hope and Empowerment,* (London: Pluto 2011), p.235.
42 Jean Zaru, *Occupied with Nonviolence: A Palestinian Woman Speaks,* Fortress: 2008).

this which I would like to develop. *Sumud,* as so many groups are demonstrating, is a spirituality with an important cultural expression. Culture is the space where people meet others and themselves, where they can discover a language that is local yet universal. Sabeel has celebrated that through these 25 years. We just witnessed it with dance, with art, with music, with poetry, in a vital, uplifting manner. But I think that *sumud* goes deeper, and I want to spend a few minutes on this. I think that the practice of *sumud* is part of a mystical, prophetic theology on which Sabeel has always focused. Two days ago, Naim called for a renewed stress on the prophetic. But the prophetic is balanced by its other side, the mystical. As the French philosopher, Charles Péguy wrote: "All things begin in politics, end in mysticism, only to begin again!"

Speaking in his panel, Fr. Peter Du Brul drew us to this special place of the mystical when he spoke of God as completion, of the experience of the completeness of God, the fullness of God, but also the absence of God. In this, the "dark night" of the Palestinian people, I suggest a mystical turn to St. John of the Cross in his *Dark Night of the Soul,* written from a Spanish prison at the time of the Inquisition. And from my own country, Julian of Norwich, who wrote just after the despair of the Black Death in the fourteenth century, when a third of the clergy in Europe were wiped out. Mystical saints speak to our desolation with hope of light and the intensity of God's love despite the dark night.

And now I want to thank Sabeel for the way it sends us back with a mission and a commitment to develop our own prophetic liberation theology in our own countries, through the publications emerging from conferences and other ways it has been able to spread the message. In the UK, one outcome of this is our response to the Kairos Palestine Document from December 2009. Some here among us, like Anne Clayton and the Rev. Warren Bardsley, led the UK team and were part of its dramatic launch at the Greenbelt Festival in August 2013. We end our UK document by affirming what was said in 2009: "*We can be silent no longer. It is time for prophetic faithfulness. It is time for action.*"

I cite this as an example that PLT is bearing fruit in other countries. Another initiative is the Balfour Project. In 1917, the Balfour Declaration was sent to Lord Rothschild, offering a home for the Jews in Palestine, ignoring the fact that the land was already inhabited by the Arabs. Following PLT's stress on reconciliation and forgiveness, The Balfour Project[43] seeks to mark the centenary of the Balfour Declaration by:

- acknowledging Britain's actions at the time of the Balfour Declaration and throughout the Mandate, and particularly the deceit surrounding our nation's true intentions;
- asking pardon from Palestinians for our nation's wrongdoing, for having intentionally ignored their legitimate aspirations;
- asking pardon from Jews for our part in the centuries of anti-Semitism;
- and exhibiting integrity in our nation's future dealings with Jews, Palestinians, and all peoples.

I see this as a way to develop the vision of PLT for the future. Liberation theology has always made the distinction between victim and oppressor. The Palestinian people are crying out for justice. We, the British, who have historically been part of the oppression, not only here but in other lands, have the moral obligation to act in reparation and in action for peace.

I end with the words written for the Balfour Project by Bishop John Austin Baker, former Bishop of Salisbury:

*There is no **peace** without repentance;*
*There is no **repentance** without knowledge;*
*There is no **knowledge** without education.*

Sabeel's inspiration in developing PLT for over 25 years has taught us in Britain that there is work that only we can do, and that is the true meaning of our solidarity with the Palestinians. My hope is that if we all recognize and commit to the task that is uniquely ours, the wall will come down, the occupation will end, and the Holy Land will at last enjoy peace with justice.

---

43 For more information, see: www.balfourproject.org

"When I Look Forward"

Bo Forsberg

As many others have done this past week, I have to begin by saying, from the bottom of my heart, thanks to Naim Ateek for everything he has done. He is a calm, humble man with a very strong message, and I love that combination. But I think you'll agree, also, if I add one comment that Sabeel wouldn't have been Sabeel without the strong women we have seen today: Cedar Duaybis, Samia Khoury, and Jean Zaru. They have written books, they have written articles. Brave women, strong women, smart women. So, thank you to all of you, the whole team, that you've made this possible.

I'm working for an organization in Sweden called Diakonia, which has about 400 partner organizations around the world, working for democracy, economic justice, human rights, and peace. Four hundred organizations, but the one I love most is Sabeel. It's really true, because Sabeel has a wonderful way of combining life for everyone in dignity, telling the truth based on international rules and laws, and, in the middle of it all, Jesus Christ. It's a wonderful combination. That's how the Gospel should be preached. When I look forward, and yes, some of us are wondering what will happen when the elders leave, I'm sure that Sabeel is stable enough to go on.

We had a youth conference in Palestine last year, sponsored by Diakonia Sweden and Sabeel. We invited youth from all over the world to come to Bethlehem, read the Gospel, and get involved in nonviolent resistance. One group built a new cave at the Tent of Nations, where some of you visited. One group rebuilt a Palestinian house that had been demolished six times; they rebuilt it in two days. You should have seen it. Young people from Cuba working, young people from Burma, Mozambique, you name it. Wonderful. And all so committed to what they were doing. Can you imagine people coming from Burma, with all their problems, and suddenly the cause of the Palestinians is their cause? It was wonderful to see, and so there is a future because there are so many committed young people from around the world and at Sabeel.

I am sure, and this has been mentioned before, that "people power" is the strongest power in the world. I am old enough now, with my grey hair, to have seen its impact, and I'm sure that changes will also come here. I was in the Philippines the week after Ferdinand Marcos fell, and people said to me, "Bo, you should have seen it last week. You should have been here and seen the crowd, hundreds and thousands of people, going up the boulevard to the presidential palace, and in front of the crowd were nuns, priests and pastors, hand-in-hand." So when they arrived at the palace, the soldiers were there with their machine guns, but when they saw the priests and nuns and hundreds and thousands of people, they couldn't shoot. They took their weapons and laid them down. And Marcos was standing in the palace and looking at what the military was doing, and he had to leave. He took his helicopter and left.

I was the chairperson of the anti-apartheid movement in Sweden during apartheid in South Africa. I remember that we wrote articles, so tired of sitting and discussing with nothing happening, nothing changing. And then suddenly it happened. Nelson Mandela was freed, the whole group around him was freed, and the changes came. I've seen it in Chile; I've seen it in El Salvador. And it's going to happen here also. Because that's the experience: it's impossible to build a state on violence, oppression, and segregation walls. Such a state cannot remain.

But the world is dense, you know. I thought that when the wall between West and East Berlin fell and people took it down stone by stone that *now* we have learned that you can't build physical walls between people. There's a wall in the U.S. separating it from

Latin America, and India is building a wall on the border with Bangladesh because it knows that, with the climate changes, the refugees will come soon. Europe has built a wall in Northern Africa, saying, "Don't come here." And then, we have *this* wall in Palestine.

People still believe that physical walls can solve the problem. Of course not. Of course not. The only way is the Sabeel way: building respect, telling the truth, building on solidarity and the idea that every human being should live life with dignity. And preaching Jesus' way of doing justice. Because what did Jesus say when he saw the Roman occupation? He challenged the religious leaders and the political leaders and he said, "Don't you see the people? Don't you see the suffering of the people? I'm going to tell you the truth." And that's exactly our duty also.

You have seen. You have listened. You know all the stories. Every Palestinian can tell their story about the oppression, about the violence, about the stealing of land—we have seen it. Now it's our duty, friends. And every time I visit Palestine, I get so angry, but I know that anger can't change anything. But, I'm also very inspired. And you are the ones who are inspiring us. Go home and do your duty, because our governments are a part of this conflict so we all have homework to do together.

Ending this conference I would like to say "thank you" for another week of inspiration. Now we go home ready to engage and do something. Naim asked this afternoon, after sharing the challenges, "Are we ready to work?" I can answer: We are ready! Here we are. Let's work together. And we are strong because there is no stronger force in the world than people working together with one vision, one goal, and that's where we are going.

APPENDICES

APPENDIX I: "Conference Prayer"

Bo Forsberg

God of peace and opportunity, our Creator and Redeemer, we come to you to pray for your mercy, forgiveness, and a new start. Instead of overcoming evil with good, we have stood by while goodness has been affronted. We ask for your help to give peace a new chance to thrive in our world.

Give us the courage to expose evil thoughts and deeds, and to speak the truth. We do not believe in the right of the strong, the strength of armies, or the power of oppression. We believe in the equal value of all people, the power of nonviolence, and solidarity based on justice.

We pray for your Holy Spirit to join our hearts and minds with the way of peace, so that our hearts may become a place where your mercy reigns.

God of justice, make us tools of your peace so that we may do your will and create a just future.

Lord, awaken your church, starting with me.

Lord, bring your flock to life, starting with me.

Lord, bring peace to the whole world, starting with me.

Lord, afford your love and truth to all people, starting with me.

APPENDIX II: "Litany for Peace and Justice"

This work is hard. It is demanding, time consuming, and sometimes tedious. Will we recommit ourselves to working for peace and justice?

We will.

This work can cause tensions and rifts. This work can drive wedges between people. But this work needs us to stick together. Will we dedicate ourselves to doing our best to work together?

We will.

This work for peace and justice is more effective when we embrace and respect diversity. Will we recommit ourselves to embracing and respecting difference?

We will.

This work requires creativity. This work demands that we push ourselves to look for new possibilities. Will we dedicate ourselves to thinking and acting creatively for peace and justice?

We will.

This work for peace and justice requires faith and hope that a better tomorrow is possible. Will we dedicate ourselves to find sources of faith and hope in our lives?

We will.

This work for peace and justice calls us to find inner peace. Will we recommit ourselves to promoting peace both within and without?

We will.

APPENDIX III: "Baptismal Covenant Renewal"

Leader 1	Do you believe in God the Father?
People	**I believe in God, the Father almighty, creator of heaven and earth.**

Leader 1	Do you believe in Jesus Christ, the Son of God?
People	**I believe in Jesus Christ, his only Son, our Lord.** **He was conceived by the power of the Holy Spirit and born of the Virgin Mary.** **He suffered under Pontius Pilate, was crucified, died, and was buried.** **He descended to the dead. On the third day he rose again.** **He ascended into heaven, and is seated at the right hand of the Father.** **He will come again to judge the living and the dead.**

Leader 1	Do you believe in God the Holy Spirit?
People	**I believe in the Holy Spirit, the holy catholic Church, the communion of saints, the forgiveness of sins, the resurrection of the body, and the life everlasting.**

Leader 2	Will you continue in the apostles' teaching and fellowship, in the breaking of bread, and in the prayers?
People	**I will, with God's help.**

Leader 2	Will you persevere in resisting evil, and, whenever you fall into sin, repent and return to the Lord?
People	**I will, with God's help.**

Leader 2	Will you proclaim by word and example the Good News of God in Christ?
People	**I will, with God's help.**
Leader 3	Will you seek and serve Christ in all persons, loving your neighbor as yourself?
People	**I will, with God's help.**
Leader 3	Will you strive for justice and peace among all people, and respect the dignity of every human being?
People	**I will, with God's help.**
Leader 3	Will you rededicate yourself to these goals with a particular emphasis on the present crisis in Israel and Palestine?
People	**I will, with God's help.**

Dr. Rosemary Radford Ruether speaks at the Celebration of 25 years of Palestinian Liberation Theology at the Notre Dame Center in Jerusalem.

Past and present International Friends of Sabeel coordinators are recognized during the conference.

The conference choir sings at the Church of the Ascension, Augusta Victoria, in Jerusalem.

Celebration of 25 years of Palestinian Liberation Theology at the Intercontinental Hotel in Jericho

The Rev. Dr. Naim Ateek and Archbishop Elias Chacour at the Celebration of 25 years of Palestinian Liberation Theology at the Intercontinental Hotel in Jericho

Mr. Bo Forsberg speaks at the Celebration of 25 years of Palestinian Liberation Theology at the Notre Dame Center in Jerusalem.

Professor Mary Grey speaks at the Celebration of 25 years of Palestinian Liberation Theology at the Notre Dame Center in Jerusalem.

Dr. Mustafa Barghouti gives his presentation, "The Status Quo in Israel and Palestine." (Conference moderator, Ambassador Hind Khoury, pictured right.)

The panel "Perspectives from Gaza-Palestine and Israel"

The panel "International Law and Religion"

The panel "Does the Bible Have a Future?"

The panel "The Land of Promise"

The panel "Biblical Authority"

Jim and Jean Strathdee (USA) sing during the conference opening worship.

The Rev. Dr. Donald Wagner gives the final sermon during the conference closing worship.

Professor John Quigley gives his presentation, "International Law and the Palestine-Israel Conflict."

Sabeel 9ᵗʰ International Conference participants at the Notre Dame Hotel and Conference Center in Jerusalem

Conference participants at the Notre Dame Conference Center

The panel "The Bible and the Occupation of Palestine"

The panel "Occupation of the Bible"